# *Skin Deep*

## *How Race and Complexion Matter in the "Color-Blind" Era*

❖❖❖

To Marsha, Ray, and Darlene

❖❖❖

# *Skin Deep*

## *How Race and Complexion Matter in the "Color-Blind" Era*

**Cedric Herring**
**Verna Keith**
**Hayward Derrick Horton**

Institute for Research on Race and Public Policy
University of Illinois at Chicago

University of Illinois Press
2004

Co-published by:

Institute for Research on Race and Public Policy

University of Illinois at Chicago

University of Illinois Press

Urbana and Chicago

**Printed in the United States of America.**

**Library of Congress Cataloging-in-Publication Data**

Herring, Cedric.
  Skin deep : how race and complexion matter in the "color-blind" era / Cedric Herring, Verna Keith, Hayward Derrick Horton.
    p. cm.
  Includes bibliographical references and index.
  ISBN 1-929011-26-1 (alk. paper)
    1. Racism. 2. Human skin color--Social aspects. 3. Human skin color--Psychological aspects. 4. Racism--United States. 5. United States--Race relations. I. Keith, Verna. II. Horton, Hayward Derrick. III. Title.
  HT1521 .H43 2004
  305.8--dc21
  2003010648

# Contents

# Chapter 1

## Skin Deep:
### Race and Complexion in the "Color-Blind" Era

**Cedric Herring**
University of Illinois at Chicago

F ew Americans would take exception to the dream put forth by the Rev. Dr. Martin Luther King, Jr. that all people should be judged by the content of their character rather than the color of their skin. Regrettably, however, people are still judged, at least in part, by the color of their skin. Much historical work by social scientists such as Drake and Cayton, E. Franklin Frazier, W.E. B. Du Bois, Anna Julia Cooper, and Oliver C. Cox showed that skin tone has been a predictor of educational attainment, occupational status, and income. More contemporary research has also shown that light skin color consistently provided higher status than darker skin color among African Americans. Some of my previous work with Verna Keith (Keith and Herring, 1991) showed that African Americans with lighter skin complexions were more likely to have higher social and economic statuses than their darker skinned counterparts in terms of educational attainment, occupational status, and income.

Skin color stratification is not a new phenomenon in the United States. Colorism in the U.S. dates back at least to the colonial era. For the most part though, it has been overshadowed by or subsumed within more general issues of racism and race relations. Nevertheless, skin tone, per se, has historically played a significant role in determining the life chances of African Americans and other people of color. The legacy of colonialism, racial oppression during slavery, legalized discrimination in the Jim Crow era, and *de facto* segregation in the post-civil rights era have all functioned to create and perpetuate skin color stratification in communities of color.

But what does the relationship between skin tone and stratification outcomes mean? Is skin tone correlated with stratification outcomes because people with darker complexions experience more discrimination than those of the same race with lighter complexions? Is skin tone differentiation a process that operates external to communities of color and is then imposed on people of color externally? Or, is skin tone stratification an internally driven process that is actively aided and abetted by members of communities of color themselves? Does the color stratification process work the same for African Americans, Hispanics, and Asian Americans?

Most Whites believe that in America, race is no longer a relevant factor because people generally receive what they deserve based on their talents and efforts. Indeed, according to a 2001 Gallup survey, 7 out of 10 Whites said that Blacks are treated "the same as Whites." But as Eduardo Bonilla-Silva (2001) puts it, despite Whites' "sincere fictions," racial considerations shade almost everything that happens in this country. Blacks–and dark-skinned racial minorities–lag well behind Whites in virtually every relevant social indicator. As he points out, Blacks tend to be poorer, earn less, and to possess significantly less wealth than Whites. They also receive impolite and discriminatory treatment in stores, at restaurants, when trying to catch a cab, while driving, and in a host of other commercial and social transactions.

Even within "racial groups," skin color matters. People who are usually considered to be of the same race are judged by the hue and shade of their skin.

**Colorism in Historical and Contemporary Perspective**

Skin tone has historically played a significant role in determining the life chances of African Americans and other people of color. It has also been important to our understanding of race and racialization processes.

"Colorism" is the discriminatory treatment of individuals falling within the same "racial" group on the basis of skin color. It operates both intraracially and interracially. Intraracial colorism occurs when members of a racial group make distinctions based upon skin color between members of their own race. Interracial colorism occurs when members of one racial group make distinctions based upon skin color between members of another racial group. Much of the recent research on colorism has focused on patterns in the African American community. It is plausible, however, that similar issues exist within the Latino, Asian American, and even the White communities.

We must understand that colorism–much like the notion of race itself–is historically contingent on supremacist assumptions. In the United States, color preferences are typically measured against putative European (i.e., White) standards. These preferences have involved physical features including skin color, hair texture, thickness of lips, eye color, nose shapes, and other phenotypical features. For centuries, African Americans with European features have been exalted above those with dark or black complexions. People with straight or "good" hair have been admired above those with nappy, kinky, or "bad" hair.[1]

During the American colonial period, interracial unions between Blacks and Whites led to a population with varying skin tones. As the number of children from these relationships grew, the colonies were faced with deciding whether these children were Black (and therefore typically slaves) or White (and therefore potentially free). The decision regarding whether the children of these couplings could ever be free gave birth to the "one drop" rule of racial assignment to protect the notion of "whiteness." This rule suggested that no matter how White a person looked, if he or she had at least one Black ancestor, that person was to be considered Black. The way in which colonial legislatures responded to this question varied widely. The treatment of mixed-race individuals varied depending on who was participating in the miscegenation and the region of the country in which the practice occurred.

# Skin Deep

During the colonial era outside the Deep South, miscegenation was generally viewed as abhorrent or morally repugnant. It primarily involved White male indentured servants and Black slave women. Because these Whites shared a similar lot and lifestyle to Black slaves, they came into close contact with Black slaves. Sometimes members of the two groups became friends or even lovers. The children of such unions were typically poor, and they were basically treated the same as Blacks.

In contrast, at the same time, much of the Deep South rejected the one drop rule and instead treated free Mulattoes as a third, intermediate class between Blacks and Whites. Mulattoes were often the children of wealthy White men as opposed to White indentured servants. Some of these men freed their mixed-race offspring and even helped them develop trades and businesses. Even among those enslaved, slave owners sometimes displayed a preference for Mulattoes by assigning them to coveted indoor jobs on plantations, while leaving the more arduous field work to darker-skinned slaves. Thus, Mulattoes in the Deep South benefitted from the socioeconomic status of their White fathers.

E. Franklin Frazier (1957), in his seminal work, *The Black Bourgeoisie*, argued that lighter skinned Blacks (i.e., Mulattoes) enjoyed a privileged status that was far beyond the reach of their darker skinned counterparts. He explored extensively the experiences of light and dark skinned Blacks and showed how skin tone permitted access to some privileges. During slavery, these fair-skinned people were at times emancipated by their White fathers. In some states such as Louisiana, more than 80 percent of the free population was of mixed ancestry (Landry, 1987). After slavery, their kinship ties to Whites gave them an advantage over other Blacks in obtaining education, higher status occupations, and property. Although the initial origin of this preferential treatment is in dispute, Gunnar Myrdall (1944) suggested that Whites probably found Mulattoes more attractive, as they often possessed some European characteristics. He also suggested that since Whites were believed to be intellectually superior, those Blacks of mixed heritage were advantaged.

Mulattoes maintained their elite position in the Black community for at least fifty years following Emancipation. They passed their advantages on to their children by continuing their close association with Whites, and by avoiding intermarriage with darker Blacks (Frazier 1966; and Landry, 1987). In his 1903 essay, "The Talented Tenth," W.E.B. Du Bois referred to the "educated Mulattoes [who] sprang up to plead for Black men's rights." He saw this talented tenth as those worthy of leadership who would elevate and lead the masses. So, light skin color continued to be a distinctive characteristic of elite status and shaped the opportunity structure in the Black community into the 20th century.

Frazier (1957) argued that the influence of White ancestry on social status had declined significantly by the first World War, and that the Mulatto elite's near monopoly on the upper ranks of Black society was disappearing. Access to elite status, according to Frazier, became increasingly dependent on professional standing, education, and economic success. This transformation in the basis of social status and prestige was facilitated by the gradual extension of educational opportunities to the Black masses, growing competition from White immigrants for service jobs historically held by Mulattoes, and mass migration of southern Blacks to urban areas (Landry, 1987). The latter created an enormous demand for Black professionals to meet the needs of a rapidly increasing Black population. As darker Blacks became more educated and economically successful, they began to marry into the old Mulatto families, and the complexion of the Black elite darkened (Landry, 1987).

The civil rights movement and the rise of Black nationalism ushered in the "Black is beautiful" sentiment. Nevertheless, studies published during the 1960s and 1970s reported that skin tone within the Black community continued to be an issue and continued to have an impact on stratification outcomes (Edwards, 1972; Freeman, Ross, Armor, and Pettigrew, 1966; Udry, Bauman and Chase, 1971; and Ransford, 1970). Even studies published during the last decade continued to suggest that skin tone does matter among African Americans (e.g., Hughes and Hertel, 1990;

Blackwell, 1991; Keith and Herring, 1991; Russell, Wilson, and Hall, 1992; Allen, Telles, and; Hunter, 2000; and Hill, 2000a). For example, Keith and Herring (1991) explored the effects of skin color on stratification outcomes such as education, occupation and income. The study included controls for factors such as parental socioeconomic status, sex, age, urbanization, marital status and region of residence. The results suggested that skin tone had significant effects on education, occupation and income; in fact, skin tone was a better predictor of stratification outcomes than such factors as parental socioeconomic status.

Similarly, Hughes and Hertel (1990) found that the impact of skin color gradation on the socioeconomic status of Blacks is as strong as the impact of race itself. They carried out an analysis of African Americans to determine whether the socioeconomic statuses of respondents' spouses were correlated with respondents' skin tones. They found that light skinned Blacks were more likely to have spouses with higher socioeconomic statuses than darker skinned Blacks. This finding was consistent even after statistically controlling the socioeconomic statuses and socioeconomic backgrounds of the respondents themselves.

Johnson, Bienenstock and Stoloff (1995) investigated the cultural capital hypothesis that the high rate of joblessness in urban America is due to cultural deficiencies among inner city residents that preclude them from competing effectively in the labor market. When they included race and skin tone in their analysis, the result was that darker skinned males were 52% less likely to be employed than their lighter-skinned counterparts.

Today, a variety of sociological and psychological factors converge to give skin color the meaning it has. For example, skin tone influences the attractiveness ratings assigned to Black women, but has much less impact on African American men (Hill, 2002b). Such findings suggest the pervasiveness of Eurocentric standards of beauty, but they make it difficult to sort out which factors may be at work in any given situation. Colorism may arise from, among other things, racist ideology, class-based assumptions, the symbolism of the colors white and black, or from a combination of these things. Knowledge of the complexity of colorism, however, is essential if we are to advance our comprehension of the increasingly diverse society in which we live. This knowledge may help us understand why, for example, Michael Jackson's complexion apparently became lighter as he became more rich and famous, why *Time* magazine chose to darken its cover photo of O.J. Simpson during his criminal trial, why the sale of skin-bleaching products is a multi-million dollar industry within the U.S., and perhaps more importantly, why there is an earnings gap between lighter and darker-skinned African Americans.

What about for other racial and ethnic groups? Colorism with respect to Latinos dates back to the historic conquest of the Americas by European powers. When European soldiers began to establish themselves in the New World, they also took part in creating a new race. Mestizos–the people of the mixed indigenous and European blood–were born to the Americas. European features, including light skin, light-colored eyes and pale hair color, were introduced into the mestizo mix. Eurocentric favoritism toward mestizos of a lighter complexion became imbedded in several Latin American societies. Those mestizos and indigenos with darker features were viewed with less regard and denigrated by the elite and powerful for centuries.

Recent studies of Mexican Americans by Walter Allen and his colleagues (Allen, Telles, and Hunter, 2000), Ed Murguia and Edward Telles (Murguia and Telles, 1996; and Telles and Murguia, 1990), and Carlos Arce and others (Arce, Murguia, and Frisbie, 1987; and Cotton, 1985) have also documented within-group differences. These studies show that darker skinned Mexican Americans with more indigenous Native Indian features as opposed to those of lighter complexion with more European characteristics are disadvantaged. Specifically, Telles and Murguia (1990) found that Mexican Americans of darker complexion with Native American phenotypic characteristics receive significantly lower earnings than those with lighter and more European phenotypes. They also found that (1) the lightest skin toned and most European looking Mexican

Americans achieved more schooling than their darker and more "Indian-looking" counterparts; (2) these relationships persisted even when other correlates of educational attainment were taken into account; and (3) phenotype was especially important for those cohorts educated before World War II, but the findings still held for later cohorts as well. Such results suggest that similar social processes that continue to rank darker-skinned African Americans below those of lighter complexion also structure stratification outcomes for Mexican Americans (Vazquez, Vazquez, Bauman, and Sierra, 1997).

Emergent research suggests that color bias also exists with respect to other people of color. Ronald Hall (1995) explains that among Indian Hindus there exists a prejudice against darker skinned Indians. Light skinned spouses are preferred. For example, light skinned wives are so preferred among Hindu men that those from upper levels within the caste system will marry women from lower caste levels, exchanging her skin tone for his caste position.

In *Caste, Class and Race*, Oliver C. Cox (1948) points out that this has not always been the case. He suggests that "white complexion was not always the most popular and the most admired one among the Hindus" (Cox, 1948:95). Rather, he quotes passages that admire Hindu Divine Incarnations and human heroes who are "dark-cloud-faced," "dusky," and "dark-blue." But he goes on to say that "since the belief in White superiority–that is to say, White nationalism–began to move over the world, no people of color has been able to develop race prejudice independent of Whites" (1948: 346).

So it appears that skin color is one of the ways that people of color have been differentiated. Still, the contemporary reasons for such dif-ferentiation are not altogether clear. Does systematic bias against individuals of darker complexion exist? Is there a systematic bias in favor of individuals who more closely approximate the traditional European standard of beauty? Or is it possible that there is bias against those with light complexions because of the perception that they are not authentic (i.e., legitimate) members of their "racial" groups?

## Skin Tone and Discrimination

When we look to the literature, while some things are clear, we still find many holes. For example, past research shows that skin color has played a major role in shaping both the social and economic structure within the Black community. Several early studies by scholars such as Drake and Cayton and Myrdal documented the importance of light skin tone in obtaining prestige within the Black population. These studies demonstrated that higher status Blacks tended to be of lighter skin tone than lower status Blacks. Moreover, they demonstrated how lighter skinned Blacks were extended more social and economic amenities than the larger group. This translated over successive generations into the Black elite being of fairer complexion.

But these patterns are also historically contingent. For example, as mentioned previously, among Blacks during the 1960s and 1970s, dark skin coloring lost its negative connotations and associated stereotypes. The term "Black" became a unifying description of the entire race rather than a divisive term used in a derogatory manner. Moreover, while many members of the African American community reject the rigidity of such precepts as the one drop rule, especially when they are imposed from outside the African American community, they are still suspicious of those who have any African ancestry but do not identify themselves as Black (Hunter, 2001). As well, some African Americans might view their light-skinned co-ethnics as inferior because of their mixed ancestry. This response may be a defense against the dominant tendency to prize lighter skin–an effort to counter the stigma of not being White enough. It may also be a form of nationalism–a manifestation of the belief that visibly unmixed Blacks are culturally and intellectually superior. In any case, this type of intraracial colorism can also lead to discrimination.

But does skin tone mediate the likelihood of being discriminated against in the 21st century? The evidence with respect to color-differentiated stratification *outcomes* is fairly clear. Empirically, skin color has been a consistent predictor of education, occupation, and income even when taking into consideration social class differences in the respondents' backgrounds. These findings appear to hold true for African Americans, Mexican Americans, and certain Asian groups. But what is the cause of the relationship between skin tone and stratification outcomes? Can such differences be linked to discrimination, per se?

Some researchers doubt the continuation of racial discrimination, much less the existence of colorism. Commentators like Denish D'Souza tend to believe that American society has made great progress in combating discrimination and that the nation is well on its way to becoming a color-blind society (D'Souza, 1995). These arguments are defended by claims that most overt discrimination has been eliminated and that the residual is not worthy of "elimination by state coercion" (Epstein, 1990). If America is as "color blind" across racial lines as these writers believe, then intraracial differences by color should also be minimal.

Prior research, although documenting intraracial *stratification* by skin tone among African Americans and Hispanics, has not explicitly examined the link between skin color and *discrimination.* So, although the preference for lightness and whiteness over darkness is a practice with much history behind it, there is no research to date that documents colorism as a function of discrimination. So, although skin color stratification occurs within communities of color, it is not clear whether discrimination, per se, helps re-create the skin color hierarchy.

It is important not only to document perceptions about colorism, but also to document experiences with discrimination because of colorism. If "gatekeepers" continue to hold color preferences and act in discriminatory bases as a consequence of such preferences, then we can expect skin tone to influence the treatment of people of color even if there has been a declining significance of intraracial colorism among members of these communities.

Is there a relationship between skin tone and reports of job discrimination? Data from the Multi-City Survey of Urban Inequality provide some answers. Figure 1.1 shows that generally, those with dark complexions report higher rates of job discrimination. Among African Americans, the real contrast appears to be between those with dark

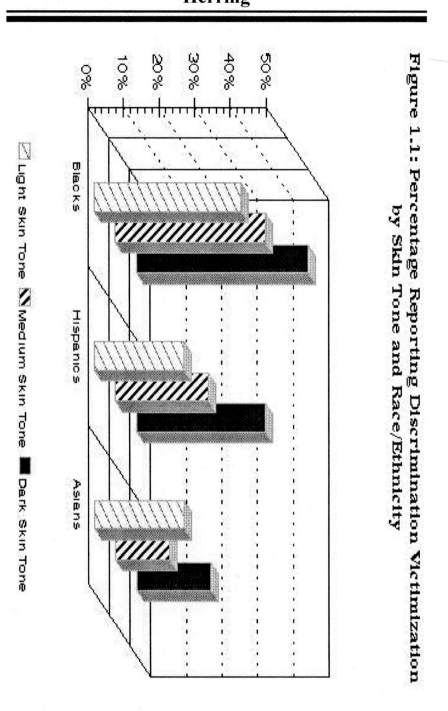

**Figure 1.1: Percentage Reporting Discrimination Victimization by Skin Tone and Race/Ethnicity**

complexions and others. Nearly half (48%) of those with dark complexions report experience with job discrimination. This contrasts with 42% of those with medium and light complexions. These differences, while not massive, are statistically significant. Generally, Hispanic respondents also exhibit the same basic pattern: 36% of those with dark complexions report experiences with job discrimination. This contrasts with 26% of Hispanics with medium and 27% of those with light complexions who report job discrimination.

In multivariate analyses of these data, my colleagues and I (Herring, Carter, and Edwards, 2000; and Herring, Thomas, Durr, and Horton, 1998) found that Asians with dark skin tones are significantly more likely to report that they have experienced job discrimination than are those with medium complexions, and those with light complexions are much less likely to report experience with job discrimination.

So, the results from statistical analysis suggest that skin tone is associated with reports of job discrimination among African Americans, Hispanics, and Asians. We also found, however, that these patterns of discrimination varied by subgroups. For example, among African Americans, the relationship between skin tone and reported discrimination also varied by gender, by marital status, by age, and by city of residence. Nevertheless, in each case, those with dark skin complexions were more likely than those with medium and those with light complexions to say that they experienced job discrimination.

But again, what does the relationship between skin tone and stratification outcomes mean? *Skin Deep: How Race and Complexion Matter in the "Color-Blind" Era* provides answers to this question. In doing so, it addresses issues such as the relationship between skin tone and self-esteem and identity, marital patterns, interracial relationships, and socioeconomic attainment. In addition, it examines intraracial class distinctions and within-race attitudinal differences along the color spectrum. It also examines some implications of colorism for our understanding of race in the 21st century.

In the next chapter, Margaret Hunter explores the advantages and disadvantages of light skin for women of color. Unlike most studies that have only focused on the advantages of light skin tones, she discloses the often hidden disadvantages of light skin, particularly in relation to identity and ethnic group membership. She shows that light skin is associated with Whites, assimilation, and a lack of racial consciousness, and thus, leaves some light skinned people of color to feel unwelcome in their own communities. This is a dilemma of ethnic authenticity that leads to a feeling that one is, or is not, "Black enough" or "Chicano enough." She points out that light skinned African Americans and Mexican Americans are often judged as lacking loyalty and lacking racial consciousness. Because they are seen as not ethnically authentic enough–not truly Black or truly Mexican–they may be ostracized from community organizations and gatherings. Although these disadvantages may not necessarily be economic in nature, the social psychological toll it takes on light skinned African Americans and Mexican Americans can be quite high. Finally, she points out the paradox between light skin as beautiful, and light skin as not ethnically authentic.

Maxine Thompson and Verna Keith examine life at the other end of the color spectrum in Chapter 3. In "Copper Brown and Blue Black: Colorism and Self Evaluation," they suggest that gender–mediated by socioeconomic status variables such as education, occupation, and income–socially constructs the importance of skin color evaluations of self esteem and self efficacy. The effects of skin color on self-esteem (i.e., feeling good about oneself) and self-efficacy (i.e., feelings of competency from undertaking challenges and succeeding at them) are different for women and men. Skin color is an important predictor of perceived efficacy for Black men but not Black women. And skin color predicts self esteem for Black women but not Black men. Their analysis supports much of the anecdotal information from clinical studies of clients in psychotherapy which have found that "dark skinned" Black women have problems with self worth and confidence. Thompson and Keith's findings suggest that this pattern is not limited to experiences of women who are in therapy, but that colorism is part of the everyday reality of Black women more generally.

In Chapter 4, Korie Edwards, Katrina Carter-Tellison, and I use data from the Multi-City Study of Urban Inequality (1992-94) to show that light skin tone is associated with a greater likelihood of being married, and to demonstrate that those with lighter skin tones have higher earning spouses. We show the degree to which the relationships among skin tone, marital status, and spousal earnings vary by gender for African Americans, Latinos, and Asian Americans. Generally, the results suggest that skin tone has, at best, a modest relationship to spousal earnings. The results vary by racial/ethnic and gender subgroups. We conclude that skin tone, although historically important in determining the life chances of people of color, is not strongly related to marital patterns among African Americans. African American women with dark complexions are as likely as other African American women to be married. Additional analysis does, however, suggest that darker African American women get married later than their lighter counterparts. Still, there is at best a modest relationship between spousal earnings and skin tone. In other words, people of color do not appear to bring about color stratification through their mate selections.

The fifth chapter, entitled "Mama Are You Brown?: Multiracial Families and the Color Line," is by Heather M. Dalmage. This chapter shows how the experiences of multiracial family members expose the active link between our views of the social structure–its demography, its laws, its customs, its threats–and our conceptions of what race means. These links, Dalmage argues, highlight the individual and institutional effort expended in maintaining the color line. She maintains that the experiences of multiracial families indicate that dominant racial ideologies in the United States continue to be fed by essentialist understandings of race that maintain a color line to the advantage of Whites, even as those advantages are being masked by color-blind rhetoric. Dalmage provides poignant examples of the many ways the color line is maintained, the discrimination faced by multiracial family members, and some potential pitfalls of the racial thinking currently guiding the collective multiracial response to discrimination.

In "Beyond Black?: The Reflexivity of Appearances in Racial Identification Among Black/White Biracials," Kerry Ann Rockquemore and David L. Brunsma examine the relationship between appearance and racial identity. They explain that racial identity is much more than meets the eye. They show how appearances are related to biracial identity. In doing so, they trace the history and legacy of the "one drop rule." They show just how fluid and context sensitive racial identity can be among biracial individuals. They show how the debate about adding a multiracial category to the 2000 census forced the nation to reflect upon important questions concerning the possibility of multiracialism and the reality of racial categories. At the heart of this controversy was the question of what it means to be multiracial in the U.S., and how individuals with one Black and one White parent understand their racial identities. Rockquemore and Brunsma document how biracial people develop several different racial identities and how these self-understandings are rooted in intriguing social, psychological, and cultural processes. They provide a new and complex foundation for future debates about the efficacy of multiracialism and the future of racial categorization in America.

In Chapter 7, Phillip J. Bowman, Ray Muhammad, and Mosi Ifatunji explore the potential moderating role of a polarizing class structure among African Americans on the relationship between skin tone and race-related attitudes. Their findings revealed dramatic differences by skin tone in class standing. For example, they found that 40 percent of those with light skin tones had incomes much above poverty compared with 31 percent of those with medium skin tone and only 25 percent of those with dark skin tones. In contrast, 37 percent of those with dark skin tones had incomes below the poverty line compared with 23 percent of those with light skin tone. They also found that these class-differentiated patterns of skin tone effects also manifest themselves as differences in racial consciousness (i.e., attitudes about the nature and causes of racial inequalities between Whites and Blacks in the U.S. and related collective action strategies) and racial and ethnic affinity (i.e., feelings of closeness to other Blacks outside the U.S. as well as other racial and ethnic groups within the United States).

Hayward Derrick Horton and Lori Latrice Sykes offer a provocative essay in Chapter 8. They focus on what they term "neo-Mulattoes." They argue that "multiracialism" is best understood in the context of changes in the social structure relative to racism and gender dynamics. Unlike many contemporary analysts of the changing terrain of race, Horton and Sykes argue that much like Mulattoes in bygone eras, the "mixed-race" or biracial population in the 21st century is attempting to put distance between themselves and their Black identity. Thus, they believe the term "neo-Mulatto" is appropriate. What has changed, they claim, is the role of White women in American society. This is evident in White women's dramatic movement into the labor force, and the subsequent increase in their levels of economic independence from White men. Consequently, White women are no longer the primary symbols of the White man's power, and the relationship between White males and White females has changed dramatically. Black men are engaging in unions with White women at a time when these women are no longer the prized possessions of White men. Thus, more often than not, neo-Mulattoes are the products of White mothers and Black fathers. This population has access to "whitespace," but is at the same time not immune from experiences associated with racism. So, while neo-Mulattoes may experience racism in more subtle forms, the experiences of this population may forecast what is to come for the general Black population.

In Chapter 9, Kimberly Ebert argues that, although America is an extremely race-conscious society, "color-blind" ideology has emerged as the dominant ideology in the post-civil rights era. Persistent racial inequalities confirm that race remains extremely significant in the distribution of life chances. She suggests that color blindness is illogical in a society where socioeconomic stratification is and has historically been based on ascribed status. But by embracing such beliefs, Whites are able to deny to themselves that their everyday lives are based on the oppression of other races. They are able to justify housing, schooling, and work preferences through the use of stereotypes without having to admit the racial nature of these stereotypes. Moreover, because these images are based in the structure and are supported and re-created by the media, politicians, and other institutions, the stereotypes become hegemonic and accepted even by oppressed social groups who act upon these stereotypes.

In "Race South of the Equator," Vânia Penha-Lopes examines Wilson's arguments about the relative importance of race and class. Wilson argues that social class becomes paramount for the status of African Americans after affirmative action policies are implemented; i.e., after Blacks can take advantage of educational opportunities and gain access to better-paying jobs. Drawing parallels between the case of the United States and Brazil, Penha-Lopes examines aspects of Wilson's thesis in the Brazilian context. She provides an overview of the myth of racial democracy and Brazil's fluid racial classification. She then reviews Wilson's thesis, drawing comparisons with the Brazilian situation. Next, using social indicators such as educational attainment, income, unemployment rates, and other social indicators based on data from the 2000 Brazilian Census and other sources, she shows that race and color continue to seriously affect life chances in Brazil, which points to the continuing necessity for governmental intervention in Brazil.

In the final chapter, Eduardo Bonilla-Silva forecasts the future of race in 21st century America. In "From Biracial to Tri-Racial: The Emergence of a New Racial Stratification System in the United States," Bonilla-Silva argues that race relations in the United States are steadily becoming "tri-racial," much like they are in Latin America, South Africa, and other regions of the world. Specifically, he argues that the U.S. is developing a tri-racial system with "Whites" at the top, an intermediary group of "honorary Whites"–similar to the coloreds in South Africa during formal apartheid, and a nonwhite group or the "collective Black" at the bottom. The "White" group will include "traditional" Whites, new "White" immigrants and, in the near future, assimilated White Latinos and other groups. The intermediate racial group or "honorary Whites" will be comprised of most White middle class Latinos (e.g., most Cubans and segments of the Mexican and Puerto Rican communities), Japanese Americans, Korean Americans, Asian Indians, Chinese Americans, and possibly Arab Americans. Finally, the "collective Black" will include Blacks, dark-skinned Latinos, Vietnamese, Cambodians, Laotians, and possibly Filipinos. As "honorary Whites" grow in size and social importance, they are likely to buffer racial conflict–or derail it–as intermediate groups do in many Latin American countries. The ideology of "color-blind" racism will become even more salient among Whites and honorary Whites and will also affect members of the collective Black. He argues that if the state decides to stop gathering racial statistics–as proponents of color-blind ideology are calling for–the struggle to document the impact of race in a variety of social venues will become monumental. Nevertheless, the deep history of Black-White divisions and disparities in the United States will not dissipate but will be masked. Thus, the new racial stratification system will be more effective in maintaining "White supremacy."

*Skin Deep* is a brief, nontechnical volume that brings clarity and insight to the role of race and skin complexion in the so-called color-blind era. Its contributors include some of the leading scholars who have written about racial identity and colorism. But, we have tried to write it in a way so that it is as jargon-free as possible. If you are a member of the educated and informed public who wants more insight into the complexities and controversies surrounding race, multiracialism, and color in an era that purports that such things no longer matter, you have found the right book.

### Endnote

[1] It should also be noted that skin color is correlated with other phenotypic features such as eye color, hair texture, broadness of nose, and fullness of lips (Russell, Wilson, and Hall, 1992). Along with light skin tone, blue and green eyes, European shaped noses, and straight as opposed to "kinky" hair are all accorded

higher status both within and beyond the African American community (Thompson and Keith, 2000). "Colorism" incorporates preference for both light skin as well as these other attendant features. Hair, eye color and facial features function along with color in complex ways to shape opportunities, norms regarding attractiveness, self-concept, and overall body image (Thompson and Keith, 2000). Yet, it is skin tone that has received the most attention in research, as it is the most visible physical feature and is also the feature that is most enduring and difficult to change (Russell, Wilson, and Hall, 1992)

## References

Allen, Walter; Edward Telles, and Margaret Hunter. 2000. "Skin Color, Income and Education: A Comparison of African Americans and Mexican Americans." *National Journal of Sociology* 12: 129-180.

Arce, Carlos H., Edward Murguia, and W. Parker Frisbie. 1987. "Phenotype and Life Chances Among Chicanos." *Hispanic Journal of Behavioral Sciences* 9: 19-32.

Blackwell, James E. 1991. *The Black Community: Diversity and Unity.* New York: HarperCollins.

Bonilla-Silva, Eduardo. 2001. *White Supremacy and Racism in the Post-Civil Rights Era.* Boulder, CO: Lynne Rienner Publishers.

Cotton, Jeremiah. 1985. "More on the Cost of Being a Black or Mexican American Male Worker". *Social Science Quarterly* 66: 867-885.

Cox, Oliver C. 1948. Caste, Class, and Race: A Study in Social Dynamics. New York and London: Modern Reader Paperbacks.

Drake, St. Clair and Horace Cayton. 1945. *Black Metropolis.* New York: Harcourt Brace.

Du Bois, W. E. Burghart. 1903. "The Talented Tenth." Chapter 2 of *The Negro Problem*. New York: James Pott and Company.

Edwards, Ozzie L. 1972. "Skin Color as a Variable in Racial Attitudes of Black Urbanites." *Journal of Black Studies* 3: 473-483.

Epstein, Richard. 1990. "The Paradox of Civil Rights." *Yale Law and Policy Review* 8:299-319.

Frazier, E. Franklin. 1966. *The Negro Family in the United States.*

Chicago: University of Chicago Press.

Frazier, E. Franklin. 1957. *The Black Bourgeoisie*. New York: Free Press.

Freeman, Howard E., J. Michael Ross, David Armor, and Thomas F. Pettigrew. 1966. "Color Gradations and Attitudes Among Middle-Income Negroes." *American Sociological Review* 31: 365-374.

Hall, Ronald, 1995. "The Bleaching Syndrome African Americans' Response to Cultural Domination vis-à-vis Skin Color." *Journal of Black Studies* 26:172-184.

Herring, Cedric, Korie Edwards, and Katrina Carter. 2000. "Not by the Color of Their Skins: Skin Tone Variations and Discrimination Against People of Color." Paper presented at the annual meeting of the Association of Black Sociologists in Washington, DC.

Herring, Cedric, Melvin Thomas, Marlese Durr, and Hayward Derrick Horton. 1998. "Does Race Matter?: The Determinants and Consequences of Self-Reports of Discrimination Victimization." *Race & Society* 1:109-123.

Hill, Mark E. 2002a. "Race of the Interviewer and Perception of Skin Color: Evidence from the Multi-City Study of Urban Inequality." *American Sociological Review* 67: 99-108.

Hill, Mark E. 2002b. "Skin Color and the Perception of Attractiveness Among African Americans: Does Gender Make a Difference? " *Social Psychology Quarterly* 65: 77-91.

Hill, Mark E. 2000. "Color Differences in the Socioeconomic Status of African American Men: Results of a Longitudinal Study." *Social Forces* 78:1437-1460.

Hughes, Michael and Bradley Hertel, 1990. "The Significance of Color Remains: A Study of Life Chances, Mate Selection, and Ethnic Consciousness Among Black Americans." *Social Forces* 69:1105-1120.

Hunter, Margaret L. 1998. "Colorstruck: Skin Color Stratification in the Lives of African American Women." *Sociological Inquiry* 68:517-535.

Johnson, James H., Elisa Jayne Bienenstock, and Jennifer A. Stoloff. 1995. "An Empirical Test of The Cultural Capital Hypothesis." The Review of Black Political Economy 23: 7-27.

Keith, Verna M. and Cedric Herring. 1991. "Skin Tone and Stratification in the Black Community." *American Journal of Sociology* 97:760-778.

Landry, Bart. 1987. *The New Black Middle Class.* Berkeley and Los Angeles: University of California Press.

Murguia, Edward. and Edward E. Telles. 1996. "Phenotype and Schooling among Mexican Americans." *Sociology of Education* 69: 276-289.

Myrdal, Gunnar. 1944. *An American Dilemma: The Negro Problem and Modern Democracy* New York: Harper and Row.

Ransford, Edward H. 1970. "Skin Color, and Life Chances, and Anti-White Attitudes." *Social Problems* 18: 164-178.

Russell, Kathy, Midge Wilson, and Ronald Hall. 1992. *The Color Complex: The Politics of Skin Color Among African Americans.* New York: Harcourt Brace Jovanovich.

Telles, Edward E. and Edward Murguia. 1990. "Phenotypic Discrimination and Income Differences among Mexican Americans." *Social Science Quarterly* 71: 682-696.

Thompson, Maxine S. and Verna M. Keith. 2000. "The Blacker the Berry: Gender, Skin Tone, Self-Esteem, and Self-Efficacy." Unpublished Manuscript.

Udry, J. Richard, Karl E. Bauman and Charles Case, 1971. "Skin Color, Status and Mate Selection." *American Journal of Sociology* 76: 722-733

Vazquez, Luis A., Enedina Garcia-Vazquez, and Arturo S. Sierra. 1997. "Skin Color, Acculturation, and Community Interest Among Mexican American Students: A Research Note." *Hispanic Journal of Behavioral Sciences* 19: 377-386.

# Chapter 2

# *Light, Bright, and Almost White*
## *The Advantages and Disadvantages of Light Skin*

**Margaret Hunter**
Loyola Marymount University

Skin color politics have long plagued minority communities in the United States. Lighter skinned African Americans earn more money and complete more years of education than do darker skinned African Americans (Hughes and Hertel, 1990; Keith and Herring, 1991) and lighter skinned Mexican Americans maintain similar advantages over darker skinned Mexican Americans (Allen, Telles, and Hunter, 2000; Arce, Murguia, and Frisbie, 1987; Telles and Murguia, 1990). The long history of skin color stratification for both of these groups has its roots in their colonization and enslavement by Europeans, but it is also maintained through internalized racism in each community (Barerra, 1979; Fanon, 1967). Based on a growing body of literature on skin color discrimination, this chapter explores both the advantages and disadvantages of light skin color for Mexican Americans and African Americans.

Discussions of skin color hierarchies have frequently been swept under the rug and avoided by public speakers and scholars for years. Considered by many to be "airing dirty laundry," public conversations about inequality and skin tone were glossed over in favor of discussing racism and discrimination against African Americans and Mexican Americans in general. However, over the past twenty-five years, scholars and public intellectuals have developed a significant body of literature that investigates the specificities of skin tone stratification in communities of color. From movies such as *School Daze* by Spike Lee, a commentary on skin tone and class in a Black college setting, to books such as *The Color Complex*, a comprehensive journalistic discussion of colorism in the Black community, skin color stratification has moved from "dirty laundry" to "dinner table conversation."

This chapter describes some of the advantages and disadvantages of light skin for women of color. Most studies to date have focused on the advantages of light skin tones including higher incomes, more years of education, and higher status occupations. In this chapter I will describe how light skin is a benefit in the dating and marriage market for women because light skin is described as more "beautiful" both inside and outside of the African American and Mexican American communities.

Beauty has recently become an object of sociological study, reflecting the growing trend of the theorization of everyday life from the perspective of women (Smith, 1987). Women are often evaluated by their physical appearance and are measured against culturally constructed norms of beauty (Baker, 1984; Banner, 1983; Ferguson, 1985; Freedman, 1986; Lakoff and Scherr, 1984; Wolf, 1991). Freedman describes how important physical appearance can be in women's lives, "because beauty is asymmetrically assigned to the feminine role, women are defined as much by their looks as by their deeds" (1986:1). In a sexist society such as the United States, women's bodies serve as an indication of their worth, as opposed to their minds or actions. Because beauty is a social construction, it is informed by other societal status characteristics including race. This helps explain why, in the U.S., where White racism still operates, light skin is defined as more beautiful and more desirable than dark skin, particularly in women.

In addition to examining the privileges of light skin, this chapter will also unearth the often hidden disadvantages of light skin, particularly in relation to identity and ethnic group membership. I will demonstrate that light skin is associated with Whites, assimilation, and a lack of racial consciousness, thus leaving some light skinned people to feel unwelcome in their own communities. This is a dilemma of ethnic authenticity. The term "ethnic authenticity" connotes the idea of "legitimate membership" in an ethnic minority community. Ethnic authenticity is often described as a feeling that one is, or is not, "Black enough" or "Chicano enough." Light skin color serves as a liability in creating a sense of ethnic authenticity. Light skinned people from both communities report feeling like outsiders, unaccepted, or even pushed out of their own communities and community organizations based on skin tone (Hunter, 1999). These characterizations of light skinned people may not be completely far-fetched, however. Many researchers report lower levels of race-consciousness, more conservative political attitudes, and less ethnic group involvement among lighter skinned African Americans and Mexican Americans when compared to their darker counterparts (Hughes and Hertel, 1990; Hall, 1994).

Why study these two minority populations? The African American and Mexican American communities are the basis for this chapter for two reasons. First, they are currently the two largest racial-ethnic groups in the U.S. and their experiences with skin color politics should shed light on how these social processes operate for other racial minority groups. Second, both groups have a history of colonial domination by Europeans: Africans were stolen from Africa, brought to the Americas and enslaved, and Mexicans were colonized by Spain and later dominated by the U.S. Their histories of European domination provide both groups with a cultural backdrop for the privileging of white skin. That is, both groups had interactions with Whites which compelled the creation of racist ideologies that, in turn, devalued Black and Mexican identities and valorized White identities. The comparative nature of this analysis helps shed light on the intricacies of skin tone hierarchies, and shows how these hierarchies manifest differently in each community.

Racism and colorism are both central to understanding skin color stratification. Colorism, a derivative of White racism, is the process of differentially allocating resources and value among people of the same racial-ethnic group according to skin tone. Individuals and institutions inside and outside of the Mexican American and African American communities perpetuate colorism. That means that Whites, as well as people of color, act in ways that maintain white and light skin privilege, and continue to devalue dark skin. Although colorism has been widely documented in the African American community, it continues to be a perplexing phenomenon in the Mexican American community that maintains the ideology of *mestizaje*–a belief system that values the mixture of races and cultures and creates an inclusive and hybrid national Mexican identity (Vasconcelos, 1925; Knight, 1990). Although Mexico is certainly not free of racial inequalities, colorism is inconsistent with the belief in *mestizaje*. Colorism focuses on status differences tied to races: indigenous groups, Africans, and Europeans, while *mestizaje* focuses on the idealized universal hybrid and equality. This seeming paradox may be the result of a culture that maintains vestiges of its racial order from Spanish colonization and American imperialism. Although many Mexican Americans are no longer an active part of contemporary Mexican society, the cultural traditions that Mexican Americans brought with them to the U.S. include ideas about race and status.

## Historical Context for Skin Color Stratification

No discussion of skin color hierarchies is complete without an understanding of the historical context for this stratification. Both African Americans and Mexican Americans were dominated by European colonists and explorers. The Europeans created racist ideologies that served to justify the colonial and slave trade projects as rational and morally defensible actions. In order to accomplish this, the ideologies relied on constructions of the Other that diminished the humanity of each colonized group.

Throughout slavery in the U.S., Whites used color differences among Blacks as a "divide and conquer" strategy to prevent revolts. Whites encouraged distrust and rancor among the enslaved Blacks on their plantations by assigning different work tasks by color: lighter skinned Blacks were often assigned to chores in the slave owner's home and darker skinned Blacks were often assigned to the fields, thought to be the harder and more unpleasant work. However, scholars later reported that working in the slave owner's home was often dangerous, alienating and more highly monitored than was fieldwork, making it not necessarily a better option. In addition to light skin privilege on the plantation, owners and overseers sometimes gave racially mixed children special status because they were usually the offspring of the slave owner. Opportunities for manumission, less violent treatment by overseers, less stressful work tasks, limited access to reading and writing skills, and opportunities for skilled labor are all examples of the privileges that some lighter skinned Black children might have received (Billingsley, 1968; Frazier, 1951; Stevenson, 1996). This practice perpetuated the color-caste system on the plantation.

Contemporary manifestations of skin color hierarchies in the Black community were established during slavery. The aesthetic notion that dark skin represents savagery, irrationality, ugliness, and inferiority was established as a justification for the brutal slave system and as a response to the abolitionists who demanded Black freedom. On the opposite side of the same coin, white skin, and thus whiteness itself, was defined by the opposite traits: civility, rationality, beauty, and superiority (Memmi, 1965; Fanon, 1967; Jordan, 1968; Ernst, 1980; Drake, 1987). These meanings were infused into actual body types to create the systems of racism and colorism still with us today.

> Racist ideology usually involves an aesthetic appraisal of physical features, a mythology about traits of mind and personality correlated with physical features, and an almost mystical belief in the power of 'blood' to elevate or to taint (Drake, 1987:23).

In this quote Drake explains the historical context for the Rule of

Hypodescent (the one-drop rule) that defined every person with any Black ancestry as Black. The Rule of Hypodescent helped perpetuate the myth of White racial purity and created a pathological fear of Black "blood" and miscegenation.

The African American community has always reflected a wide spectrum of colors, in part due to miscegenation, and a wide variety of class positions. There was a small, but influential community of African Americans, primarily from the North who were never enslaved. This group, along with a growing number of freed Blacks in the South created a small cadre of African Americans who would later serve the community as business and civic leaders. The light skinned leadership that began to emerge was, however, interpreted by many Whites as confirmation that White blood and lineage were superior to Black. Many Whites saw the notable success of mixed race and light skinned people as evidence that only those with "White blood" had the capacity to lead. Reuter's (1918) (in)famous work entitled, *The Mulatto in the United States,* is an example of that type of racist thinking. He asserted that mixed race African Americans emerged as leaders of the Black community because of their genetic likeness to Whites instead of because of increased opportunities available to them as light skinned people. This kind of genetic thinking explains why light skin is associated with superior abilities, particularly intellectual ones.

Skin color stratification has an equally long history for Mexican Americans. The historical context of skin color differentiation and stratification began with the Spanish colonization of Mexico. Spain was involved in the creation of a colonial, racist ideology that justified its movement into the Americas as a noble cause to spread Catholicism and to civilize. "New Spain" was a hierarchical, multi-ethnic society that included the Spanish, indigenous peoples, and Africans. Through typical colonial actions, the Spanish stole land, demolished governments, repressed religions, and continuously suppressed the indigenous peoples. As was true for most European colonizers, the Spanish justified their pillaging of the land and people with an ideology that portrayed themselves as civilized Christians on a mission to redeem the savage and heathen dark Other (Almaguer, 1994).

Similarities to the previous discussion of the racialization of Africans in the U.S. are obvious. However, one of the major differences in the development of the two societies was the level of intermarriage and mixture of the ethnic/racial groups. During slavery, any consensual relationships between Blacks and Whites were illegal, but many Black women were victims of rape and sexual abuse by White men. In New Spain, interracial relationships were tolerated, but like the situation for Black women, many indigenous women were victimized in violent relationships with White men. There were many "reports of atrocities committed against the native populations, especially against the Indian women" (Blea, 1992:43). Rape was a common form of Spanish social control in New Spain, and indigenous women were the most common victims (Blea, 1992; Castañeda, 1993). These consensual and violent practices resulted in a racially mixed population like no other, and the "mestizo" was born.

Eventually, the Spanish were overthrown, and in 1821, Mexico won the revolution and re-established itself as an independent nation. Mexico began to re-create its own national identity in a historical period dominated by the discourse of European scientific racism. Scientific racism purported that races were biological and hierarchical, and that Europeans were the superior race above all darker races (Gossett, 1963; Kevles, 1985). Mexico wanted to be considered a country of leadership and intelligence, but it also had many brown skinned peoples–mestizos–in its citizenry. Jose Vasconcelos, a famous Mexican philosopher, developed the theory of la raza cosmica–the cosmic race (Vasconcelos, 1925). "The social genius of *La Raza* as Vasconcelos envisioned it was in the model (the attitude) that it embraces the four major races of the world... *La Raza's* contribution was its concept of *mestizaje*. It was an inclusive model of social-racial integration" (Guerrero, 1987, p.123). Because the mestizo was a hybrid,

Vasconcelos believed it to be a superior race that would develop to exceed the limits of all other races including the White Europeans.

Meanwhile, the U.S., true to its Puritan ideology of Manifest Destiny, was waiting for the right opportunity to increase its land mass and take over part of Mexico. "European Americans saw it as their providential mission to settle the entire North American continent with a homogenous White population, bringing with them their superior political institutions, notions of progress and democracy, and economic system" (Almaguer, 1994:32). The idea of Manifest Destiny, as articulated through White racism, rests on the assumption of White superiority over all other peoples of color, including Mexicans (Acuña, 1988).

After the takeover, White Americans debated the incorporation of Mexicans into the newly expanded United States. Although Whites recognized Mexican people as "racially different" they saw enough similarity with them to consider maintaining economic and social relation-ships. "The Mexicans' mixed European ancestry, romance language, Catholic religious practices, and familiar political-economic institutions elevated them above all other cultural groups in the White man's eyes" (Almaguer, 1994:8).

Despite the similarities with other European cultures, the Mexican population in the southwest was split between a light skinned, monied, ranchero class and a darker skinned, poorer class of workers. This color and class distinction complicated the debate over the race and citizenship of Mexicans. Anglos were more willing to grant citizenship to light skinned wealthy, land-owning Mexican people than they were the dark skinned disadvantaged class. The debate over the racial status of Mexican Americans continued throughout the twentieth century. The various legal cases dealing with the racial identity of Mexican Americans have been extremely inconsistent. Anglo judges declared Mexicans as Whites when it disabled them from demanding minority rights and the same judges would declare them non-White when it restricted their access to rights reserved for Whites only (Martinez, 1997). The ambiguous history of

Mexican Americans and whiteness is still debated today and light skin privilege is a legacy of that history.

### The Advantages of Light Skin: Beauty and the Marriage Market

Scholars have widely demonstrated that light skin tone for African Americans and Mexican Americans is correlated with higher incomes, higher levels of educational attainment, more integrated housing options, more occupational choices, higher levels of self esteem, and fewer mental health problems (Allen, Telles, and Hunter, 2000; Arce, Murguia, and Frisbie, 1987; Codina and Montalvo, 1994; Edwards, 1959; Edwards, 1973; Hughes and Hertel, 1990; Hunter, 1998; Keith and Herring, 1991; Murguia and Telles, 1996; Relethford et al., 1983; Udry, Baumann, and Chase, 1971). Light skin provides more opportunities and greater access to resources in almost all of the major categories of life chances. One under-explored area of privilege is the dating/marriage market. How does skin color affect a woman's status in the marriage market? Unsurprisingly, light skinned African American women have a higher status in the marriage market and are more likely to marry high status men than are darker skinned women with the same educational credentials (Hunter, 1998). How does skin color get translated into status? Is it through the racially informed notion of beauty?

Beauty is not objective, nor is it neutral. However, beauty is also not in the eye of the beholder, as the common saying goes. Beauty is ideological and serves to support White supremacy and male dominance. In the U.S. beauty is usually defined, in part, by white or light skin and Western-European features (Lakoff and Scherr, 1984; Wolf, 1991; Zavella, 1997). "There is a surprisingly high level of agreement about who is beautiful and who is not" (Freedman, 1986:6). Although the overt racial standards of beauty are often unspoken, people across ethnic groups and class levels tend to agree about who possesses beauty and who does not. This upsets the old adage that beauty is in the eye of the beholder, and instead supports the notion that beauty is only in the eye of those beholding

Whites. Although race does not exclusively define beauty, most women who are labeled as beautiful are White; few women of color don that label unless they physically emulate Whites with European facial features, long light hair, or light skin.

Why does beauty matter? Beauty is a crucial resource for women because it operates as a form of social capital. It is transformable into other types of capital, through access to high status occupations, higher educational attainment, and even higher incomes. Wolf (1991) argues that by the 1980s, when women had made significant inroads into corporations and management positions, beauty became as important as intellectual qualifications for employment. "Beauty was no longer just a symbolic form of currency; it literally *became* money" (Wolf, 1991:21).

Beauty as capital operates similarly to Harris's (1995) conception of "whiteness as property." In discussing the phenomenon of racially "passing" she describes the, "valorization of whiteness as treasured property in a society structured on racial caste... the set of assumptions, privileges, and benefits that accompany the status of being White have become a valuable asset - one that Whites sought to protect and those who passed sought to attain, by fraud if necessary." (Harris, 1995: 277). Harris succinctly illustrates the importance of seeing whiteness as property, as a form of capital, by using terms such as "value" and "asset" when describing it. I suggest that beauty operates as a form of capital much in the way that whiteness does.

In this economic context women's bodies are manipulable commodities objectified for male consumption. More specifically, the entire beauty industry is built on the foundational principle that women will alter their bodies, through make-up, hair coloring, colored contact lenses, body hair removal, and plastic surgery to increase their amount of beauty, or capital (Chorlton, 1988). The racial implications are obvious. Women of color, like White women, spend millions of dollars every year on beauty products. However, unlike White women's products, many products for women of color are geared toward whitening as a part of the beautifying process. Hair straighteners, light colored contacts, and even some skin creams and bleaches all help women of color become more beautiful by becoming more White. Cosmetic surgery is also a tool used by many to whiten and beautify. The industry itself reports that procedures to alter typically "ethnic" characteristics in order to make them more "mainstream" (read White) are on the rise (Davis, 1995).

Similar messages about color and status are prevalent in the Mexican American community. Ruiz's study of advertising campaigns reveals that the beauty industry marketed skin bleaching creams to Mexican American women as early as the 1940s. Major cosmetic companies told Mexican American women, "Those with lighter, more healthy skin tones will become much more successful in business, love, and society" (Ruiz, 1998: 57). Although messages like this might seem capricious, there was certainly a kernel of truth in the idea that those with lighter skin tones received privileges in education, employment, and even in choosing a marital partner. "The popularity of bleaching creams offers a poignant testament to color consciousness in Mexican communities, a historical consciousness accentuated by Americanization through education and popular culture" (Ruiz, 1998:57).

Unfortunately, color consciousness did not disappear after the "Black is beautiful" and "Brown power" sentiments of the civil rights movements of the 1960s and 70s. In 1984, Lakoff and Scherr, found that Mexican American women still reported strong community and family norms valuing white or light skin. One interviewee said, "'I was called 'indita' or 'negrita'... I was ugly, no doubt about that... so ugly and so dark that I wasn't to go out in the sun" (Lakoff and Scherr, 1984:258). This quotation illustrates the conflation of dark skin and "ugliness" that is so common in mainstream discourse.

In their study of Black women's attitudes about race and body image, Bond and Cash (1992) found that many women expressed satisfaction with their skin colors, but those who did wish to change their skin colors, wished to be lighter. These findings reveal that the desire for light or white skin is not all-consuming and that many women feel good about the colors that they are. However, Bond and Cash also found that some women in their study described themselves as lighter in skin color than the interviewers did. This subtle finding highlights the fact that being "light skinned" is still a socially desirable identity for many women of color.

Leeds' (1994) study of young Black women and their beauty practices revealed the same ambiguity found in Bond and Cash's research. Young women shared their values in a Black aesthetic and acknowledged that "White" standards of beauty were unfair to Black women. Yet, at the same time, these young women also participated in practices and expressed attitudes that valued mainstream definitions of beauty.

These students frequently stated that there was a beauty standard that valued lighter skin and longer and straighter hair. They distanced themselves from that standard and articulated a more inclusive idea of beauty. Yet their own taunts about skin color and hair length indicate that they, to some degree, accept a Eurocentric ideal. (Leeds, 1994:6)

When asked if they would change their appearance, several of the young women reported wanting longer hair, lighter skin, or lighter eyes. Their responses reflect the persistent quest for White-like traits prevalent in many communities of color. I think that Leeds' analysis of the young women's ambivalence toward beauty and race reflects a similar ambivalence in the larger population. Many African American and Mexican American women negotiate between buying into traditional Eurocentric ideals of beauty and racial-ethnic pride. Many women (and men) are able to see beauty in traditionally Black identities or Mexican identities including dark skin color, but they may also never fully release the power of the White beauty standards. In fact, one may wonder if it is even possible, while constantly bombarded with media images of White beauty, to ever fully embrace an alternative beauty aesthetic.

Beauty ideals are informed by White privilege, but how does that translate into real life benefits or disadvantages for people of color?

Physical descriptions of beauty are still linked to beliefs about competence and intelligence. Unfortunately, many Americans are still debating racial differences in intelligence and ability–just look to Herrnstein and Murray's (1994) account of genetic racial differences in intelligence. In a climate where racial differences in intelligence are still being debated to the detriment of children of color, it is only a small step to see how ideas about phenotype can influence teachers' perceptions of who the smart kids and the not-so-smart kids are. Ideas about who "looks smart" and who does not are heavily influenced by race, gender, and skin color. Individuals who have skin colors and facial features associated with Whites, and thus associated with rationality and civility, are more likely to be perceived as intelligent, competent, trustworthy, and friendly than individuals with skin colors and features more closely resembling another ethnic group. The conceptual leap from phenotype to ability accounts for much of the correlation between skin color and income, occupation, and educational attainment.

In addition to the privileges of added wealth and education that light skin accrues, light skin tone also provides an advantage for women in the marriage market. This kind of aesthetic "commodifies women by measuring various quantities of beauty that women broker in the marital marketplace" (Collins, 1991:88). Beauty is centrally important then, not simply to self-esteem or peer group acceptance, but beauty actually has a relationship to the types of economic capital available to women of color. In this way, beauty matters significantly in affecting a woman's life chances. Lighter skinned Black women have an advantage in the marriage marketplace over darker skinned women with similar backgrounds. The "traditional status advantage of light skinned [African American] women holds for all cohorts, with little indication of change" (Udry, Baumann, and Chase, 1971:722). Advantage in choosing a mate is no small matter. Advantages in the marriage market often translate into real material advantages where light skinned women have access to higher status spouses with more education and presumably higher incomes (Hunter, 1998).

Research on Mexican American women has shown that despite popular understandings of light skin privileges, light skin does not significantly affect Mexican American women's spouses' status (Hunter, 2002).

Light skin color does not provide the same level of consistent advantage for men in the marriage market as it does for women. In fact, for Black men, light skin has a much less pronounced effect on mate selection. Light skinned men are not more likely to have higher status wives than are dark skinned men when socioeconomic status is controlled (Udry, Baumann, and Chase, 1971). Mexican American men's spousal status has not yet been researched, but it is likely that no relationship exists between color and spousal status since there is also no relationship between those two variables for Mexican American women. Future research should investigate this possibility.

**The Disadvantages of Light Skin: Ethnic Identity and Legitimacy**

Despite the many advantages of light skin, there is also one notable disadvantage: the perception of ethnic legitimacy. Skin color has long been tied to notions of "race purity," and in more recent contexts, has been associated with group membership and "ethnic legitimacy." In both the Mexican American and African American communities, dark skin is usually perceived to be more ethnically authentic than light. Women and men with dark skin are more likely to be seen and accepted as legitimate members of their ethnic groups, are less likely to have their group loyalty questioned, are more likely to be perceived as "racially-conscious," and are less likely to be accused of trying to assimilate or "wanting to be White." Ethnic authenticity or ethnic legitimacy are primarily in-group issues where members of the African American or Mexican American communities are generally accepted by others and viewed as legitimate members of their communities or not. Many light skinned members of these groups, especially if they are multiracial, report feeling excluded from their ethnic groups and viewed as not "Black enough" or not "Chicano enough" (Hunter, 1999).

Perceptions of light skinned people as less connected with or loyal to the Black and Mexican American communities is not necessarily based in myth. Hughes and Hertel (1990) found that light skinned African Americans reported less Black pride, more openness toward racial integration, and less concern with racial discrimination than dark skinned Blacks. Skin tone is associated with both internal and external evaluations of racial identity. Psychologists have found that physical appearance is a significant predictor of racial identity for biracial people. Biracial people are likely to identify with the ethnic group they most closely resemble. Because many lighter skinned people are seen as "closer to White" at least phenotypically, and sometimes politically, many members of racial minority communities believe that light skinned people are less ethnically authentic, and therefore less worthy of in-group validation.

Despite the fact that light skin tone is associated with less racial consciousness for Blacks and Mexican Americans, there is also a historical precedent for the community leaders to be very light skinned. F. James Davis writes, "Many of the nation's black leaders have been of predominantly White ancestry" (1991:6). He goes on to describe people such as Robert Purvis, W.E.B. Du Bois, and Walter White, as examples of influential Black leaders for civil rights who were all light skinned African Americans (Davis, 1991). This seeming contradiction highlights the paradoxical role that skin color plays in this country. On the one hand, light skin affords more privileges and access to resources for people of color that could hasten assimilation. On the other hand, light skin color affords privileges and status that have been used to call attention to the plight of African Americans and Mexican Americans and to work against the persistent problem of American racism.

A similar paradox is at work in the Mexican American community. For Mexican Americans ethnic authenticity is closely tied to Mexican cultural practices, especially the use of the Spanish language. Many Mexican Americans, though not all, are relatively recent immigrants to the U.S. having been here for two to three generations. Consequently, concerns about Anglo assimilation are strong within a community trying to preserve its homeland culture, while also trying to be upwardly mobile in an Anglo controlled society. Many believe that ethnic authenticity is defined by dark skin, indigenous features, and Spanish language use. For Mexican Americans, skin color and Spanish language use interact to create an ideal of ethnic legitimacy in the community (Hunter, 1999). Much like African Americans, Mexican Americans believe that lighter skinned people are less likely to be supporters of Chicano political movements, of Spanish language maintenance, and are more likely to be assimilated into Anglo culture. These beliefs are consistent with much of the research on this topic that links light skin color to less salient ethnic identities, less radicalism, and less interest in racial politics (Hall, 1994).

Despite the common beliefs that many hold about light skinned people and their lack of racial consciousness, many light skinned and biracial African Americans and Mexican Americans report being very proud of their ethnic group and having high levels of political activism and racial consciousness. There is a constant tension in the literature between the survey research that supports the contention that lighter skin results in less salient ethnic identities, and the majority of influential leaders in both communities having been light skinned people.

**Conclusions**

Skin color hierarchies have a long history in the United States and are rooted in the histories of slavery and colonialism. In the African American and Mexican American communities, light skin is privileged in that it provides access to higher incomes, better jobs, more education, more housing, higher status spouses, and better mental health. Of all these privileges, skin color and its relationship to definitions of beauty is one of the least explored. Beauty, defined in part by light skin, is a valuable resource for women who are often judged and evaluated by the physical appearance of their bodies rather than their abilities. Because of that reality, light skin operates as a form of social capital, through beauty, that provides

African American and Mexican American women access to additional resources out of reach of their darker sisters.

Alongside the clear advantages of light skin, there is one glaring disadvantage. Light skinned members of racial minority communities are less likely to be seen as legitimate members of those groups, and are often judged as lacking loyalty and lacking racial consciousness. Because they are seen as not ethnically authentic enough–not truly Black or truly Mexican–they may be ostracized from community organizations and gatherings. Although this disadvantage may not necessarily be economic in nature, the social psychological toll it takes on light skinned African Americans and Mexican Americans has yet to be determined.

One of the most interesting aspects of skin color stratification is the paradox between light skin as beautiful, and light skin as not ethnically authentic. This points to the fact that the African American and Mexican American communities most highly revere an aesthetic that least resembles most members of those communities. The "most beautiful" African Americans and Mexican Americans are those who look least like most African American and Mexican American people. The female celebrities and other icons of beauty are often light skinned people with European features. There is a paradox of color where on one hand, we name beauty only in European looking people, and on the other hand we tell light skinned people they are not ethnic enough. This may best be explained by the simultaneous processes of ethnic pride and racism. Ethnic pride in each community values people who most resemble that community's ancestors. Racism, on the other hand, devalues those people and values those who look most White. The interplay of these social processes is an area for future theorization and research.

Some attempts to counter Eurocentric beauty standards have simply inverted those standards to elevate all things African or Indian, and to denigrate all things European. As Leeds (1994) points out, this too is a short-sighted goal.

The establishment of an Afrocentric [or Chicano-centric] beauty standard was a limited and problematic goal. It was limited because changing the definition of beauty would do little to restructure institutional racism. It was problematic because even a redefinition of beauty reinforced the exaggerated importance of beauty for women, upsetting the racial order, while validating gender hierarchies (Leeds, 1994:1).

Leeds' assertion is directly on point. It is not adequate to simply change the standards of beauty. The fact that there are standards at all is problematic. Furthermore, changing beauty standards is a far cry from breaking the clutch of institutional racism in the U.S. Instead, people must change the way they think about beauty altogether.

Combating colorism and racism is a slow and long battle for both ethnic communities. Changes within social structures must take place and must be accompanied by individual daily acts of resistance. African Americans and Mexican Americans can begin that change process by examining language. There is much reference to color in our daily language that glorifies whiteness and denigrates darkness. We need only look as far as the Mexican custom of showing pleasure at the whiteness of a new baby, or the Black saying, "She's dark, but she's pretty." Eliminating value-laden language about skin color in daily vocabularies should be a top priority. In addition, members of both groups can embrace ethnic authenticity in its aesthetic as well as its politics. That means finding beauty in things African and Indian, as well as recognizing work for the liberation of both communities as ethnically legitimate regardless of the color of the person doing it.

Finally, comparing colorism in the Mexican American and African American communities is useful because it provides further evidence that colorism is not unique to either group but an outgrowth of European racial ideologies. Skin color remains an important status distinction within the African American and Mexican American communities. Stratification by color is an outgrowth of the colonial and slave histories of each group and their contact with Europeans. Light skin offers many advantages, both economic and social to people of color. Light skin also has a few disadvantages, although those may be less directly linked to socio-economic success and more linked to in-group membership. This discussion reveals that the legacies of slavery, colonialism, and modern day racism still inform contemporary discussions of status and skin color.

## References

Acuña, Rodolfo. 1988. *Occupied America.* New York: Harper and Row.

Allen, Walter, Edward Telles, and Margaret Hunter. 2000. "Skin Color, Income and Education: A Comparison of African Americans and Mexican Americans." *National Journal of Sociology* 12:129-180.

Almaguer, Tomás. 1994. *Racial Fault Lines*. Berkeley: University of California Press.

Arce, Carlos, Edward Murguia, and W. Parker Frisbie. 1987. "Phenotype and Life Chances Among Chicanos" in *Hispanic Journal of Behavioral Sciences* 9:19-32.

Baker, Nancy C. 1984. *The Beauty Trap*. New York: Franklin Watts.

Banner, Lois. 1983. *American Beauty*. New York: Knopf.

Barrera, Mario. 1979. *Race and Class in the Southwest*. Notre Dame: University of Notre Dame Press.

Billingsley, Andrew. 1968. *Black Families in White America*. Englewood Cliffs, NJ: Prentice Hall Inc.

Blea, Irene. 1992. *La Chicana and the Intersection of Race, Class, and Gender*. Westport, Connecticut: Praeger.

Bond, Selena and Thomas Cash. 1992. "Black Beauty: Skin Color and Body Images among African American College-Age Women" *Journal of Applied Social Psychology* 22:874-888.

Castañeda, Antonia. 1993. "Sexual Violence in the Politics of and Policies of Conquest: Amerindian Women and the Spanish Conquest of Alta California" in *Building With Our Hands: New Directions in*

*Chicana Studies.* Adela de la Torre and Beatríz M. Pesquera (Eds.). Berkeley: University of California Press.

Chorlton, Penny. 1988. *Cover-up: Taking the Lid Off the Cosmetics Industry.* Wellingborough, England: Grapevine.

Codina, E. and F. Montalvo 1994. "Chicano Phenotype and Depression." *Hispanic Journal of Behavioral Sciences* 16:296-306.

Collins, Patricia Hill. 1991. *Black Feminist Thought.* New York: Routledge.

Davis, F. James. 1991. *Who Is Black? One Nation's Definition.* University Park, PA: Pennsylvania State University Press.

Davis, Kathy. 1995. *Reshaping the Female Body.* New York: Routledge.

Drake, St. Clair. 1987. *Black Folk Here and There, Volume One.* CAAS: University of California Press.

Edwards, G.F. 1959. *The Negro Professional Class.* Glencoe, IL: The Free Press.

Edwards, Ozzie. 1973. "Skin Color as a Variable in Racial Attitudes of Black Urbanites" *Journal of Black Studies* 3:473-483.

Ernst, Klaus. 1980. "Racialism, Racialist Ideology, and Colonialism, Past and Present" in *Sociological Theories: Race and Colonialism.* United Kingdom: UNESCO.

Fanon, Frantz. 1967. *Black Skin White Masks.* New York: Grove Weidenfeld.

Ferguson, Marjorie. 1985. *Forever Feminine: Women's Magazines and the Cult of Femininity.* Brookfield, England: Gower.

Frazier, E. Franklin. 1951. *The Negro Family in the United States.* New York: The Dryden Press.

Freedman, Rita. 1986. *Beauty Bound.* Lexington, MA: Lexington Books.

Gossett, Thomas F. 1963. *Race: The History of an Idea in America.* Dallas: Southern Methodist University Press.

Guerrero, Andrés. 1987. *A Chicano Theology.* New York: Orbis Books.

Hall, Ronald. 1994. "'The Bleaching Syndrome': Implications of Light Skin for Hispanic American Assimilation" *Hispanic Journal of*

*Behavioral Sciences*16(3):307-314.

Harris, Cheryl. 1995. "Whiteness as Property" in *Critical Race Theory*. Kimberlé Crenshaw, Neil Gotanda, Gary Peller, and Kendall Thomas. (Eds.). New York: The New Press.

Herrnstein, Richard J. and Charles Murray. 1994. *The Bell Curve: Intelligence and Class Structure in American Life*. New York: The Free Press.

Hughes and Hertel. 1990. "The Significance of Color Remains: A Study of Life Chances, Mate Selection, and Ethnic Consciousness Among Black Americans" *Social Forces* 68(4):1105-20.

Hunter, Margaret. 1998. "Colorstruck: Skin color stratification in the lives of African American women." *Sociological Inquiry* 68(4): 517-535.

Hunter, Margaret. 1999 "The *Lighter* the Berry? Race, Color, and Gender in the Lives of African American and Mexican American Women." Unpublished Dissertation at UCLA: UMI.

Hunter, Margaret. 2002. "'If you're light you're alright': Light skin color as social capital for women of color." *Gender & Society* 16(2): 171-189.

Jordan, Winthrop. 1968. *White Over Black*. Chapel Hill: University of North Carolina Press.

Keith, Verna and Cedric Herring. 1991. "Skin Tone and Stratification in the Black Community" *American Journal of Sociology* 97:760-778.

Kevles, Daniel. 1985. *In the Name of Eugenics: Genetics and the Uses of Human Heredity*. New York: Knopf.

Knight, Alan. 1990. "Racism, Revolution, and Indigenismo: Mexico, 1910-1940" *in The Idea of Race in Latin America*. Richard Graham (ed.). Austin, Texas: University of Texas Press.

Lakoff, Robin and Racquel Scherr. 1984. *Face Value: The Politics of Beauty*. Boston: Routledge.

Leeds, Maxine. 1994. "Young African-American Women and the

Language of Beauty" in Ideals of Feminine Beauty: Philosophical, Social, and Cultural Dimensions. Ed. Karen Callaghan. London: Greenwood Press.

Martinez, George. 1997. "Mexican Americans and Whiteness" in *Critical White Studies*. Richard Delgado and Jean Stefancic. (Eds.). Philadelphia: Temple University Press.

Memmi, Albert. 1965. *The Colonizer and the Colonized*. Boston: Beacon Press.

Murguia, Edward and Edward Telles. 1996. "Phenotype and Schooling among Mexican Americans." *Sociology of Education* 69:276-289.

Relethford, J., P. Stern, S.P. Catskill, and H.P. Hazuda. 1983. "Social Class, Admixture, and Skin Color Variation in Mexican Americans and Anglo Americans Living in San Antonio, Texas" *American Journal of Physical Anthropology* 61:97-102.

Reuter, E.B. 1918. *The Mulatto in the United States*. New York: Negro University Press.

Ruiz, Vicki. 1998. *From Out of the Shadows: Mexican Women in Twentieth Century America*. New York: Oxford University Press.

Russell, Kathy and Midge Wilson and Ronald Hall. 1992. *The Color Complex*. New York: Doubleday.

Smith, Dorothy. 1987. "Women's Perspective as Radical Critique of Sociology" in *Feminism and Methodology*. Sandra Harding (ed.). Bloomington: Indiana University Press.

Stevenson, Brenda. 1996. *Life in Black and White: Family and Community in the Slave South*. New York: Oxford University Press.

Telles, Edward and Edward Murguia. 1990. "Phenotypic Discrimination and Income Differences among Mexican Americans" *Social Science Quarterly* 71: 682-696.

Udry, Richard, Karl Baumann, and Charles Chase. 1971. "Skin Color, Status, and Mate Selection" *American Journal of Sociology* 76(4):722-33.

Vasconcelos, José. 1925. *La Raza Cósmica, Misión de la Raza*

*Iberoamericana*. Paris: Agencia Mundial de Librería.

Wolf, Naomi. 1991. *The Beauty Myth: How Images of Beauty are Used Against* Women. New York: Doubleday Books.

Zavella, Patricia. 1997. "Reflections on Diversity Among Chicanas" in *Challenging Fronteras: Structuring Latina and Latino Lives in the U.S.* Mary Romero, Pierrette Hondagneu-Sotelo, and Vilma Ortiz. (Eds). New York: Routledge.

# Chapter 3

# *Copper Brown and Blue Black:*
## *Colorism and Self Evaluation*

**Maxine S. Thompson**

North Carolina State University

and

**Verna M. Keith**

Arizona State University

W e begin this chapter with comments about the experience of growing up "copper brown and blue black" in the Black community from the perspectives of two African Americans employed in professional occupations. One interviewee is female, and the other is male.

**Carolyn:** *The first time I asked my mother "why am I so dark? She replied, "Oh, you're special! . . . And you look just like your daddy! I knew by the smile on her face that I must be special! That was until I entered school and then, the derisive comments began: "She's dark, but smart! She's dark but pretty and she's dark but . . . Or "you're the first dark skinned girl that I ever dated!" The message was clear, in order to be accepted I'd have to compensate for my dark skin color by being better than average!*

**Mike:** *I was always singled out or suspected for doing "bad things, being a trouble maker or fighting in my community!" I remember this particular incident happened on a rainy day. My friends and I were walking down the hall of our middle school,* *and this curly haired boy walking ahead of us slipped on the wet floor. His mother ran over, grabbed me by the shirt, took me to the principal's office, and accused me of "pushing her son." The only thing that saved me was "I was smart." I had a good reputation in school. The principal and teachers liked me. I had already been skipped a grade and a half. . . . Later in high school, the girl that I had been dating for several years, skipped over me for her escort to the "Cotillion". Her escort was a lighter skinned guy. . . . I thought that I had gotten away from that backward thinking until the birth of my daughter, the darkest of three siblings, when the wife of our African American neighbors commented "It's a shame that she's so dark!"*

**Carolyn:** *Yea, it's not behind us! My niece in elementary school came home one day and asked "Mama, why can't I be light brown like you and grandma?"*

The above comments illustrate the influence of dark skin tone on African Americans' self perceptions. Colorism, the prejudicial treatment of individuals falling within the same racial group on the basis of skin color, has now become part of the public discourse in the academy as well as in the African American community. No longer an unspoken taboo, color prejudice within the African American community has been a "hot" topic of talk shows, novels, and movies. It is also a popular discussion issue for web sites, and the subject of a court case on discrimination in the workplace (Russell, Wilson and Hall, 1992).[1]

In addition to discussions within lay communities, research scholars have had considerable interest in the importance of skin color. At the level of social institutions, studies have noted that skin color is an important determinant of educational and occupational attainment. Lighter skinned Blacks complete more years of schooling, have more prestigious jobs and earn more than darker skinned Blacks (Hughes and Hertel, 1990;

Keith and Herring, 1991). In fact one study notes that the effect of skin color on earnings of "lighter" and "darker" Blacks-is as great as the effect of race on the earnings of Whites and all Blacks (Hughes and Hertel, 1990).

The most impressive research on skin tone effects are studies on skin tone and blood pressure. Using a reflectometer to measure skin color, research has shown that dark skin tone is associated with high blood pressure in African Americans with low socioeconomic status (Klag et al., 1991; Tryoler and James, 1978). And at the individual level, studies find that skin color is related to feelings of self-worth and attractiveness, self control, satisfaction and quality of life (Bond and Cash, 1992; Boyd Franklin, 1991; Cash and Duncan, 1984; Chambers et al., 1994; Neal and Wilson, 1989; Okazawa Rey, Robinson and Ward, 1987).

It is important to note that skin color is highly correlated with other phenotypic features-eye color, hair texture, broadness of nose, and fullness of lips. Along with light skin, blue and green eyes, European shaped noses, and straight as opposed to "kinky" hair are all accorded higher status, both within and beyond the African American community. Colorism embodies preference and desire for both light skin as well as these other attendant features. Hair, eye color and facial features function, along with color in complex ways, to shape opportunities, norms regarding attractiveness, self-concept, and overall body image. Yet, it is color that has received the most attention in research on African Americans.[2] The reasons for this emphasis is not clear, although one can speculate that it is due to the fact that color is the most visible physical feature and is also the feature that is most enduring and difficult to change.

As Russell, Wilson, and Hall (1992) point out, hair can be straightened with chemicals, eye color can be changed with contact lenses, and a broad nose can be altered with cosmetic surgery. Bleaching skin to a lighter tone, however, seldom meets with success (Okazawa Rey, Robinson and Ward, 1987). Ethnographic research also suggests that the research focus on skin color is somewhat justified. For example, it played the central role in determining membership in the affluent African American clubs. In the *Black Bourgeoisie*, Frazier (1957) describes affluent organized clubs within the Black community called "blue vein" societies. To be accepted into these clubs, skin tone was required to be lighter than a "paper bag" or light enough for visibility of "blue veins" (Okazawa Rey, Robinson and Ward, 1987). Preferential treatment given by both Black and White cultures to African Americans with light skin have conveyed to many Blacks that if they conformed to the White majority standard of beauty, their lives would be more rewarding (Bond and Cash, 1992; Gatewood, 1988).

Although colorism affects attitudes about the self for both men and women, it appears that these effects are stronger for women than men. In earlier studies, dark skinned women were seen as occupying the bottom rungs of the social ladder, least marriageable, having the fewest options for higher education and career advancement and as more color conscious than their male counterparts (Parrish, 1944; Warner, Junker and Adams, 1941). There is very little empirical research on the relationship between gender, skin color, and self concept development. In this paper we describe our findings from research on the importance of skin color to feelings about the self for men and women within the African American community (Thompson and Keith, 2001). Before sharing our findings we present a brief review of studies that suggest that one should expect gender differences in the impact of skin tone on self evaluation.

## Skin Tone and Gender

The bleak prospects of being female and dark skinned resonates in the life experiences of Wallace Thurman's (1929:4) character Emma Lou in his novel, *The Blacker the Berry*:

> *She should have been a boy, then color of skin wouldn't have mattered so much, for wasn't her mother always saying that a*

*boy could get along, but that a Black girl would never know
anything but sorrow and disappointment?*

Issues of skin color and physical attractiveness are closely linked
and because expectations of physical attractiveness are applied more
heavily to women across all cultures, stereotypes of attractiveness and color
preference are more profound for Black women (Warner, Junker and
Adams, 1941). In the clinical literature (Boyd Franklin, 1991; Grier and
Cobbs, 1968; Neal and Wilson, 1989; Okazawa Rey, Robinson and Ward,
1987) issues of racial identity, skin color, and attractiveness were central
concerns of women. The "what is beautiful is good" stereotype creates a
"halo" effect for light skinned persons. The positive glow generated by
physical attractiveness includes a host of desirable personality traits.
Included in these positive judgments are beliefs that attractive people
would be significantly more intelligent, kind, confident, interesting, sexy,
assertive, poised, modest, and successful and they appear to have higher
self esteem and self worth (Dion, Berscheid and Walster, 1972). When
complexion is the indicator of attractiveness similar stereotypic attributes
are found.

There is evidence that gender difference in response to the
importance of skin color to attractiveness appears during childhood. Girls
as young as six are twice as likely as boys to be sensitive to the social
importance of skin color (Porter, 1971; Russell, Wilson and Hall, 1992:
68). In a study of facial features, skin color and attractiveness, Neal (1988,
cited in Neal and Wilson, 1989) found that "unattractive women were
perceived as having darker skin tones than attractive women and that
women with more Caucasoid features were perceived as more attractive to
the opposite sex, more successful in their love lives and their careers than
women with Negroid features" (Neal and Wilson, 1989: 328).

Frequent exposure to negative evaluations can undermine a
woman's sense of self. "A dark skinned Black woman who feels herself

unattractive, however, may think that she has nothing to offer society no matter how intelligent or inventive she is" (Russell, Wilson and Hall, 1992: 42). A diminished sense of self is described in the following quotation as Emma Lou ponders the failure of bleaching agents to lighten her complexion:

> *There is no place in the world for a girl as black as she anyway. Her grandmother had assured her that she would never find a husband worth a dime, and her mother had said again and again, "Oh if you had only been a boy!" until Emma Lou often wondered why it was that people were not able to effect a change of sex or at least a change of complexion* (Thurman, 1929:18).

Several explanations are proffered for gender differences in self esteem among Blacks. One is that women are socialized to attend to evaluations of others and are vulnerable to negative appraisals. Women seek to validate their selves through appraisal from others more than men. And the media has encouraged greater negative self appraisals for dark skinned women. One recent study examined the gender and skin tone of the lead character cast in 46 romantic music videos aired on cable television (Little, 1997). Overwhelmingly, they found that the female lead character is lighter in skin color than the male lead character. A darker skinned female cast with a lighter skinned male was found in only four of the 46 videos. The message is even more explicit when one examines the content of the lyrics of one popular song:

> *"Woman, my love for you is deep as can be,*
> *And I know my love is real 'cause you're lighter than me"*
> (Little, 1997).

A second explanation is that colorism and its associated stressors are not the same for dark skinned men and women. For men, stereotypes associated with perceived dangerousness, criminality and competence are associated with dark skin tone, while for women the issue is attractiveness (Russell, Wilson and Hall, 1992:38). Educational attainment is a vehicle by which men might overcome skin color bias but changes in physical features are difficult to accomplish. Third, women may react more strongly to skin color bias because they feel less control over their lives. Research studies show that women and persons of low status tend to feel fatalistic (Pearlin and Schooler, 1978; Turner and Noh, 1983) and to react more intensely than comparable others to stressors (Kessler and McLeod, 1984; Pearlin and Johnson, 1977; Turner and Noh, 1983; Thoits, 1982; 1984). This suggests a triple jeopardy situation: Black women face problems of racism and sexism and when these two negative status positions-being Black and being female-combine with colorism, a triple threat lowers self esteem and feelings of competence among dark Black women.

## How Does Skin Tone Influence Attitudes about the Self?

Self evaluations are seen as having two dimensions, one reflecting the person's moral worth and the other reflecting the individual's competency or agency (Gecas, 1989). The former refers to self esteem and indicates how we feel about ourselves. The latter refers to self efficacy and indicates our belief in the ability to control our own fate.

Self esteem is influenced by both the social comparisons we make of ourselves with others and by the reactions that other people have toward us (i.e., reflected appraisals). The self concept depends also on the attributes of others who are available for comparison. Self evaluation theory argues that Blacks will compare themselves to other Blacks in their community. Significant others will provide affirmation of one's identity. That similarity between one's self and others shapes the self. Thus, a sense of personal connectedness to other African Americans is most important for fostering and reinforcing positive self evaluations. This explains why the personal self esteem of Blacks, in spite of their lower status position, was as high as that of Whites (Porter and Washington, 1989; Rosenberg and Simmons, 1971).[3] It does not explain the possible influence of colorism on self esteem within the African American community. Evidence suggests that conflictual and dissonant environments have negative effects on self esteem, especially within the working class (Porter and Washington, 1989; Verna and Runion, 1985). The heterogeneity of skin tone hues and colorism create a dissonant racial environment and become a source of negative self evaluation.

In contrast, performance influences self efficacy, the belief that one can master situations and control events, such that when faced with a failure, individuals with high self efficacy generally believe that extra effort or persistence will lead to success (Bandura, 1982). However, if failure is related to some stable personal characteristic such as "dark skin color," or social constraints such as blocked opportunities resulting from main-streaming practices in the workplace, then one is likely to be discouraged by failure and to feel less efficacious than his or her lighter counterparts. In fact, Pearlin and colleagues (1981) argue that stressors which seem to be associated with inadequacy of one's efforts or lack of success are implicated in a diminished sense of self. Problems or hardships "to which people can see no end, those that seem to become fixtures of their existence" pose the most sustained affront to a sense of mastery and self worth (Pearlin et al, 1981:345).

For Bandura, however, individual agency plays a role in sustaining the self. Individuals actively engage in activities that are congenial with a positive sense of self. Self efficacy results not primarily from beliefs or attitudes about performance but from undertaking challenges and succeeding. Thus, darker skinned Blacks who experience success in their everyday world (e.g., work, education etc.) will feel more confident and empowered. Now, we turn to a summary of our research findings.

## Our Research Findings

Our study used data from the National Survey of Black Americans (NSBA) (Jackson and Gurin, 1987). The sample for the survey was drawn to ensure that every Black household in the United States had an equal probability of being selected for the study and is representative of the national Black population enumerated in the 1980 census. Face-to-face interviews were carried out by trained Black interviewers, yielding a sample of 2,107 respondents. Our analyses employed objective reliability measures of skin tone, self concept and adequate control variables for socioeconomic status (for more details see Thompson and Keith, 2001).

Skin tone had a significant positive effect on self efficacy for both men and women. Lighter complexion was associated with higher feelings of perceived mastery. The skin tone effect on self efficacy was much stronger for men. In fact, the effect for the skin tone predicting self efficacy for men was almost twice that of the effect for women. Socioeconomic status, body image (represented by attractiveness, weight, and disabled health conditions) did not alter the skin tone effect. By contrast, the determinants of self efficacy for women in this study were age, education, income, disability and urban residence. Among women, the skin tone effect on self efficacy is largely indirect, via its consequence for income and education.

A similar analysis for the self esteem measure was also conducted and showed that the effect for skin tone on self esteem was not statistically important for Black men in this study. Conversely, among Black women skin tone had a positive association with self esteem, even after taking into account education, income and body image characteristics.

More importantly the results indicated that the relationship between skin tone and personal income is strongest among women with the lowest incomes. In other words, among women with the lowest levels of income, self esteem increases as color lightens. The relationship is also positive and significant for women with average levels of income, although the relationship is not as strong. There is no relationship between skin tone and self esteem among women with the highest incomes. Thus, women who are dark and successful evaluate themselves just as positively as women who are lighter and successful. Similar to the findings for income, skin color has a significant positive effect on self esteem among women evaluated as having low and average levels of attractiveness, although the effect is stronger for the former. Self esteem increases as skin color becomes lighter among women judged unattractive or average. There is no relationship between skin tone and self esteem for women who are judged highly attractive. In other words, skin tone does not have much relevance for self esteem among women who have higher levels of income and who are attractive. Education, unlike income, has no significant effect on women's self-esteem. We are at a loss to explain this finding. Perhaps income is more important because it permits women to obtain more visible symbols of success such as clothing, cars, and living quarters. We discuss this further in the concluding section.

For males in our study, body image, particularly weight, seems to tailor the effects of skin tone on attitudes about the self. Skin tone has a significant impact on self esteem for men who are either under weight or over weight. Among under weight males, self esteem decreases as skin tone becomes lighter. But among over weight males, self esteem increases as skin tone becomes lighter. We suggest that cultural definitions of weight probably interact with those of skin color and health as explanations of the observed effects. In our culture, a robust athletic body is associated with masculinity, and a thin body frame combined with light complexion might be viewed as ill health. And negative stigma of both weight and complexion impact on self esteem for men who are overweight and dark skinned. It seems that light skin compensates for the negative stigma of weight for large body frames but enhances the negative stigma for thin frames. Similarly for self efficacy, our findings show that among those judged over weight, lighter men are more likely to have high self efficacy.

## Conclusions

The data in this study indicate that gender - mediated by socioeconomic status variables such as education, occupation, and income - socially constructs the importance of skin color evaluations of self esteem and self efficacy. Self efficacy results not primarily from beliefs or attitudes about performance but rather, reflects an individual's competency or agency from undertaking challenges and succeeding at overcoming them. Self esteem consists of feeling good about oneself, as well as being liked and treated favorably by others. However, the effect of skin color on these two domains of self is different for women and men. Skin color is an important predictor of perceived efficacy for Black men but not Black women. And skin color predicts self esteem for Black women but not Black men. This pattern conforms to traditional gendered expectations (Collins, 1990:79-80). The traditional definitions of masculinity demand men specialize in achievement outside the home, dominate in interpersonal relationships, and remain rational and self-contained. Women, in contrast, are expected to seek affirmation from others, to be warm and nurturing. Thus, consistent with gendered characteristics of men and women, skin color is important in self domains that are central to masculinity (i.e. competence) and femininity (i.e., affirmation of the self).

Turning our attention to the association between skin color and self concept for Black men, the association between skin color and self efficacy increases significantly as skin color lightens. And this is independent of the strong positive contribution of education - and ultimately socioeconomic status - to feelings of competence for men. We think that the effect of skin tone on self efficacy is the result of widespread negative stereotyping and fear associated with dark skinned men that pervades the larger society and operates independent of social class. Correspondingly, employers view darker African American men as violent, uncooperative, dishonest and unstable (Kirschenman and Neckerman, 1998). As a consequence employers exclude "darker" African American men from employment and, thus, block their access to rewards and resources.

Evidence from research on the relationship between skin tone and achievement supports our interpretation. The literature on achievement and skin tone shows that lighter skinned Blacks are economically better off than darker skinned persons (Hughes and Hertel, 1990; Keith and Herring, 1991). Hughes and Hertel (1990), using the NSBA data, present findings that show that for every dollar a light skinned African American earns, the darker skinned person earns 72 cents. Thus, it seems colorism is operative within the workplace. Lighter skinned persons are probably better able to predict what will happen to them and what doors will open and remain open, thus leading to a higher sense of control over their environment. Our data supports this finding and adds additional information on how that process might work, at least in the lives of Black men.

Perhaps employers are looking to hire African American men who will assimilate into the work environment, who do not alienate their clients (Kirschenman and Neckerman, 1998) and who are nonthreatening. One consequence of mainstreaming the workplace is that darker skinned Black men have fewer opportunities to demonstrate competence in the breadwinner role. It is no accident that our inner cities, where unemployment is highest, are filled with darker skinned persons, especially men (Russell, Wilson and Hall, 1992, 38). During adolescence, lighter skinned boys discover that they have better job prospects, appear less threatening to Whites and have a clearer sense of who they are and their competency (Russell, Wilson and Hall, 1992:67). In contrast, darker skinned African American males may feel powerless and less able to affect change through the "normal" channels available to lighter skinned African American males (who are able to achieve a more prestigious socioeconomic status).

While skin color is an important predictor of self-efficacy for African American men, it is more important as a predictor of self esteem for African American women. These data confirm much of the anecdotal information from clinical studies of clients in psychotherapy which have found that "dark skinned" Black women have problems with self worth and confidence. Our findings suggest that this pattern is not limited to experiences of women who are in therapy, but that colorism is part of the everyday reality of Black women. Black women expect to be judged by their skin tone. No doubt, messages from peers, the media and family show a preference for lighter skin tones. Several studies cited in the literature review point out that Black women of all ages tend to prefer lighter skin tones and believe that lighter hues are perceived as most attractive by their Black male counterparts (Bond and Cash, 1992; Chambers et al., 1994; Porter, 1971; Robinson and Ward, 1995).

Evidence from personal accounts reported in research on the impact of racism in the everyday lives of Black women by St. John and Feagin (1998) support this interpretation. One young woman describes her father's efforts to shape her expectations about the meaning of beauty in our society-and where Black women entered this equation:

> Beauty, beauty standards in this country, a big thing with me. It's a big gripe, because I went through a lot of personal anguish over that, being Black and being female, it's a real big thing with me, because it took a lot for me to find a sense of self . . . in this White=male-dominated society. And just how beauty standards are so warped because, like my daddy always tell me, "white is right." The whiter you are, somehow the better you are, and if you look White, well hell, you've got your ticket, and anything you want, too (St. John and Feagin, 1998:75).

Nevertheless, the relationship between skin color and self esteem among African American women is moderated by socioeconomic status. For example, there is no correlation between skin color and self esteem among women who have a more privileged socioeconomic status. Consequently, women who are darker and "successful" evaluate themselves just as positively as women of a lighter color. On the other hand, the relationship between skin color and self esteem is stronger for African American women from the less privileged socioeconomic sectors. In other words, darker skinned women with the lowest incomes display the lowest levels of self esteem, but self esteem increases as their skin color lightens.

Why does skin color have such importance for self regard in the context of low income or poverty? Low income shapes self esteem because it provides fewer opportunities for rewarding experiences or affirming relationships. In addition, there are more negative attributes associated with behaviors of individuals from less privileged socioeconomic status than with those of more prestigious ones. For example, the derisive comment, "ghetto chick," is often used to describe the behaviors, dress, communication, and interaction styles of women from low income groups. Combine stereotypes of classism and colorism and you have a mixture that fosters an undesirable, if not malignant, context for self esteem development.

An important finding of this research is that skin color and income determine self worth for Black women, and especially that these factors can work together. Dark skin and low income produce Black women with very low self esteem. Accordingly, this data helps refine our understanding of gendered racism, and of "triple oppression" involving race, gender, and class that places women of color in a subordinate social and economic position relative to men of color and the larger White population as well (Segura, 1986). More important, the data suggest that darker skinned African American women actually experience a "quadruple" oppression originating in the convergence of social inequalities based on gender, class, race, and color. Earlier we noted that the relationship between skin tone and self esteem is not moderated by education and that we can only speculate on the explanation for this non-finding. Perhaps education does not have the same implications for self-esteem as income because it is a less visible symbol of success. Financial success affords one the ability to purchase consumer items that tell others, even at a distance, that an individual is successful. These visible symbols include the place where we live, the kind of car we drive, and the kind of clothing that we wear. Educational attainment is not as easily grasped, especially in distant social interactions such as passing on the street, walking in the park, or attending a concert event. In other words, for a dark-skinned African American woman, her M.A. or Ph.D. may be largely unknown outside her immediate friends, family, and coworkers. Her Lexus or Mercedes, however, is visible to the world and is generally accorded a great deal of prestige.

Finally, the data indicate that self esteem increases as skin color becomes lighter among African American women who are judged as having "low and average levels of attractiveness." There is no relationship between skin color and self esteem for women who are judged "highly attractive," just as there is no correlation between skin color and self esteem for women of higher socioeconomic status. That physical attractiveness influenced feelings of self worth for Black women is not surprising. Women have traditionally been concerned with appearance, regardless of ethnicity. Indeed, the pursuit and preoccupation with beauty are central features of female sex-role socialization. Our findings suggest that women who are judged "unattractive" are more vulnerable to color bias than those judged attractive.

## Endnotes

1. In 1990 a workplace discrimination suit was filed in Atlanta Georgia, on the behalf of a light skinned Black female against her dark skinned supervisor on the charge of color discrimination (see Russell, Wilson and Hall, 1992 for a discussion).

2. Skin color bias has also been investigated among Latino groups, although more emphasis has been placed on the combination of both color and European phenotype facial characteristics. Studies of Mexican Americans have documented that those with lighter skin and European features attain more schooling (Telles and Murguia, 1990) and generally have higher socioeconomic status (Arce, Murguia, and Frisbie, 1987) than those of darker complexion with more Indian features. Similar findings have been reported for Puerto Ricans

(Rodriguez, 1989), a population with African admixture.

3. Self concept theory argued that the experience of social inequality would foster lower self concept of persons in lower status positions compared to their higher status counterparts. However, when comparing the self concept of African American school boys and girls, Rosenberg and Simmons (1971) found that their self feelings were as high and in some instances higher than that White school children. This "unexpected" finding was explained by strong ties and bonds within the African American community as opposed to identifying with the larger community.

## References

Acre, Carlos, Edward Murguia and W. P. Frisbie. 1987. "Phenotype and Life Chances Among Chicanos." *Hispanic Journal of Behavioral Sciences* 9:19-32.

Bandura, A. 1982. "Self Efficacy Mechanism in Human Agency." *American Psychologist* 37:122-147.

Bond, S. and T. F. Cash. 1992. "Black Beauty: Skin Color and Body Images among African-American College Women." *Journal of Applied Social Psychology* 22:874-888.

Boyd Franklin, N. 1991. "Recurrent Themes in the Treatment of African-American Women in Group Psychotherapy." *Women and Therapy* 11:25-40.

Cash, T. S. and N. C. Duncan. 1984. "Physical Attractiveness Stereotyping Among Black American College Students." *Journal of Social Psychology* 1:71-77.

Chambers, J. W., T. Clark, L. Dantzler and J. Baldwin. 1994. "Perceived Attractiveness, Facial Features, and African Self-Consciousness." *Journal of Black Psychology* 20:305-324.

Collins, Patricia Hill. 1990. *Black Feminist Thought: Knowledge, Consciousness, and the Politics of Empowerment*. Boston: Unwin

Hyman.

Dion, K., E. Berscheid and E. Walster. 1972. "What is Beautiful is Good." *Journal of Personality and Social Psychology* 24:285-290.

Frazier, E. Franklin. 1957. *Black Bourgeoise: The Rise of the New Middle Class*. New York: The Free Press.

Gatewood, W. B. 1988. "Aristocrat of Color: South and North and the Black Elite, 1880-1920." *Journal of Southern History* 54:3-19.

Gecas, Viktor. 1989. "The Social Psychology of Self-Efficacy." *Annual Review of Sociology* 15:291-316.

Grier, W. and P. Cobbs. 1968. *Black Rage*. New York: Basic Books.

Hughes, M. and B. R. Hertel. 1990. "The Significance of Color Remains: A Study of Life Chances, Mate Selection, and Ethnic Consciousness among Black Americans." *Social Forces* 68:1105-1120.

Jackson, J. and G. Gurin. 1987. *National Survey of Black Americans, 1979-1980* (machine readable codebook). Inter-University Consortium for Political and Social Research, University of Michigan.

Keith, V. M. and C. Herring. 1991. "Skin Tone and Stratification in the Black Community." *American Journal of Sociology* 97:760-778.

Kessler, R. C. and J. D. McLeod. 1984. "Sex Differences in Vulnerability to Undesirable Life Events." *American Sociological Review* 49:620-31.

Kirschenman, J. and Neckerman, K.M. 1998. "We'd Love to Hire Them, But..." In *The Meaning of Race for Employers in Working in America: Continuity, Conflict, and Change*, edited by Amy S. Wharton. Mountain View, CA: Mayfield.

Klag, Michael, Paul Whelton, Josef Coresh, Clarence Grim and Lewis Kuller. 1991. "The Association of Skin Color with Blood Pressure in US Blacks with Low Socioeconomic Status." *Journal of*

*American Medical Association* 65:599-602

Little, M.G. 1997. "What Color is Black Love? HYPE: Monitoring the Black Image in the Media. Center on Blacks and the Media." (http://pan.afrikan.net/hype/cover1.html).

Neal, A. and M. Wilson. 1989. "The Role of Skin Color and Features in the Black Community: Implications for Black Women in Therapy." *Clinical Psychology Review* 9:323-333.

Okazawa Rey, Margo, Tracy Robinson and Janie V. Ward. 1987. *Black Women and the Politics of Skin Color and Hair.* New York: Haworth.

Parrish, Charles. 1944. *The Significance of Skin Color in the Negro Community.* Unpublished Doctoral Dissertation. University of Chicago.

Pearlin, L. I. and J. S. Johnson. 1977. "Marital Status, Life Strains, and Depression." *American Sociological Review* 42:704-15.

Pearlin, L. I., M. A. Liberman, E. G. Menaghan and J. T. Mullan. 1981. "The Stress Process." *Journal of Health and Social Behavior* 22:337-356.

Pearlin, L. I. and C. Schooler. 1978. "The Structure of Coping." *Journal of Health and Social Behavior* 19:2-21.

Porter, J. 1971. *Black Child, White Child: The Development of Racial Attitudes.* Cambridge: Harvard.

Porter, J. R. and R. E. Washington. 1989. "Developments in Research on Black Identity and Self Esteem: 1979-88." *Review of International Psychology and Sociology* 2:341-53.

Porter, J. R. and R. E. Washington. 1989. "Developments in Research on Black Identity and Self Esteem: 1979-88." *Review of International Psychology and Sociology* 2:341-53.

Rodriguez, Clara. 1989. *Puerto Ricans in the USA*. Boston: Unwin Hyman.

Rosenberg, M. and R. Simmons. 1971. *Black and White Self-Esteem: The Urban School Child*. Washington, D.C.: American Sociological Association.

Russell, Kathy, Midge Wilson and Ronald Hall. 1992. *The Color Complex: The Politics of Skin Color Among African Americans*. New York: Harcourt Brace Jovanovich.

Segura, Denise. 1986. "Chicanas and Triple Oppression in the Labor Force." In *Chicana Voices: Intersections of Class, Race and Gender*, edited by Teresa Cordova et al. Austin Texas: Center for Mexican American Studies.

St. John, Y. and J. R. Feagin. 1998. *Double Burden: Black Women and Everyday Racism*. New York: M.E. Sharpe Inc.

Telles, Edward E. and Edward Murguia. 1990. "Phenotypic Discrimination and Income Differences Among Mexican Americans." *Social Science Quarterly* 71:682-695.

Thompson, Maxine and Verna Keith 2001. "The Blacker the Berry: Gender, Skin Tone, Self-Esteem and Self Efficacy." *Gender and Society* 15: 336-357.

Thoits, Peggy A. 1982. "Life Stress, Social Support, and Psychological Vulnerability: Epidemiological Considerations." *Journal of Community Psychology* 10:341-62.

Thoits, Peggy A. 1984. "Explaining Distributions of Psychological Vulnerability: Lack of Social Support in the Face of Life Stress." *Social Forces* 63:452-81.

Thurman, Wallace. 1929. *The Blacker the Berry-A Novel of Negro Life*. New York: McMillan.

Turner, R. J. and S. Noh. 1983. "Class and Psychological Vulnerability

Among Women: The Significance of Social Support and Personal Control." *Journal of Health and Social Behavior* 24:2-15.

Tyroler, H. A. and S. A. James. 1978. "Blood Pressure and Skin Color." *American Journal of Public Health* 58:1170-1172.

Verna, G. and K. Runion. 1985. "The Effects of Contextual Dissonance on the Self Concept of Youth from High vs. Low Socially Valued Group." *Journal of Social Psychology* 125:449-458.

Warner, W. L., B. H. Junker and W. A. Adams. 1941. *Color and Human Nature.* Washington, D.C.: American Council on Education.

# Chapter 4

# For Richer, For Poorer, Whether Dark or Light:
## Skin Tone, Marital Status, and Spouse's Earnings

**Korie Edwards**
University of Illinois at Chicago
**Katrina M. Carter-Tellison**
University of Miami
and
**Cedric Herring**
University of Illinois at Chicago

Skin tone has historically played a significant role in determining the life chances of African Americans and other people of color. Research shows that light skin color has consistently provided higher status than darker skin color (Davis, Gardner, and Gardner, 1941; Billingsley, 1968; Hughes and Hertel, 1990; Blackwell, 1991; Keith and Herring, 1991; Russell, Wilson, and Hall, 1992; and Hill, 2000). This is especially true for women of color, as much research reveals that physical appearance and racialized notions of beauty matter significantly in the lives of U.S. women (Baker, 1984; Lakoff and Scherr, 1984; and Collins, 1990). Beauty ideals usually include phenotypical traits such as whiteness and European features (Wolf, 1991; and Lakoff and Scherr, 1984).

But what does the relationship between skin tone and stratification outcomes mean in contemporary America? To what degree are stratification outcomes the byproducts of complexion-related mate selection processes? One of the most significant and recurring themes in the area of racial and ethnic inequality is that of differential marital patterns. To the degree that people with lighter complexions are more often chosen as husbands and wives, such patterns signal that the color complex is related to mate selection. Moreover, if high earners select mates with lighter complexions (from various racial and ethnic groups), we can think of the skin tone stratification process as being one that is at least in part driven by considerations that are internal to a community. To the degree that those with darker complexions have lower prospects for marriage or fewer options in terms of mate selection, we might think of the racialization of skin color as a phenomenon that, despite its externally imposed origins, has been internalized.

Is there a link between skin complexion and mate selection? If so, does the color-mate selection nexus operate the same for African Americans, Hispanics, and Asian Americans? This chapter presents evidence concerning the relationship between skin color and marital status among these three groups. It also presents information about skin tone and the earning power of the spouses of African Americans, Hispanics, and Asian Americans. We use data from the Multi-City Study of Urban Inequality (1992-94) to examine these relationships net of other factors which affect marital status. We also examine the degree to which the relationships among skin tone, self-esteem, and spousal earnings vary by gender for these various racial and ethnic groups. First, however, we summarize the literature on the importance of skin tone variation within communities of color.

## Skin Color and the Life Chances of People of Color

The literature on skin tone variations and mate selection has generally shown that lighter skin is preferred within darker subordinate racial groups (Drake and Cayton, 1945; Udry, 1997; Sahay and Piran, 1997; and Ross, 1997). This "bleaching syndrome" is attributed to subordinate group members taking on the dominant group values in order to assimilate into the dominant group. Among African American women, for example, even when they do not believe that lighter skin is better or more beautiful, they are still aware that other people do hold such beliefs. Research by Sahay and Prian (1997) has shown that some of these same basic patterns hold true for other groups of color. They demonstrated that some South Asians were primarily influenced by White Western culture as a result of British colonization. Even after South Asian countries regained their independence, they continued to hold on to White Western values. And those South Asians who have immigrated to Western countries continue to be directly influenced by the Western dominant culture. African Americans are also influenced by the dominant American (White) culture due to their subordinate group status within American society.

A number of writers have suggested that skin tone and stratification outcomes are not related in the same manner for all African Americans (e.g., Drake and Cayton, 1945; Frazier 1957a; 1957b; 1966; Blackwell 1975; Landry 1987; Hughes and Hertel, 1990; and Keith and Herring, 1991). It is reasonable to expect that such differences might exist among other groups as well. This is in addition to the idea that skin color may have different consequences for people from various racial and ethnic groups.

It is also possible that the relationship between skin tone and how other people think about a person may differ from the relationship between skin color and how that person thinks about himself or herself. Accordingly, we briefly review the literature on skin tone and mate selection as well as the literature on skin tone and self-perceptions.

*Mate Selection and Marital Patterns*

One of the earlier studies done on the effects of skin color on mate selection within the Black community was done by Udry and his colleagues (Udry, Bauman and Case, 1971). That study of African American married couples aimed to determine whether the effects of skin color had changed as a result of the "Black is beautiful" movement in the late sixties and seventies. Udry and his colleagues found that light skin remained an advantage for women in the mate selection process and that, at least for those men married during the sixties, darker skin proved to be advantageous. In a more recent study comparing the importance of attractiveness versus educational attainment of women as a predictor of women marrying husbands with higher socioeconomic status, Udry (1997) found that the effects of attractiveness varied for Black and White women. Although attractiveness is a strong predictor for lower status White women marrying husbands with high socioeconomic status, it is not a strong predictor for higher status White women. For Blacks, the importance of attractiveness does not disappear with the increase in woman's socioeconomic status. Attractiveness is important for Black women with lower educational attainment to marry an upwardly mobile husband. But, attractiveness becomes an even stronger predictor for women with higher educational attainment to marry upwardly mobile husbands.

Ross (1997) conducted a study of Black college students to determine if skin color was a significant factor in mate selection. The study attempted to measure students' willingness to date or marry people from a lower socioeconomic level, preference for dating or marrying persons with lighter skin, and importance of marrying people with higher socioeconomic levels. It was hypothesized that men and women would differ on their willingness and preferences to date "down" (marrying darker skinned Blacks or people with lower socioeconomic status) and that physical attractiveness is more important for men than for women when selecting a mate. The study presumed that light skin is considered an attribute of beauty for African Americans. The results showed that about one out of six of the women preferred to date (16%) or marry (17%) light skinned men. One out of three of the men preferred to date (33%) or marry (38%) light skinned women. The study also found that those with higher socioeconomic backgrounds were less concerned with marrying someone who was upwardly mobile than those with lower socioeconomic backgrounds.

Hughes and Hertel (1990) carried out an analysis of African

Americans to determine whether the socioeconomic statuses of respondents' spouses were correlated with respondents' skin tones. They found that light skinned Blacks were more likely to have spouses with higher socioeconomic statuses than darker skinned Blacks. This finding was consistent even after statistically controlling the socioeconomic statuses and socioeconomic backgrounds of the respondents themselves. These relationships were the same for both males and females.

Hunter (1998), also using national data, found that light skinned African American women had higher educational attainment, higher personal incomes, and were more likely to marry high-status husbands than were darker-skinned African American women. These patterns persisted even after controlling for background characteristics.

Finally, Hall (1995) explains that among Indian Hindus there exists a prejudice against darker skinned Indians. Light skinned spouses are preferred. For instance, light skinned wives are so preferred that Hindus from upper levels within a caste system will marry women from lower caste levels, exchanging her skin tone for his caste position. This preference is not as strong for Hindu men. Dark skinned Hindu men, who are of high status, can exchange their wealth for a light skinned wife. This is not as probable for dark skinned women.

*Skin Tone and Self-Perceptions*

Generally, the relationship between skin tone and self-perceptions exhibits patterns that differ from those demonstrated by skin tone and mate selection. For example, in a study of the self-perceptions of dark and light skinned Blacks, Wade (1996) found that dark-skinned males had more favorable self-perception of their sexual attractiveness relative to light skinned men. Self-perception of sexual attractiveness did not vary by skin color among women. Physical attractiveness did not vary by skin color for men nor women.

To determine differences in Black women's perception of body image, Bond and Cash (1992) asked African Americans about their satisfaction with their own skin colors. They found that 70% of the women in the sample believed lighter skin to be preferred by Black men. Medium skinned women idealized light skin. But, both light and dark skinned women considered their own skin tones to be ideal. Thirty-six percent of the women reported that, if given the chance, they would lighten their skin color. Seventeen percent said that they would darken their skin color. Nearly half (47%) said they would not choose to change their skin color. Furthermore, dissatisfaction with one's skin color was strongly correlated with dissatisfaction with one's body in general.

In a similar study of South Asian and European Canadian women's satisfaction with their bodies and skin colors, Sahay and Piran (1997) found that South Asian Canadian women desired to have lighter skins (not so light as to be considered White) relative to European Canadian women. European Canadian women, however, preferred to have darker skins (not so dark as to be considered non-White). The preference for lighter skins was greatest for darker skinned South Asian Canadians. As for body satisfaction, "medium skinned South Asian Canadians had lower body satisfaction than darker skinned South Asian Canadians." Both light skinned South Asian and European Canadian women had similar ratings for body satisfaction.

In a study using data from the National Survey of Black Americans, Thompson and Keith (forthcoming), found that skin tone has negative effects on self-esteem and self-efficacy but operates in different domains of the self for Black men and for Black women. They found that skin color is an important predictor of self-esteem for Black women but not for Black men. Conversely, they found that color predicts efficacy for Black men but not Black women. In other words, the effects of skin tone were gendered and conformed to traditional gendered expectations of masculinity and femininity.

In short, for both African Americans and South Asians, skin color is important. Skin color has played an important role in mate selection as well as one's self-perceptions. Among both groups, light skinned women are preferred for spouses. Research suggests, however, that this preference for lighter complexions is not as important to women in selecting their mates. Furthermore, light skinned women are more capable of exchanging their skin color for higher status husbands. Also, women's body satisfaction has varied by skin color. Both light and dark skinned women appear to be more satisfied with their bodies than medium skinned women.

It should also be noted that skin color is correlated with other phenotypic features such as eye color, hair texture, broadness of nose, and fullness of lips (Russell, Wilson, and Hall, 1992) . Along with light skin tone, blue and green eyes, European shaped noses, and straight as opposed to "kinky" hair are all accorded higher status both within and beyond the African American community (Thompson and Keith, forthcoming). "Colorism" incorporates preference for both light skin as well as these other attendant features. Hair, eye color and facial features function along with color in complex ways to shape opportunities, norms regarding attractiveness, self-concept, and overall body image (Thompson and Keith, forthcoming). Yet, it is skin tone that has received the most attention in research, as it is the most visible physical feature and is also the feature that is most enduring and difficult to change (Russell, Wilson, and Hall, 1992).

Below, we demonstrate how skin color affects the marital patterns of African Americans, Hispanics, and Asian Americans. We also discuss the relationship between skin tone and spousal earnings.

## The Color of Marriage
Is there a relationship between skin tone and marital status? Figure 4.1 shows that the answer is a decided yes. While 27% of those with dark complexion are currently married, 42% of those with light skin tone are currently married. These patterns are parallel for men and women, but the marriage rates are substantially higher for men. In particular, nearly half (47%) of men are currently married, but less than a third of women (31%) report that they are married. Men with dark complexions are much less likely (36%) to report that they are currently married than are other men

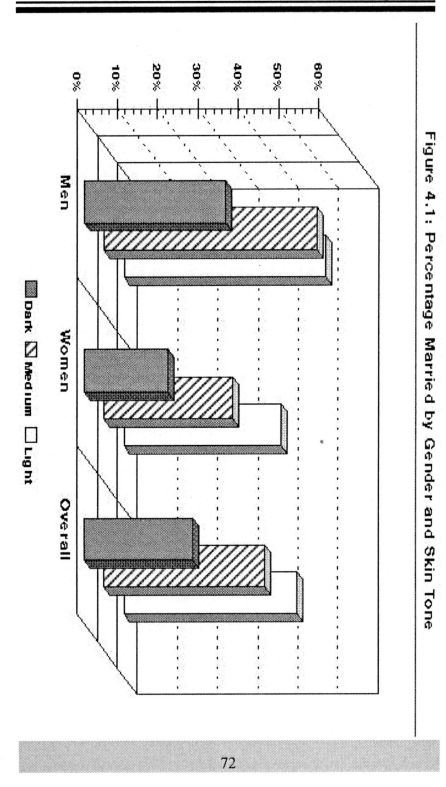

Figure 4.1: Percentage Married by Gender and Skin Tone

(52%). Women with dark complexions are also much less likely (21%) than are other women (35%) to report that they are married.

These marital patterns differ by gender, race and ethnicity. In particular, Figure 4.2 shows that among African Americans, men with light complexions (40%) are slightly more likely than are other African American men (32%) to be married. Among African American women, however, there are no systematic differences by skin tone, as roughly 19% of African American women of all skin tones are currently married. Additional analysis does, however, suggest that darker African American women get married later than their lighter counterparts. Only 12% of African American women with dark complexions were married by the median marital age. This compares to 20% of those with light complexions.

For Latinos, the relationship between skin tone and marital status also is different for men and women. Among Latina women, those with lighter complexions are more likely to be married. Among Latino men, it is those with medium complexions who are most likely to be married.

The relationship between skin complexion and marital status is also different for Asian men and women. Among Asian women, the lighter their complexions, the more likely are they to be married. Among Asian men, it is those with medium complexions who are most likely to be married.

Among those who are married, do those with lighter complexions tend to marry those who are more financially successful? Do they, for example, tend to marry those with higher incomes? Figure 4.3 shows that lighter skin tone is associated with higher spousal earnings overall. The spouses of those with dark complexions had average earnings of $17,510. This compares with $20,332 for the spouses of those with medium complexions, and $21,540 for the spouses of those with light skin tones. When race is taken into consideration, however, differential patterns emerge. Among African Americans, those with medium skin color have spouses with the highest average earnings ($24,096), followed by those with light skin tone ($21,093), and then those with dark complexion ($20,323). For Hispanics,

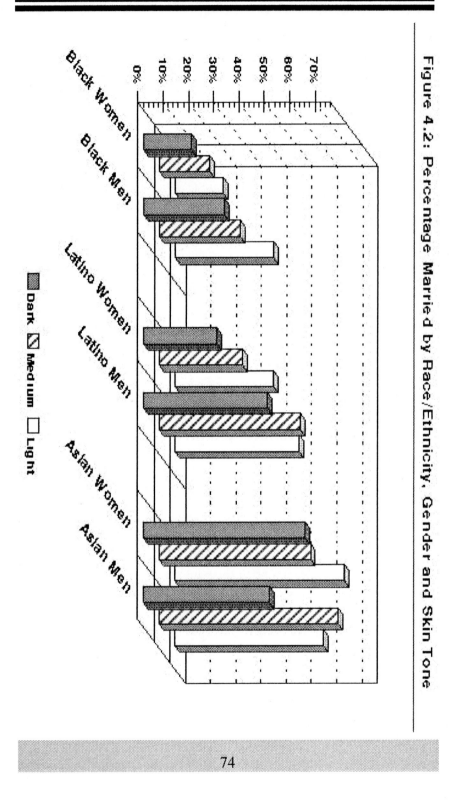

Figure 4.2: Percentage Married by Race/Ethnicity, Gender and Skin Tone

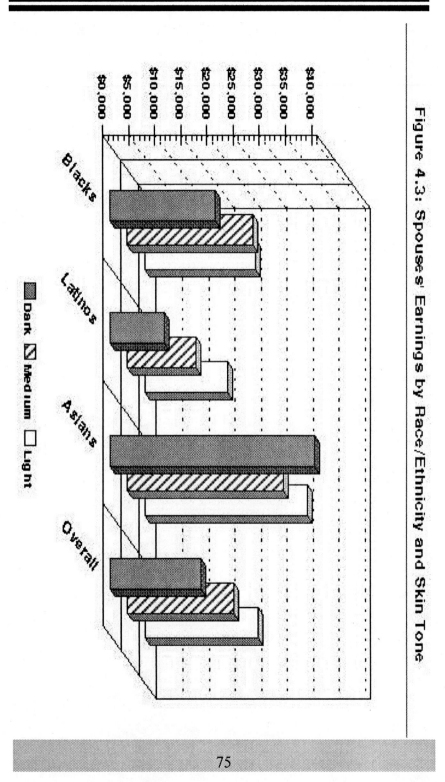

Figure 4.3: Spouses' Earnings by Race/Ethnicity and Skin Tone

lighter complexions are associated with spouses with (significantly) higher earnings, as those with dark complexions have spouses who earned $10,458 on average. Hispanics with medium skin tones had spouses who earned $13,193 on average, and those with light skin had spouses who earned $15,761 on average. Among Asians, those with dark complexions had spouses who averaged $39,286; those with medium complexions had spouses who averaged $29,823; and those with light complexions had spouses who earned $31,159 on average.

When other factors are included in our statistical analysis, there is a curvilinear (bell-shaped) relationship between skin tone and spousal earnings. Generally, the earnings of the spouses of those with light skin colors *and* dark skin colors are *lower* (about $3,000 lower) than the earnings of the spouses of those with medium skin tones. This is true even after we take into consideration the effects of other factors such as race. Among African Americans, the spouses of those with light complexions earn $8,620 less than the spouses of those with medium skin complexions. Among Hispanics, the spouses of those with fair complexion earn $6,626 less than those with medium complexions. These patterns suggest that spousal earnings are *not* associated with one's skin tone in a fashion whereby those with light complexions are more likely to be married to higher earners.

But do these patterns differ by gender? Because the literature suggests that there are often gender differences in the relationship between skin tone and stratification outcomes, we present the average spousal earnings by skin tone from a race-by-gender stratified analysis in Figure 4.4. This chart shows that among African American men, the wives of those with medium skin complexion are the highest earners. Similarly, among African American women, those with medium skin tones have the highest earning husbands. In other words, there are no discernible gender differences among African Americans. There is little to suggest that those with men with lighter complexions have higher income wives, and there is little to

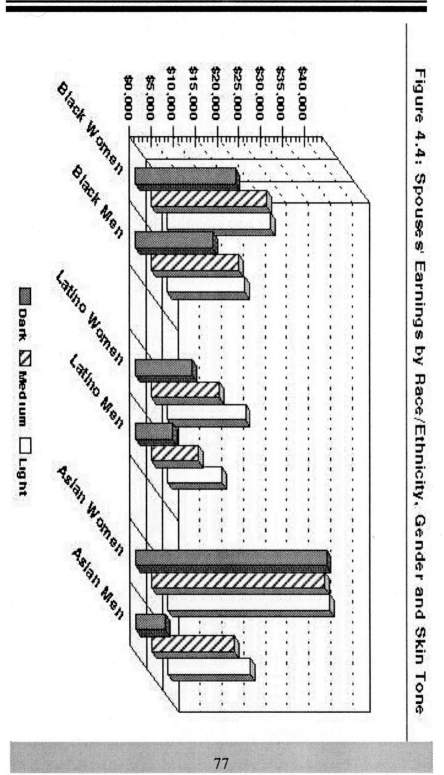

Figure 4.4: Spouses' Earnings by Race/Ethnicity, Gender and Skin Tone

suggest that those women with lighter complexions have higher income husbands.

The patterns for Hispanics, however, are different. Among Hispanic men and women, the lighter one's complexion, the higher are the earnings of one's spouse. Among Asian American men, it is those with light complexions who have the highest earning wives. But among Asian American women, it is those with medium complexions who have the highest earning husbands.

Generally, these results suggest that skin tone has, at best, a very modest relationship to spousal earnings. The results vary by racial/ethnic and gender subgroups. Among African Americans, there is little to suggest that mate selection follows the "bleaching syndrome," and there is little to suggest that men with lighter complexions are more likely to have higher earning wives or that women with lighter complexions are more likely to have higher earning husbands.

## Summary and Conclusions

This chapter began with the observation that skin tone has historically played a significant role in determining the life chances of people of color. Our central questions have been: "Are complexion-related outcomes the products of mate selection processes?" and "Do complexion-related outcomes operate in the same fashion for different racial/ethnic and gender groups?"

We conclude that skin tone, although historically important in determining the life chances of people of color, is not strongly related to marital patterns among African Americans. African American women with dark complexions are as likely as other African American women to be married. They do, however, appear to get married somewhat later than their lighter counterparts. There is at best a modest relationship between spousal earnings and skin tone. In other words, people of color do not bring about color stratification through their mate selections.

As Keith and Herring (1991) argued, these facts suggest that it is not primarily people of color who are involved in discriminating on the basis of skin color. Rather, it is more likely that color stratification comes about as a consequence of discrimination against people with darker complexions by those outside of their communities.

Because skin color stratification is the manifestation of a racialized ideology, it is not self-sustaining and must constantly be reinforced and recreated. If Whites, particularly in their roles as gatekeepers to jobs and education, continue to exercise color preferences, then we can expect skin tone to influence the status attainment of people of color in spite of diminished importance within these communities.

## References

Allen, Walter; Edward Telles, and Margaret Hunter. 2000. "Skin Color, Income and Education: A Comparison of African Americans and Mexican Americans." *National Journal of Sociology* 12:129-180.

Baker, Nancy C. 1984. *The Beauty Trap*. New York: Franklin Watts.

Bell, Yvonne R. and Cathy L. Bowie and Joseph A. Baldwin. 1990. "Afrocentric Cultural Consciousness and African-American Male-Female Relationships." *Journal of Black Studies* 21:162-189.

Billingsley, Andrew. 1968. *Black Families in White America*. NJ: Prentice-Hall.

Blackwell, James E. 1991. *The Black Community: Diversity and Unity*. New York: HarperCollins.

Bond, Selena and Thomas F. Cash, 1992. "Black Beauty: Skin Color and Body Images among African-American College Women." *Journal of Applied Social Psychology* 22:874-888.

Collins, Patricia Hill. 1990. *Black Feminist Thought: Knowledge, Consciousness, and the Politics of Empowerment*. New York: Routledge.

Davis, Allison, Burleigh R. Gardner, and Mary R. Gardner. 1941. *Deep South*. Chicago: University of Chicago Press.

Drake, St. Clair and Horace Cayton. 1945. *Black Metropolis*. New York: Harcourt Brace.

Frazier, E. Franklin. 1966. *The Negro Family in the United States*. Chicago: University of Chicago Press.

Frazier, E. Franklin. 1957a. *The Black Bourgeoisie*. New York: Free Press.

Frazier, E. Franklin. 1957b. *The Negro in the United States*. New York: Macmillan.

Hall, Ronald, 1995. "The Bleaching Syndrome African Americans' Response to Cultural Domination vis-à-vis Skin Color." *Journal of Black Studies* 26:172-184.

Hill, Mark E. 2000. "Color Differences in the Socioeconomic Status of African American Men: Results of a Longitudinal Study." *Social Forces* 78:1437-1460.

Hughes, Michael and Bradley Hertel, 1990. "The Significance of Color Remains: A Study of Life Chances, Mate Selection, and Ethnic Consciousness Among Black Americans." *Social Forces* 69:1105-1120.

Hunter, Margaret L. 1998. "Colorstruck: Skin Color Stratification in the Lives of African American Women." *Sociological Inquiry* 68:517-535.

Keith, Verna M. and Cedric Herring. 1991. "Skin Tone and Stratification in the Black Community." *American Journal of Sociology* 97:760-778.

Lakoff, Robin Tolmach and Racquel Scherr. 1984. *Face Value: The Politics of Beauty*. Boston: Routledge & Kegan Paul.

Landry, Bart. 1987. *The New Black Middle Class*. Berkeley and Los Angeles: University of California Press.

Ross, Louie E., 1997. "Mate Selection Preferences Among African-American College Students." *Journal of Black Studies* 27:554-569.

Russell, Kathy, Midge Wilson, and Ronald Hall. 1992. *The Color Complex: The Politics of Skin Color Among African Americans*. New York: Harcourt Brace Jovanovich.

Sahay, Sarita and Niva Piran, 1997. "Skin Color Preferences and Body Satisfaction among South-Asian Canadian and European-Canadian Female University Students." *Journal of Social Psychology* 137:167-171.

Thompson, Maxine Seaborn and Verna M. Keith. 2001. "The Blacker the Berry: Gender, Skin Tone, Self-Esteem, and Self-Efficacy." In *In and Out of Our Right Minds*. D. Brown and V. Keith (eds.). Cambridge, MA: Oxford University Press.

Udry, J. Richard, 1997. "The Importance of Being Beautiful: A Re-examination and Racial Comparison." *American Journal of Sociology* 83:154-160.

Udry, J. Richard, Karl E. Bauman and Charles Case, 1971. "Skin Color, Status and Mate Selection." *American Journal of Sociology* 76: 722-733.

Wade, T. Joel, 1996. "The Relationship Between Skin Color and Self-Perceived Global, Physical and Sexual Attractiveness, and Self-esteem for African-Americans." *Journal of Black Psychology* 22: 358-373.

Wolf, Naomi. 1991. *The Beauty Myth: How Images of Beauty are Used Against Women*. New York: Doubleday.

# Chapter 5

## *"Mama, Are You Brown?"*
### *Mutiracial Families and the Color Line*

**Heather M. Dalmage**
Roosevelt University

In *The Book of Life*, Barbara Katz Rothman observes that "Seeing race is always about . . . a discriminating, discerning, trained eye recognizing the "essential" or defining characteristic(s) in the individual that confer(s) race categorization" (Rothman, 2001:51). The "reading" of skin color and other discernible indicators of race guides most interactions. But what does skin color really tell us? Skin color can provide clues about what social situations a person might face in a racist society but it does not tell us about an individual's culture, politics, morals, education, intelligence, athletic ability, or class. For instance, we know that, based on skin color, a White male will have a much better chance of catching a cab than will a Black male. In this case, skin color gives us a clue that White men do not have to spend as much time or energy getting from one location to another. We can also surmise that these cab-catching White men don't have to worry about being late for an appointment because of racism. Skin color does not, however, tell us who is rich or poor; who is a Republican, Democrat, or Socialist. It does not tell us who is xenophobic, sexist, or homophobic. It does not tell us who can dance well, who is uptight, who is smart, or who can jump. Skin color actually tells us very little (Dalmage, 2000).

Our physical bodies mediate our experiences in the world and serve to place us in to particular categories. Of central concern to many multiracial family members I have interacted with and interviewed is of the disharmony between their physical appearance and societal expectations in a way that highlights the persistence of essentialist thinking in society. For instance, Whites in multiracial families talk about shifting racial locations and feeling like they are 'passing for White' (Lazarre, 1996; Reddy, 1994). Multiracial women with light skin and ambiguous features express a strong desire to have children who are visibly African American (Dalmage, 2000). Black members of multiracial families who had come to expect acceptance from other Blacks find that their choice of a White partner often makes them on outsider within Black communities. Physical bodies are categorized and valued according to socially constructed rules about privilege, power and domination.

The typologies created through western thought, first written by Linneaus, and used to maintain the color line to Whites' advantage have been dismissed by all but a fringe (Ferber, 1998; and Winant, 2001). Unfortunately, the underlying essentialist and racist assumptions persist and guide our social institutions and daily interactions. For instance, while most people would find it laughable to look at something like the shape of a forehead to determine predisposition to criminality, skin color coupled with other physical features are still used to provide clues about a person's place in the racial hierarchy and resulting treatment. Because of the importance of racial categories, most people do not feel comfortable until they have neatly categorized those with whom they are interacting. And yet, our bodies, politics and identities are often at odds, or more specifically, the way our bodies are read and the way we think about ourselves, are often at odds. Du Bois identified this experience many years ago as the "double consciousness," that is, we live at two levels, how we understand and value ourselves and our awareness of how others value and understand us (DuBois, 1977 [1935]; and Winant, 1997).

We can find social patterns tied to skin color and physical features, but social patterns tell us more about social structures and social inequality than about individuals within categories. Omi and Winant point out that "analyzing stereotypes reveals the always present, already active link between our view of the social structure–its demography, its laws, its customs, its threats–and our conceptions of what race means." The experiences of multiracial family members expose these links and highlight the individual and institutional effort expended in maintaining the color line. Moreover, their experiences indicate that dominant racial ideologies in the U.S. continue to be fed by essentialist understandings, that maintain a color line to the advantage of Whites, even as those advantages are being masked by color-blind rhetoric. In this chapter I will address the many ways the color line is maintained, the discrimination faced by multiracial family members, and some of the potential pitfalls of the racial thinking currently guiding the collective multiracial response to discrimination.

## Borders

Throughout U.S. history individuals invested in maintaining the color line have set up borders. Racial borders include the contested, patrolled, and often hostile spaces near the color line. Historical creations, borders have become institutionalized and internalized. They exist in how society is structured as well as in how individuals learn to think about and act on race. Borders created to protect resources such as goods and power are kept in place by laws, language, cultural norms, images, and individual action as well as by interlocking with other borders including national, religious, political, sexual, gender, racial, and age. Each has a unique history laden with power struggles. People are raised to understand their world through borders. We are taught from an early age to know where the borders exist. To young children, categories and their borders do not yet represent power and exclusion. They are just puzzles to be figured out. The construction of the puzzle takes place at the intersection of the physical body (skin color, physical features, hair texture) in interaction with family, friends, teachers, media, neighborhood, and for many, religion. How children understand the world and themselves racially is an outcome of all these interactions. As they grow, they learn about the power associated with the categories and the consequences for attempting to cross borders. The greater the power imbalance, the greater the consequences. As when touching a hot stove, we all learn where the boundaries are and avoid getting too close. We curtail our behaviors, thoughts, and desires so as not to get burned. By doing and seeing what is considered appropriate, we reinforce the strength of the categories and build borders. After learning to see categories, we internalize the borders, and assume the socially created differences and valuations of those differences are inherent and natural. In turn, we patrol ourselves and others and in the process, we strengthen the color line (Dalmage, 2000).

The other day I was shopping in the local grocery store near my home. As I pushed my daughter in her stroller through the crowded produce section she asked,

"Mama, are you brown?"

I made my way to the less crowded bread aisle so as to avoid an audience for what I thought was going to be our first "race" conversation.

"Papa is brown," I replied.

"Okay Mama. Can I get some cookies?"

I waited. That was it. End of conversation. What did this exchange mean to my almost three year-old multiracial daughter? What did the question mean to her thirty-something White Mama? If I had replied, "I'm White," I would have racialized a question that was about skin color. Yet, answering the way I did, I had left White an unnamed, universal category. As my daughter begins to put together pieces of a puzzle, I am acutely aware of the importance of helping her frame the social world in a way that doesn't reproduce White privilege and power, allows her freedom to think beyond racial borders, and have an appreciation for blackness. Being acutely aware and being acutely able are not synonymous, however, and here in lies the struggle for many multiracial family members. The color line was historically created and imposed to protect White privilege and power. Blacks have used the color line as a means for creating community in a struggle for liberation. Thus, moving beyond borders may translate into undermining those struggling for liberation, and yet, the borders impose, confine, and deflate our humanity.

Perhaps I should have made the conversation in the grocery store about race. After all, her daily existence, like all people in society, is saturated with all the signs of racial injustice. From Disney's *The Lion King* to *Cinderella* and beyond, the "bad," "evil" and "sinister" characters are given dark features. Goodness is light, and generally blond. The people in the street who ask for money and cause her to question aloud, "Mama, why does she live outside?" are Black. The homeowners on our street are disproportionately White; the renters are disproportionately Black. While she may not yet articulate what she sees, all of it informs her understandings of the world. At the same time, many of her favorite people are Black. I reason that she is observing the outcome of racial injustice, while she is learning the reality of humanity across and beyond the color line. Given the dual and opposing roles of the color line, those who cross the line through choice of partner, adoption, or birth struggle to articulate the world in a way that allows for movement beyond borders while simultaneously struggling for social justice. Exploring the experiences of multiracial family members highlights that one cannot happen without the other.

**Flipping the Script**

Nearly a hundred years ago, Du Bois addressed the problem of the color line as a central and pressing issue in society. Despite Du Bois' insights and a new century, society focuses on individuals who *cross the color line* rather than the production of the line itself. Academics, the media, and general public have constructed pictures of multiracial families as pathological. An abundance of work, particularly in the social sciences, has taken for granted that multiracial family members are "problems" to be analyzed: How do they identify and why? Who marries interracially and why? How can parents raise a healthy multiracial child? In daily interaction multiracial family members are held in suspicion by both sides. The color line remains beyond question while multiracial family members are labeled weak, neurotic, and wishy-washy.

For example, recently, a young multiracial woman who had run away from her home in the south was raped and killed by a Black man in Chicago. A local White reporter called to ask if I thought her "biracialness" was the basic problem this woman was running from and the reason she had left a party with three Black male strangers. The reporter explained that in talking with family members and friends it was apparent that this young woman was trying to get in touch with her "Black side." I was reminded of an interview I had conducted with a young multiracial woman a few years ago. She had grown tired of Blacks and Whites assuming that being "biracial" meant a difficult, internal war. When individuals asked her about the difficulty of being biracial she would sarcastically respond: "Well, yeah, you know, some mornings I wake up with this craving for fried chicken, and other mornings I just can't get the beat, I start dancing and can't get the beat" (Dalmage, 2000). The idea that multiracial people have discrete "Black sides" and "White sides" only makes sense in a society that continues to understand race as biological, static, and immutable. Irritated by the reporter's simplistic and narrow analysis I decided to "flip the script."[1] I explained to her that the media's fascination with this young woman's "biraciality" has been about maintaining racial myths. The story could have been sliced a dozen different ways. The fact that the media used it for yet another telling of the tragic Mulatto story speaks to the underlying assumptions guiding race thought in the U.S. I suggested she write about the ways the color line is reproduced thus making life more difficult for multiracial people. These ideas did not make print – not even close. The message of the story was loud and clear: White spaces are safe (albeit racially naive), Black spaces are dangerous (no place for those raised in naive White spaces), and a firm response of "tragic" was given to those who still wondered about that age-old question, "What about the children?" Nowhere did the reporter speak to the tragedy of racism and White supremacy. Perhaps one of the greatest difficulties faced by multiracial family members who attempt to think beyond borders is to challenge the current essentialist assumptions that inform U.S. racial thinking. In this case, the color line was left unexamined while the "problem" was located inside the murdered woman.

## Patrolling Borders

Individuals who comfortably claim one racial identity or think that race is something that can be observed or uncovered with enough clues may feel confusion, anger, skepticism, concern, pity, hostility, curiosity, or superiority when they meet someone who does not seem to fit neatly into a preset racial category. On both sides of the color line "border patrollers" believe the color line is static and immutable and thus they think they can distinguish between us and them. Border patrollers claim that race is a simple concept, demand that others comply, and make their presence felt through various actions (Dalmage, 2000). The most common action, by far, is the stare. Other forms of border patrolling include probing and inappropriate questions: *"Do you date Blacks or Whites?"*; expressions of concern: *"It must be so difficult"*; assumptive statements: *"I bet your parents had a problem with your relationship"*; and outright warnings by peers: *"You need to sit at our table in the lunchroom."* In rare situations the patrolling escalates to physical violence and death (Hale, 1998). Because they think they can determine "authentic" behaviors they also think they have the right to grant or withhold acceptance. Even when acceptance isn't granted, individuals are expected at act as if they belong; to do otherwise will provoke further patrolling. In *Race, Nation, Class: Ambiguous Identities*, Etienne Balibar and Immanuel Wallerstein (1991:71) note that "people shoot each other every day over the question of labels. And yet, the very people who do so tend to deny that the issue is complex or puzzling or indeed anything but self evident." In short, border patrollers simplify the complex and target those who call into question racial categories.

Everyone who has learned about race U.S. style looks for clues about how to racially categorize others. Some Whites need to take this step before they feel comfortable interacting with new people. They may sense that the color line is shifting and fear losing their racial status. Thus, until they can categorize others, they feel vague and uneasy about their own racial status and identity (Gotanda, 1995). For people of color, the desire to distinguish the color may concern a quest for allegiance and unity, a means to determine who is "us" and who is "them" politically, socially, and culturally (Dyson, 1994). While border patrolling from either side may be scary, hurtful, or annoying, Blacks and Whites are situated differently in the racial order and thus the patrolling has a very different meaning and consequence.

The color line was imposed by Whites who now have institutional means for maintaining their power; in contrast Blacks must consciously and actively struggle for liberation. Repeatedly, through my years researching and interacting with members of multiracial families I have heard, "The one thing that David Duke and Louis Farrakhan agree on is that we should not exist." Rarely analyzed is the differing historical legacies that bring each of the men to their conclusions. White border patrollers and Black border patrollers may each feel threatened by people who cross the color line, but the threat arises from different historical and material realities (Dalmage, 2000).

During slavery and Reconstruction, Blacks were denied all forms of legitimized power and were forced to struggle for physical survival. Through legal and extralegal forms of physical and psychological violence,

Whites imposed a racist system (Omi and Winant, 1994; Lopez, 1996). Any perceived transgression against the White supremacist system–against the imposed color line– was met with violence or death, a means that allowed White to create a sense of unity. Because of the terror created by violence, people defined as Black and thus as potential slaves began to suppress cultural and linguistic differences and build their own basis for unity (Levine, 1977); the color line began to be patrolled on both sides. In short, as Whites were creating a system in which White privilege would be institutionally protected, Blacks were unifying in a struggle for survival and liberation. Despite the institutional mechanisms in place to safeguard White privilege, many Whites continue to feel both the right and need to act out against those who cross the color line. Thus while Black border patrollers may be concerned about unity, belonging, and affirmation, Whites who patrol are primarily concerned with maintaining White privilege and a sense of White superiority.

The concern for multiracial family members is how to protect their families and children from the pain caused by border patrolling in ways that can transform a racist system. Attempts have been made to carve out spaces and reframe race in way that allow multiracial children and their families to live beyond borders. Unfortunately, the practice often has not been transformative, instead it has been largely invested in the same color-blind rhetoric that masks an essentialist and racist color line.

## Public Responses to the Patrolling

Through magazines, the Internet, and organizations, multiracial families have been reaching out to each other. For most people, the desire to meet others is about creating spaces in society where they do not have to fend off border patrollers. Until the 1980s most multiracial family members were forced to contend with border patrolling in isolation from other multiracial families. However, by the 1980s organizations began to arise, creating both real and imagined communities. This sense of community was developing during the Reagan years, which were marked by self-conscious efforts to create color-blind rhetoric and undermine civil rights legislation (Omi and Winant, 1996). The color-blind rhetoric resonated with many multiracial family members who knew, intimately, the hurtfulness and falseness of racial categories. Moreover, White members of multiracial families discover, often for the first time, the hurtfulness of racism. Without a connection or understanding of the richness of blackness as a social, historical, political, and cultural construction these Whites have erred in arguing for the transcending of race. Michael Eric Dyson argues that "the goal should not be to transcend race, but to transcend the biased meanings associated with race. Ironically, the very attempt to transcend race by denying its presence reinforces its power to influence perceptions because it gains strength in secrecy" (1994: 227). Unfortunately, many outspoken members of multiracial families believe that the removal of race talk from the social, legal, and political landscapes as a first step toward the acceptance of multiracial families and people in society (Dalmage, forthcoming).

Over the past twenty years, more than five dozen multiracial family organizations, numerous websites, and interested academicians and scholars have created a broadly defined *Multiracial Movement* (Dalmage forthcoming). The central rallying point for the movement has been the addition of a multiracial category to the census. Most multiracial family organizations have formally declared a desire for a socially accepted and officially recognized multiracial population. Within the multiracial movement, arguments for the addition of a multiracial category tend to fall into two overlapping groups. Each draws on liberal tenets of individual rights over group rights by suggesting that a multiracial category should be a priority despite the potential dangers such a category presents to civil rights legislation. One group argues that multiracial people constitute a new race. Some have even suggested that biological differences exist between multiracial people and others (Korgen, 1998; Project RACE, 1997). The other group asserts that a multiracial category will ultimately undermine the color line by working against the myth of White racial purity and the one-drop rule. Where the first group argues that race is essential and objective; adding a multiracial category is a way to be more accurate (Dalmage, 2000). The other group suggests that race, while historically constructed, is merely an illusion; adding a multiracial category will be an important step toward exploding the illusion. The ultimate goal for this group is to create a color-blind world and thus some have joined arms with conservatives to undermine race-based legislation. In fact, arguments on both sides fall short. Race is neither illusionary nor essential. It is a social construction that has created objective conditions of injustice. Any struggle to restructure racial categories should, at a minimum, address social justice; this may be possible only by articulating identities *within* communities that are already struggling for liberation (Dyson, 1998). A silent minority within the multiracial population has struggled to build connections in African American communities and in other communities struggling for social justice. These individuals, along with civil rights advocates, are often dismissed by outspoken members of the multiracial movement as 'missing the point' of the demands and needs of the multiracial population.

The multiracial movement continues to develop momentum from conservative racial politics, (some have actively joined arms with conservatives). Despite these allegiances, much of the rhetoric arising from the multiracial movement implies that multiracial activists have greater insight into race and a more progressive racial agenda than others. For instance, Francis Wardle, a self-proclaimed authority on multiracial issues praises "courageous people who withstood angry opposition from established civil rights groups and their intellectual and liberal supporters" (Wardle, 2001). Wardle fails to speak of the conservative support behind the "courageous people." That is, conservative political and social shifts toward color-blind ideologies that have made room for the possibility of a multiracial category are also the same shifts that are undermining civil rights legislation. Depicting the struggle for a multiracial category as one in opposition to civil rights groups implies that Blacks are the obstructionists to a more progressive understanding of race. Charles Byrd of Interracial Voice, a website that "wholeheartedly supported the initiative to establish a multiracial category on the 2000 Census," writes that "Afrocentric Nationalism by the Black community coupled with the 1967 Supreme Court decision overthrowing the remaining anti-miscegenation laws in this country are the two most important factors in the genesis of the multiracial "movement" (Byrd, 1996). Rather than acknowledging the historical context of White supremacy, Byrd's statement identifies Black nationalism as the reason a multiracial movement is necessary. Addressing the shortcomings of such a construction of history, Gary Peller writes, "To be sure, much nationalist rhetoric was reductionist with respect to the complexity of group relations . . . but through the identification of racial identity and group-consciousness as central to the structure of American social relations, the Black nationalists of the sixties also identified the particular aspect of Black liberation assumed–the commitment by Whites to deny the centrality of race as a historically constructed, powerful factor in the social structure of American life" (Peller, 1995:149). Statements such as Wardle's and Byrd's fail to grasp the complexity of race within a White supremacist society and thus cause people of color–Blacks in particular–to question the motives behind the push for a separate multiracial category.

In *The New Colored People: The Mixed-Race Movement in America*, Jon Michael Spencer calls on multiracial people with African ancestry to align with the Black community. At the same time, he points out that African Americans, "must open up new space for mixed-race Blacks to be biracially Black." He explains, "African Americans must not place membership restrictions on mixed-race people who say they are half Black. "The Black community cannot hold certain of its members in limbo, feeling uneasy about interracial marriages or their biracialness, and expect them to wait for acceptance" (Spencer, 1997: 159). Citing Itabari Njeri, he suggests that if Blacks do not open their borders, then "they are simply forcing the creation of a multiracial classification by forcing the exodus of mixed-race Blacks from even a partial Black identity" (Spencer, 1997: 159). The need for solidarity against White supremacy requires the recognition that the color line is not static and borders are not fixed and unchanging. Likewise, multiracial family members must begin to acknowledge, discuss, and act upon the connection between border patrolling and White supremacy. That is, Black communities have used border patrolling as a protection against White supremacy. If White supremacy did not exist then Black border patrolling would diminish. The central role that race, and more specifically White supremacy, has played in the U.S. must be acknowledged in any racial movement concerned with social justice. And here is precisely the point that must be addressed as various groups move to the corners waiting for the bell to ring on the next round of fights over racial categories and the meaning of race in society.

## Conclusions

Because multiracial people and often their families are visible indicators that the color line has been breached, they all will join in the discussion about multiracialism on some level (Nakashima, 1996: 80). Thus the politics of race and multiracialism extend beyond those who are active in multiracial organizations and overt politics. It includes all members of multiracial families—even those who want to opt out of racial discussions. For instance, when identifying themselves and others they may claim to be color blind, *"culture matters not race";* they may claim membership in a single racial community, *"my dad may be White, but I'm Black and that's that"*; they may advocate for a recognition of a multiracial identity, *"I have the right to identify how I choose."* In each of these examples a particular racial ideology and racial politic is being forwarded (Dalmage, forthcoming). For example, denying the significance of race also denies the significance of White supremacy and racism, while making claims to "individual rights" implies a level playing field and dismisses institutional racism (Roberts, 1997). In short, the ways we identify are intimately connected to our understandings of the world and our own role in the world.

It is one thing to seek a sense of comfort and belonging, it is another to demand that a particular identity be officially recognized. Some people hold out hope that a multiracial category will dilute racial categories into non-existence given the browning of America (Root, 1995). This category could even prove to be the unifier against a system of whiteness. However, a state legitimized multiracial classification could also function to blur clear signs of whiteness (Daniel, 1992). Attempts to redefine and transcend race must happen within the context of struggles for social justice. Multiracial family members are at a crossroads right now and must decide how to proceed. As we do, we must recognize and address race as a system of power. We must balance the desire to create spaces of comfort and the struggle for social justice and the liberation of all communities of color. Struggles for social justice must include expanded borders and attempts to move beyond borders must happen in the context of struggles for social justice.

My daughter and I were sharing fries at a local fast food joint when I noticed two pre-teen girls asking a homeless man about the open sores on his legs and feet. Kindly and gently the older Black man replied, "Comes from bein' in my shoes too long." Whether he meant to refer to his plight both as lived experience and metaphor, I do not know. I do know however, that his statement summed up well the outcome of a system of whiteness in which race pathologizes even as racial categories serve a purpose to those oppressed by whiteness. If we are concerned about humanity and social justice, we must explore the context of border patrolling and the functions of the color line protected by border patrolling. We must make clear the ways communities, identities, politics, and material realities are created and positioned by the color line. We must acknowledge the ways whiteness distorts, destroys, and dehumanizes.

The two young Black girls soon came to my table.

"Is she your daughter?" The older one asked.

"Yep." I replied.

"Where she get that hair?"

I looked at my daughter's Afro puffs springing back to life after the removal of her hat and hood.

"Her Papa's Black." I replied.

My daughter jumped up, eyes wide, "No! Papa's brown." Pointing to one of the girls, who by now had sat down with us, she said proudly, "Same, just like you."

## Endnote

1. Thanks to Tameka Elzy, a former graduate student at Roosevelt University, for suggesting this succinct phrase.

## References

Balibar, Etienne and Immanuel Wallerstein. 1991. *Race, Nation, Class: Ambiguous Identities.* New York: Verso.

Byrd, Charles Michael. 1996. *Speech.* Multiracial Solidarity March. Washington, D.C.

Cohen, Cathy J. 1996. "Contested Membership: Black Gay Identities and the Politics of AIDS." in *Queer Theory/Sociology.* Edited by Steven Seidman. Cambridge, MA.: Blackwell.

Dalmage, Heather. 2000. *Tripping on the Color Line: Black-White Multiracial Families in a Racially Divided World.* New Brunswick, NJ: Rutgers University Press.

Dalmage, Heather. Forthcoming. "Introduction," in *The Politics of Multiracialism.* Edited by Heather Dalmage. Albany, NY: SUNY Press.

Daniel, G. Reginald. 1992. "Beyond Black and White: The New

Multiracial Consciousness." Pp. 333-341 in *Racially Mixed People in America*. Edited by Maria Root. Newbury Park, CA: Sage Publications.

Dyson, Michael Eric. 1994. "Essentialism and the Complexity of Racial Identity." Pp. 218-229 in *Multiculturalism: A Critical Reader*. Edited by David Theo Goldberg. Cambridge, MA: Blackwell.

Dyson, Michael Eric. 1998. "Keynote Address." Color Lines in the 21st Century Conference. Chicago, Roosevelt University.

DuBois, W.E.B.1977 [1935]. *Black Reconstruction in America: An Essay Toward a History of the Part Which Black Folk Played in the Attempt to Reconstruct Democracy in America, 1860-1880*. New York: Atheneum.

Ferber, Abby. 1998. *White Man Falling: Race, Gender and White Supremacy*. Rowman & Littlefield: New York.

Gotanda, Neil. 1995. "A Critique of 'Our Constitution is Color-Blind.'" Pp. 257-275 in *Critical Race Theory: The Key Writings that Formed the Movement*. Edited by Kimberle Crenshaw, Neil Gotanda, Gary Peller, and Kendall Thomas. New York: New York University Press.

Hale, Grace Elizabeth. 1998. *The Making of Whiteness: The Culture of Segregation in the South, 1890-1940*. New York: Vintage.

Korgen, Kathy Odell. 1998. *From Black to Biracial: Transforming Identity Among Americans*. Westport, CT: Praeger.

Lazarre, Jane. 1996. *Beyond the Whiteness of Whiteness: Memoir of a White Mother of Black Sons*. Durham, N.C.: Duke University Press.

Levine, Lawrence. 1977. *Black Culture and Black Consciousness: Afro-American Folk Thought from Slavery to Freedom*. New York: Oxford University Press.

Lopez, Ian Haney. 1996. *White By Law: The Legal Construction of Race*. New York: New York University Press.

Nakashima, Cynthia. 1996. "Voices from the Movement: Approaches to Multiraciality," Page 80 in *The Multiracial Experience: Racial Borders as the New Frontier,* edited by Maria Root. Thousand Oaks, CA: Sage.

Peller, Gary. 1995. "Race-Consciousness." Pp. 127-158 in *Critical Race Theory: The Key Writings That Formed the Movement.* New York: The New Press.

Project RACE. 1997. "Urgent Medical Concerns." Posted on the Project RACE Website at: http://www. projectrace.home.mindspring.com.

Omi, Michael and Howard Winant. 1996. *Racial Formation in the United States: From the 1960s to the 1990s* (2nd ed.). New York: Routledge and Kegan, Paul.

Reddy, Maureen. 1994. *Crossing the Color Line: Race, Parenting, and Culture.* New Brunswick, N.J.: Rutgers University Press.

Roberts, Dorothy. 1997. *Killing the Black Body: Race, Reproduction, and the Meaning of Liberty.* New York: Pantheon.

Root, Maria. 1995. "The Multiracial Contribution to the Browning of America." Pp. 231-236 in *American Mixed Race: The Culture of Microdiversity.* Edited by Naomi Zack. Lanham, MD: Rowman and Littlefield.

Rothman, Barbara Katz. 2001. *The Book of Life.* Boston, MA: Beacon Press.

Spencer, Jon Michael. 1997. *The New Colored People: The Mixed-Race Movement in America.* New York: New York University Press.

Wardle, Francis. 2001. "Congratulations," in *newpeoplemagazine.com.*

Winant, Howard. 1997. "Behind Blue Eyes: Whiteness and Contemporary U.S. Racial Politics." Pp. 40-56 in *Off White: Readings on Race, Power, and Society.* Edited by Michelle Fine, Lois Weiss, Linda C. Powell, L. Mun Wong. New York: Routledge.

Winant, Howard. 2001. *The World is a Ghetto: Race and Democracy Since WWII.* New York: Basic Books.

# Chapter 6

# *Beyond Black?*
## *The Reflexivity of Appearances in Racial Identification Among Black/White Biracials*

**Kerry Ann Rockquemore**
Boston College
and
**David L. Brunsma**
University of Alabama at Huntsville

Both social science research and public policy on race relations in the United States collectively rest upon the one drop rule as an unquestioned assumption for establishing racial identity. This "rule" denotes that individuals with any Black ancestry whatsoever, belong to the Black "race" (Davis, 1991). Reflecting the social divisions inherent in the institution of slavery, the one drop rule emerged as a representation of the White supremacist ideological prohibition against miscegenation or "race-mixing." It was grounded in acutely eugenic racial classification schemes and hierarchies (Zuberi, 2001). The one drop rule has served as a legal, and subsequently, cultural and interactional marker, guiding the ever-changing dynamics of inter- *and* intra-racial relations. In shaping scientific research, institutional procedures, and public perceptions of race, this seemingly simple rule is *pervasive* in its scope and influence, *persistent* in staying power, and *pernicious* in its hegemonic capacity to sustain the myth of biological race.

The one drop rule has long provided a culturally sanctioned and socially supported answer to the question "who is Black?" in America. Under closer scrutiny, however, it has been found to be illogical in application, disconnected from biological reality, and a longstanding source of division within the Black community (Davis, 1991; Spencer, 1999; and Russell, Wilson and Hall, 1992). Yet, through oppressed groups' internalization of this norm (hooks, 1995), the one drop rule has forced a racialized identity on people who possess certain genealogical and/or phenotypic characteristics. For Whites, this cultural dictum has served as a way to identify and categorize individuals as "Black" by applying the criterion of that one powerful drop. Thus, socially and culturally, skin color and physical appearance have been viewed as determinative of Black group membership.

The accuracy and legitimacy of the one drop rule, as a guide for racial identification, has recently come under fire from organizations representing parents of mixed-race children and biracial people (Dalmage, forthcoming; Daniel, 2001; Root ,1996; and Spencer, 1999). Known as the "multiracial movement," they have argued that (1) increasing interracial marriage and coupling have produced a "biracial baby boom,"( 2) mixed-race people understand themselves as biracial, and (3) the U.S. government should add a "multiracial" category to the 2000 census as a reflection of changing demographic trends (Anderson and Fienberg, 1999; Spencer, 1997; and Spencer, 1999). This movement was opposed by civil rights leaders who contended that the one drop rule is alive and well as a classification norm, that an estimated 75% of the African American population has White ancestry and that, irrespective of an individual's desire for self-definition, society continues to view anyone with one drop of Black blood as a member of the Black race.

To social scientists, the existence of mixed-race people is clearly *not* a new social phenomenon. What is new, however, is the recent challenge to the one drop rule and the idea that in post-civil rights America, social forces have created a social environment in which biracial people may identify, and be identified by others, as something other than Black (Korgen, 1998). These forces include declining structural barriers (Collins, 1998; Durr and Logan 1997; Freeman, 1981; Farley, 1984), the diffusion and co-optation of Black culture (Dyson, 1997; hooks, 1992; and Rose, 1994) and increased interracial coupling and marriage (Besharov and Sullivan, 1996). These various factors have produced a great deal of within-group diversification among African Americans and increasingly frequent questions about the meaning of "Blackness," the cohesiveness of the "Black community" and the diversification of "Black culture." This fluidity has dissipated the deterministic aspects of the one drop rule and weakened its near total constraint on racial identity. As the one drop rule loses cultural support (via the emergence of self-identifying multiracial celebrities) and institutional sanctioning (via the U.S. Census), increasingly diverse racial identity choices are being observed among multiracial people.

The addition of a "check all that apply" directive in the 2000 census suggests that racial identity has shifted from caste-like rigidity to more porous and fluid notions of racial group membership. Or has it? Are appearances declining in significance for the racial identity of multiracial individuals? Do skin color and the racialized assumptions of others with whom biracial people interact determine their racial identity? We address the role that appearances play in the identity choices by focusing on those who straddle the most volatile racial divide in the United States: Black/White biracials.

## Research on Skin Color and Appearances

Throughout the history of the United States, African Americans' social status has been intimately related to the color of their skin (Hughes and Hertel, 1990). During slavery, light skinned Blacks were accorded privileges in the form of household duties, less violent treatment by overseers, better living conditions, educational opportunities, and opportunities for manumission (Billingsley, 1968; Franklin, 1980; Frazier, 1957; Keith and Herring, 1991; Landry, 1987; and Myrdal, 1944). After the Civil War, light skin became a condition for the attainment of prestige in the Black community (Davis, Gardner, and Gardner, 1941; Dollard ,1957; Drake and Cayton ,1945; and Myrdal 1944). Dark skin increasingly symbolized lower status while light skin became even more associated with high status (Herskovits, 1968; Parrish, 1944; and Warner, Junker and Adams, 1941). Because of the preference for all things that approximated whiteness, many Blacks desired fair skin, White facial features and straight hair (Johnson, 1941).

Ideologically, White supremacist logic defined Blacks as barbaric, savage and ugly, in juxtaposition to Whites who were deemed civilized, Christian, and beautiful (Fanon, 1967). Hunter (1998: 519) argues that various phenotypic traits became the symbols of racist colonial ideology, so that "dark brown skin, kinky hair, and wide noses *themselves* started to represent barbarism and ugliness. Similarly, straight blonde hair and white skin as physical traits came to represent civility and beauty." From this dichotomy, two categories emerged: (1) "good" (White) features–straight and/or long hair, a small nose, thin lips and light eyes and (2) "bad" (Black) features–short or kinky hair, full lips, and a wide nose (Neal and Wilson, 1989). Over time, nose width, lip thickness, and hair texture joined skin color as important intra-racial status markers within the Black community (Grier and Cobbs, 1968; and Gwaltney, 1980).

Social scientists studying skin color stratification have found that it affects many facets of Black people's lives. Phenotype has been associated with rates of mental illness (Boyd-Franklin, 1989; Harvey, 1995; and Neal and Wilson, 1989), body image dissatisfaction (Bond and Cash, 1992), and difficulties in self-concept and self-esteem development among those with darker skin (Smith, 1979; Clark and Clark, 1947; and Holtzman, 1973). Skin color differences have also been found to affect mate selection (Bond and Cash, 1992; Goering, 1971; Hall, 1992; and Udry, Baumann, and Chase, 1971) and friendship networks (Hallinan and Williams, 1987; and Porter, 1991). Despite the "Black is beautiful" message of the Black power movement, recent empirical research documents that light skinned Blacks continue to be evaluated as more attractive than those with dark skin (Hall, 1992; Neal and Wilson, 1989; and Russell, Wilson and Hall, 1993) and have higher personal income, educational attainment, and occupational prestige (Hughes and Hertel, 1990; and Keith and Herring, 1991).

Under the guise of the one drop rule, individuals with mixed race ancestry were considered a part of the African American population, making up a disproportionate share of those who benefitted from skin color stratification. It is only in recent literature that scholars have begun to study racial identification processes among biracial people as distinct from Blacks. This research has documented the fact that multiracial people make various choices about their racial identity. In accordance with the one drop rule, some individuals with one Black and one White parent identify exclusively as Black (Root, 1990, 1996; Rockquemore and Brunsma, 2001; Storrs, 1999). However, in complete defiance of that rule, others choose White as their racial identity (Root, 1998; and Rockquemore and Brunsma, 2001). The majority of this literature focuses on the emergence of a "border" or biracial identity that blends both of an individual's racial backgrounds into a new and unique category of self-understanding (Anzaldua, 1987; Bowles, 1993; Bradshaw, 1992; Brown, 1990; Daniel, 1996; Fields, 1996; Hall,1980; Johnson, 1992; Kerwin, Ponterotto, Jackson and Harris, 1993; Kich, 1992; King and DaCosta, 1996; Williams, 1996; Herring, 1995; Poston, 1990; Rockquemore and Brunsma 2001; Gibbs, 1997; Tizard and Phoenix, 1995; and Wardle, 1987 and 1992). Some biracial people choose not one, but several categories of identification, shifting between Black, White and biracial identities depending on the racial composition of the group they are interacting within (Daniel, 1996; Miller, 1992; Root, 1990; Stephens, 1992; Tizard and Phoenix, 1995). In addition, there are also biracial people who eschew any racial designation whatsoever and describe their identity in ways that are not racialized. These "transcendents" or "marginals" claim they have no racial identity (Daniel, 1996; Rockquemore, 1999, and Rockquemore and Brunsma, 2001).

Given the multidimensional ways in which biracial individuals understand their racial identity, and the varied of social contexts in which they interact, the link between skin color and identity is much more complex than the straightforward causal effects observed among the Black population. We turn now to the theoretical models that link appearance and identity to gain insight into how these social processes may explain the influence of appearances on racial identity construction among biracial people.

## Identity Theory and Appearances: More than Meets the Eye

Our investigation of the link between appearances and racial identity is rooted in three standard propositions of symbolic interactionism: that humans perceive things through the medium of meaning, that meaning is created through social interaction, and that meanings also change through succeeding interactions (Blumer, 1969). In terms of *identity*, actors are situated within social contexts that define the existing parameters of possible identities, the meaning of those identities, and their importance vis-à-vis one another. Identity, in this schema, refers to a validated sense of self that socially defines and places the social actor (Stone, 1962). As a result of this process of *mutual identification*, individuals construct identities, placing themselves and others, and evaluating their selves in relation to others.

According to Stone (1962), appearances not only communicate identity, but also have a reflexive relationship with identity. Through our appearances, we present our self to others, mobilizing a response (or review) from them. In addition, we have the capacity to imagine others' responses concerning our presented identity prior to that response (preview). We can, therefore, make adjustments in our presentation of self.

Stone further elaborates that in order for an identity to "achieve significance," the identity presented (through appearances) must match the review of others. If this mutual identification does not occur, then the presented identity is challenged and fails to be realized.

While Stone never intended his appearance model to apply to *racial* identities, we believe it provides a foundation for a conceptual apparatus that explains variation in racial identity among biracial individuals. In a racist social structure, race functions as a master status, making an actor's physical body a collection of cultural meanings that provide basic information to others. As previously described, skin color, hair texture and facial features are not simply construed as value-neutral bodily differences, but instead carry symbolic, and thus racialized, meanings. In the context of the one drop rule as categorization norm, physical characteristics act as inescapable signifiers used by others to define and situate an actor's identity and impute various meanings on the individuals' attitudes, values, and moral character.

If race is a master status, and appearances communicate that status, how then can individuals with Black ancestry claim any identity other than Black? What occurs in circumstances where physical characteristics are ambiguous and where an individual's presented identity may be continuously challenged? How can a person choose an exclusively Black, or exclusively White, identity if their physical appearance does not match their chosen identity? All these questions point to the critical role of social context in the process of identity construction. If, in fact, appearances do affect racial identity among multiracial individuals, it is most likely to occur in a *contextualized* manner.

Given that identity is an interactionally validated self-understanding, an identity can only be realized when both the self and others recognize a particular identity. Depending on the context and the interactions taking place within it, perceptions of appearance are primarily based on others' assumptions and the individual's understanding of those assumptions. Specifically, social context affects how we understand ourselves and how we are understood by others. Appearance in general, and skin color in particular, have both a personal and a social component: we perceive our own skin color, but also interprets our appearance through the "eyes" of others within any given interactional sphere. If a mixed-race individual is to construct a racial identity other than that dictated by the one drop rule, that alternative identity must be: (1) considered legitimate in their social context and (2) validated in their interactions with others.

## Findings

### Variation in Racial Identity

Respondents in our sample varied greatly in their choices of racial identity. In seeming contradiction to the one drop rule, only 13.7% of our sample identified exclusively as Black, while 3.7% identified exclusively as White. The majority of our respondents (64%) described their racial identity as "biracial," understanding themselves as neither Black nor White, but some distinct combination of the two. Five percent viewed themselves as possessing multiple racial identities, shifting between Black, White and biracial depending on the circumstances and another 13.7% claimed that they have no racial identity whatsoever.

### Skin Color vs. Appearance

Respondents, by their own estimation, assessed their skin color as ranging across the phenotypic spectrum (ranging from 0-12; median 6). However, the majority of respondents (56.2%) described their appearance as "ambiguous though most people assume I am Black"–despite reporting wide variation in skin color. Seventeen percent stated that they "appear Black, most people assume I am Black," while sixteen percent stated that they were "ambiguous, most people do *not* assume I am Black." Finally, ten percent of our sample said they "appear White, I could pass as White." An examination of the descriptive measures reveal two crucial facts that are important to our forthcoming analysis: (1) the sample includes variation on the two key measures of appearance set forth in our theoretical model, and (2) the differences between these two variables suggest that they are, in fact, measuring two conceptually distinct elements.

## Appearance and Biracial Identity

Respondents who chose "biracial" to describe their racial identity had a common set of social experiences. Many of them were middle- to upper-middle class, educated in private schools, raised in predominately White neighborhoods with predominately White friends and relatives composing their social networks. In many of these cases, they were the only (or one of few) non-White within their schools and communities. Many were popular and active in sports and school activities and/or held leadership positions in their educational institutions. In fact, they approximated their White peers in almost every way including their language usage, tastes, mannerisms, and style. In fact, the only differences between them and their peers was the racial group membership of one of their parents (who may, or may not, have played a role in their upbringing) and their physical appearance. In the minds of their peers, they were more like them than they were different and did not fit into their cognitive conception of "Black." Given that both the respondents and their peers had little contact with Blacks, their perceptions were largely stereotypical and media-derived. The result of this particular set of circumstances is that individuals repeatedly were told by their peers (in a complimentary fashion) "Well, I don't really think of you as Black.". This statement implies: (1) that the speaker has a cognitive perception of what "Black" is; (2) that "Black" is something different from what the speaker is ("White"); and (3) that the respondents do not fit into that category because they are more like the speaker (in the speaker's mind) than the speaker's understanding of "Black." This coincidental failure of mutual identification is for both parties to agree on a new category of identification–that being "biracial" where biracial means, for both, something between White and Black. It is within this particular type of social context, combined with a homogeneous set of social networks, that this group of respondents were able to construct and maintain a biracial identity.

Although the most common choice of racial identity among our respondents was "biracial," this group of respondents can be disaggregated into two distinct subgroups: those who have their biracial identity validated by others and those who do not. While 23.6% of the total sample identify exclusively as biracial, another 40.4% qualify that by stating "but I experience the world as a Black person." This indicates that while the racial category "biracial" may receive validation in some contexts, it is not universally accepted as a legitimate category of racial identity. When an individual's racial identity is not validated by others in their social network, they must either alter their identification or remain in a nebulous, marginal, and unresolved state with regard to their racial identity. The salient question is what difference appearance makes, if any, in the construction of a biracial identity? Are there differences, rooted in appearances that distinguish between those with a validated biracial identity versus those who remain unvalidated?

There is a wide distribution of skin tones among those who identify exclusively as biracial, with most describing themselves in the middle of the spectrum. Skin color, however, does not influence whether or not others validate their racial identity. What is more important is their socially-mediated appearance. More than twice as many of the unvalidated respondents are perceived by others to be Black than those whose biracial identity is validated. While "biracial," as a legitimate racial category, is acceptable in some of the respondents' social networks, it is not in others and though they desire a unique identity as biracial, if they appear Black to others, they are most likely to report that "I consider myself biracial but I experience the world as a Black person."

When we consider the process of mutual identification, interaction becomes difficult if individuals cannot be placed immediately and unconsciously into a particular racial group. Categorization is problematic when: (1) bodily features are ambiguous; (2) others have information about the individual that complicates categorization (such as knowing that a person has one Black and one White parent); or (3) the individual's secondary and tertiary cues (language and dress) do not fit into the other's preconceived ideas about members of a particular category. Any one or a combination of these factors can introduce difficulty into the mutual identification process. This difficulty is typically broken by directly addressing the identification problem. For example, biracial individuals often report being asked, "What are you?" to clarify an ambiguous appearance. This question and answer series often involves negotiation, resulting in the introduction of a new category of meaning–that being "biracial."

Negotiations in the identification process explain how respondents construct racial self-understandings regardless of their bodily appearances. Among the validated biracials are individuals who may be characterized from appearance alone as Black. However, their White parentage, socialization in White middle class networks, and their presentation of self allow them to understand themselves, and be validated by others, as "biracial." This category also encompasses individuals whose physical characteristics are ambiguous (but not White) with similar socialization experiences. Finally, this category includes individuals who are "light enough to pass," or look White, who also share similar social experiences. In sum, regardless of the individuals' bodily characteristics, their understanding of their racial identity as neither Black nor White derives from the complexity of the mutual identification process and the ability of individual actors to negotiate a meaningful identity with a selected subset of White others. The situation is entirely different for those respondents whose identity is not renegotiated, where the process of mutual identification is seemingly bypassed and the individual is assumed to be

Black by others – the unvalidated group. They are trapped in the gray area between the one drop rule and the multiracial movement, both of which have worked to parameterize their racial identities in opposing directions.

*Appearance and Singular Identities*

In contrast to those who choose a biracial identity, there are individuals with one Black and one White parent who identify exclusively as Black or exclusively as White. For them, "biracial" is a mere acknowledgment of the racial categorization of one of their birth parents. Their cognitive conception of what it means to be "Black" (or less commonly "White) is inclusive of a wide range of individual appearances and parental combinations. At the extreme, individuals simply admit the existence of their (White or Black) parent, but it is not salient to their self-definition and may not be offered as identifying information unless specifically requested.

John is one of our respondents who self-identifies as White. His case, while rare, is worthy of further analysis because it directly challenges the one drop rule. John was raised by his White mother and step father in an affluent White suburb. He was not told that his biological father was Black until he was 18, which did not change his racial self-understanding whatsoever. In part, John's failure to consider the race of his father as necessitating a modification of his racial identity is due to the negative association with the circumstances of his conception (his mother was raped). It is also partly due to his physical appearance and the fact that other people assume, without question, that he is White. In this case, the individual has constructed a singular racial identity as "White" without knowing that his biological father was African American. This identity was consistently validated throughout his socialization because of his appearance and social context. When the critical information was revealed, he was unable to reconcile it with his constructed identity. Instead of re-constructing his racial identity in light of the new information, he chose to have his appearance permanently altered via plastic surgery in order to solidify his whiteness.

Singular identities rely heavily on a combination of physical characteristics and the cultural availability of identity options. For many, "biracial" is simply not an available option of racial identification, either because others do not hold that category to be meaningful, or the individual's physical appearance demands adherence to traditional categories of racial grouping. Of the respondents who adopted a Black identity, ninety five percent reported that others "assume they are Black." When others assume they are Black, and particularly when they exist in a Black social network, respondents construct and maintain a Black identity. In fact, none of those choosing the Black identity said that they "appear White and could pass," even though twenty seven percent of them described themselves as having light skin color.

In the case of the singular Black identity, we see a straightforward relationship between appearance and racial identity. Our respondents who chose this identity option overwhelmingly were assumed by other people to be Black despite the fact that they described themselves as having a wide range of skin colors. Predictably, the pre-view, self-presentation and review were all Black and the mutual identification process occurred quickly, efficiently and without incident in the course of social interaction.

*Appearance and the Protean Identity*

Still other individuals in our sample understand their racial identity as characterized by their protean capacity to move between and among cultural contexts and established identities. These respondents highlight their ability to cross cultural boundaries between Black, White, and biracial–a possibility available to them because they possess the ability to present a Black, White, and biracial identities successfully. Highlighting their cultural savvy in multiple social worlds, they describe themselves as being validated, however conditionally, in varied interactional settings.

Their racial identities are accepted by members of different racial groups in diverse social contexts because their dual experiences with both Whites and Blacks have given them the ability to shift their identity according to the context of any particular interaction. Most importantly, they have learned to effectively imagine the desired racial identity of their audience and adjust their presentation of self accordingly. This contextual shifting is evidence of a complex self, one that has a heightened concomitant awareness of the self in action.

Individuals who shift their racial identity were most likely to use multiple and varied self-labels. At times, they would call themselves "Black," at others "White"ethnic, and still others "biracial." They readily admitted checking different racial identity boxes on institutional forms according to what they thought the audience would find most favorable. For example, when filling out admissions forms for colleges and universities, members of this group admitted checking "Black" as their race. They did so because of a perception that this would enhance their opportunities of gaining admission or financial aid. These individuals fall into a location that cannot be easily categorized by their appearance. Instead of constant negotiation (the strategy of those with an exclusively biracial identity), they put emphasis on playing the expected role, or allowing the pre-view to dictate their identity instead of presenting their authentic self. One cannot simply look at them and know that they are Black-Irish-biracial, or Black-German-biracial. Even if it were somehow possible to communicate this in their bodily presence, it would be an ambiguous, or meaningless, category of understanding for most others. It would not allow for the facile categorization that the general categories of placement provide. Stated simply, it would not facilitate the important process of mutual identification.

Overall, the skin color of respondents choosing this protean option is centered in the middle of the spectrum. In addition, they have a fairly wide range of appearances as understood through the reviews of others;

however, most report their appearance as "ambiguous, but assumed Black" by others. What is interesting about this option is the conscious manipulation of appearances and the use of secondary and tertiary cues. Respondents moved in and between standard and Black vernacular English with an intuitive ease. In one case, we were able to observe this during the interview. The respondent and the interviewer were seated in the main eating area on campus and several of the respondent's friends approached the table during the interview. The respondent greeted each one differently, some with standard English and some with Black vernacular English, some with a stiff body posture, some with a loose demeanor. In fact, due to the ambiguities in the interviewer's appearance, this particular respondent began the interview speaking standard English because he was unable to assess her pre-view. Several minutes into the interview, he directly inquired about her racial identity. After receiving an answer, his formal demeanor instantly slipped away and he never again used Standard English.

Renegotiating a program is, for this group, not a fundamentally problematic experience. If, for any reason, their pre-view is wrong or they misjudge the expected response of the other, they simply renegotiate. A challenge to a projected identity is not equivalent to a questioning of the self. For those who understand their racial identity as "biracial," an unvalidated identity is highly problematic. If, for example, someone were to call them a derogatory name used exclusively for African Americans and the context of the situation did not allow for renegotiating, it would call their self-understanding directly into question. For the protean group, however, no such self-questioning would be necessary. Because they are continually engaged in identity work and are not particularly wedded to any one identity, they can shift to an alternative one without great psychological cost.

*Appearance and the Transcendent Identity*

A small number of our respondents described themselves as having no racial identity (13.8%). Reminiscent of Park's "Marginal Man," they possess the qualities of the cosmopolitan stranger, one whose marginal status enables an objective view of social reality. This "transcendent" identity was most prevalent among interview respondents who appeared White. Their presentation of self was intentionally race-less because they did not consider themselves to have any racial identity whatsoever. Given that American society has a finite codification system of racial group membership, this purported race-less program was the functional equivalent to presenting a White identity. In fact, built into every interaction was the anticipation that the reviews of others would be erroneous, or an acceptance of the fact that others would assume they are White. For example, when Mike entered an interactional context, his physical features did not, in and of themselves, announce any particular racial identity (by default, he was considered White). Mike did not engage in any attempts to utilize secondary or tertiary cues, such as the purposive use of Black vernacular, or donning certain types of apparel as a cue of racial group membership. In his mind, he presented identities that were unrelated to any master status racial category. Because his bodily features were unambiguous (he looked White), he was repeatedly assumed to be White. This individual allowed miscategorization in order to facilitate and prioritize his other non-racial identities, but would reveal his parentage if the information was requested.

This type of identity has been constructed over time due to the ambiguity of the individual's appearance and parental socialization stressing the inaccuracies and ideological problematic of racial categorization. Due to his bodily ambiguities, he can go for long periods of time with the non-racial identity maintained and continuously validated. However, in some social contexts, and for some individuals, attempts to avoid, deny, or denounce categorization are unacceptable. It is intolerable in some contexts precisely because the mutual identification process that utilizes racial categorizations has meaningful consequences. Where racial group membership is a particularly salient feature of everyday life, one's group membership serves as a signifier of where one will stand on social issues; with whom one can (and cannot) have friendships, and the range of others considered acceptable in the dating pool. Upon entering this type of social context, where the race-less stranger is no longer an available possibility, the demands for self-identification are both persistent and difficult to avoid. Given that the one drop rule remains, by and large, the cultural and legal norm, the result is a grudging acceptance of categorization as Black. We refrain from saying that these respondents accept a Black *identity* because it is only the *label* "Black" that is accepted. This particular group of individuals (those who do not look Black) may also find themselves in social contexts where they experience the double bind of not being accepted as Black by either Whites or Blacks.

In sum, our results indicate that there is no association between skin color and racial identity, yet there is a strong association between socially-mediated appearance and racial identity. This is not surprising, because our appearance measure (much more so than skin color) taps into both the appraisal of others *and* the racialized assumptions others make about biracial individuals.

**Discussion**

When focusing on racial identity, the use of appearances as signifiers of group membership are not always clear cut. In fact, the relationship between appearances and racial identity choice becomes even more complex when we consider the multi-dimensionality of biracial identity. Given the various racial identity choices made by our sample of respondents, the appearance-identity link functions in different ways in different contexts. What is clear is that the basic process of mutual identification helps us to better understand two outcomes. The first is how people with the same parental background (one Black and one White parent) can make very different choices about their racial identities. The second is to try to understand why one's appearance does not always directly predict that outcome. In other words, why do we find people who appear White yet identify as Black and those who appear Black who say they are *not* Black, but biracial? Trying to interpret these cases becomes clearer if we focus on the basic processes that take place *between* individuals and *within* the individual.

The first process, mutual identification, is critical to both identity construction and maintenance. If an individual (regardless of bodily characteristics) exists within a social context where "biracial" is a meaningful identity, he or she may develop a biracial identity. If this racial category does not exist and one becomes accustomed to and adept at switching from Black to White, they will construct multiple racial identities. If an individual appears White, they may develop no racial identity, but only if their social context does not demand categorization. If none of these options are available, then the one drop rule dictates that their racial identity above and beyond (and at times in spite of) their appearance will be "Black."

The process of identity construction also involves the self functioning as subject, in such a way that we are able to reflect on our own identity-in-context. In some cases (the protean option), the self not only has the capacity for spontaneous adjustment, but it uses that concomitant awareness as a survival tool. Individuals can assess the anticipated response from an approaching other, modify their presentation of self accordingly, and continually monitor their performance for necessary renegotiating or re-formulations. This intense activity requires an ongoing subjective awareness of the self's activities and much bi-cultural (or identity) capital (see Côté, 1996). We see this same process continually at work in the other identity options, however, it takes on a slightly variant form of activity.

By focusing on the space between mutual identification and self-monitoring, we see that identity development is a dynamic journey and not a stagnant destination. This view of identity construction and maintenance highlights the importance of interactional strategies (Berzonsky, 1999c;

Blanz, 1998), negotiations (Gilliam and Gilliam, 1999; Swann, 1987), and racial narratives (Storrs, 1999). Indeed, a micro perspective highlights the way that individuals engage in "identity work" on an interaction-by-interaction basis (Storrs, 1999) by using caches of "identity capital" within a variety of salient "identity markets" (Côté, 1996, 1997). Research on biracial identity would greatly benefit from further exploration of the existence of multiple identities within one individual, the functions each plays, the contextual enactment of these identities, and how they change over time (Deaux, 1993; Deaux et al., 1995; and Ethier and Deaux, 1994).

It is still the case that racial identities are subject to a degree of constraint that ethnic identities are not. Specifically, racial identities continue to be constrained by historical stratification that is directly tied to bodily characteristics. These characteristics linger in our cultural symbols and traditional ways of thinking and being. The existence, experience and voice of biracial individuals are challenging the current categorization of race, altering the meaning of racial identity, and, in the process, altering the cultural toolkit of race in the United States. For individuals who are caught in between existing cultural categories at this time of uneven but emerging changes in those categories, appearances remain a significant constraining factor in identity construction and maintenance. While our research demonstrates that new identities are beginning to emerge, there still exist many social contexts where the biologically driven and fallacious one drop rule remains alive and well. The reality of the racial identity choices that biracial individuals make is that while they are increasingly varied, they continue to be contextually and experientially bound, and much more than skin deep.

## Methods Appendix

Much of the existing literature on biracial identity utilizes anecdotal, biographical, or small interview studies because of the difficulty of obtaining a sample of biracial individuals. In order to overcome the limitations of small sample studies, and delve more deeply into the social processes that govern racial identity construction and maintenance, we surveyed a sample of 177 individuals with one Black and one White parent and conducted interviews with a sub-sample. Our survey allowed us to inquire about racial identity, racial composition of social networks, racialized social experiences, reference groups, socioeconomic status, and appearances along with a multitude of other items (see Rockquemore and Brunsma 2001). This mixed-method approach enabled empirical testing of ideas within the literature that had previously been only anecdotally argued, theoretically postulated, and/or derived from small clinical samples.

Respondents for our survey were drawn from two colleges in metropolitan Detroit, Michigan: a private liberal arts college and a large community college. The Detroit Metropolitan Area was selected due to the large African American population and the high degree of residential segregation, while the institutions were selected to provide a sample of students who ranged in age, socioeconomic status, and life experience. Sampling from a population of college students, provided us with respondents who were comparable along the dimension of education level, but purposively stratified by socioeconomic indicators, racial composition of their social networks, and other salient dimensions of interest. Using institutional lists of students, we solicited 4532 students registered as "Black or African American," "Other," or those that left the race question blank on their college's admission forms. After cleaning the data, identifying only individuals with one Black and one White parent, and removing cases with missing data, we were left with 177 cases for the analysis.

*Measuring Racial Identity*

Given that the emerging body of literature on the multiracial experience argues that racial identity varies, we allowed for that variation in our survey. Specifically, we asked respondents: "Which of the following statements best describes your racial identity?" They chose from the following options: (1) I consider myself exclusively Black (or African American), (2) I sometimes consider myself Black, sometimes my other race, and sometimes biracial depending on the circumstances, (3) I consider myself biracial, but I experience the world as a Black person, (4) I consider myself exclusively as biracial (neither Black nor White), (5) I consider myself exclusively as my other race (not Black or biracial), (6) Race is meaningless, I do not believe in racial identities or (7) Other (fill in the blank).

*Measuring Appearances*

Measuring skin color has proven to be a difficult task for social scientists. Research that focuses on skin color stratification within the Black community has ranged from self-perception items that allow the respondent to choose between defined categories of skin tone from lightest to darkest (Hall, 1992; Wade, 1996), to more sophisticated measures such as the *Skin Color Assessment Procedure* that allows respondents to choose their actual, self-perceived, and idealized skin color from a randomized color wheel (Bond and Cash, 1992), to interviewers' observations of respondents' skin color (Hunter, 1998; Hughes and Hertel, 1990).

In order to measure phenotype in such a way that is consistent with our theoretical framework and allows for reflexivity, we measured both self-perceived *skin color* and how the respondent *appears* to others. To measure skin color, we provided respondents with a twelve-category continuum that used the following terms and codes: 12=Black, 10=Dark Brown, 8=Medium Brown, 6=Light Brown, 4=Yellow, 2=Olive, and 0=White. This measure resulted in an ordinal level self-perceived skin color variable. In contrast, our "appearance" measure captures respondents' estimates of how other people categorize them based on their physical features. The distinction lies between the respondents' self-assessment (skin color) and their understanding of others' assessments (appearance).

Specifically, we asked respondents to select which of the following statements best described their physical appearance: (1) "I look Black and most people assume that I am Black", (2) "My physical features are ambiguous, people assume I am Black mixed with something else", (3) "My physical features are ambiguous, people do not assume that I am Black", (4) "I physically look White, I could pass."

### References

Anderson, Margo J. and Stephen E. Fienberg. 1999. *Who Counts? The Politics of Census-Taking in Contemporary America.* New York: Russell Sage Foundation.

Anzaldua, Gloria. 1987. *Borderlands/La Frontera: The New Mestiza.* San Francisco: Spinsters/Aunt Lute Foundation.

Berzonsky, M. 1999a. "Identity Styles and Hypothesis-Testing Strategies.". Journal of Social Psychology 139: 784-789.

Berzonsky, M. 1999b. "Identity Processing Style and Cognitive Attributional Strategies: Similarities and difference Across Different Contexts". *European Journal of Personality* 13:105-120.

Berzonsky, M. 1999c. "Reevaluating the Identity Status Paradigm: Still useful after 35 years." *Development Review* 19:557-590.

Berzonsky, M. 1994. "Individual Differences in Self-Construction: The Role of Constructivist Epistemological Assumptions." *Journal of Constructivist Psychology* 7: 263-281.

Berzonsky, M. 1992. "Identity Style and Coping Strategies." *Journal of Personality* 60: 771-788.

Berzonsky, M. 1989. "The Self as Theorist: Individual Differences in Identity Formation." *International Journal of Personal Construct Psychology* 2: 363-376.

Besharov, Douglas and Timothy Sullivan. 1996. "One Flesh." *The New Democrat* 8(4).

Billingsley, Andrew. 1968. *Black Families in White America*. Englewood Cliffs, NJ: Prentice Hall.

Blanz, M. et al. 1998. "Responding to Negative Social Identity: A Taxonomy of Identity Management Strategies." *European Journal of Social Psychology* 28: 697-729.

Blumer, Herbert. 1969. *Symbolic Interactionism: Perspective and Method*. Englewood Cliffs, N.J.: Prentice-Hall

Bond, Selena and Thomas Cash. 1992. "Black Beauty: Skin Color and Body Images among African American College Women." *Journal of Applied* Social Psychology 22:874-888.

Bowles, Dorcas D. 1993. "Bi-racial identity: Children born to African-American and White couples." *Clinical Social Work Journal*. 21(4): 417-428.

Boyd-Franklin, N. 1989. *Black Families in Therapy: A Multisystems Approach*. New York: Guilford.

Bradshaw, Carla. 1992. "Beauty and the Beast: On Racial Ambiguity." In Maria Root (Ed.), *Racially Mixed People in America*. Newbury Park, CA: Sage.

Brown, Philip M. 1990. "Biracial identity and social marginality." *Child and Adolescent Social Work Journal* 7(4): 319-337.

Brunsma, David and Kerry Ann Rockquemore. 2001. "The New Color Complex: Phenotype, Appearances, and (Bi)racial Identity." *Identity* 3(1):225-246.

Clark, K.B. and M. P. Clark. 1947. "Racial Identification and Preference in Negro Children." Pp. 159-169 in T.M. Newcombe and E. L. Hartley (eds.) *Readings in Social Psychology*.

Collins, Sharon. 1998. *Black Corporate Executives: The Making and Breaking of a Black Middle Class*. Philadelphia: Temple University Press.

Côté, J. E. 1997. "An Empirical Test of the Identity Capital Model." *Journal of Adolescence* 20: 577-597.

Côté, J. E. 1996. "Sociological Perspectives on Identity Formation: The Culture-Identity Link and Identity *Capital." Journal of Adolescence* 19: 417-428.

Dalmage, Heather (Ed.) (forthcoming). *The Politics of Multiracialism.* Albany, NY: State University of New York Press.

Daniel, G. Reginald. 2001. *More Than Black? Multiracial Identity and the New Racial Order.* Temple University Press.

Daniel, G. Reginald. 1996. "Black and White Identity in the New Millennium: Unsevering the Ties that Bind." In Maria Root (Ed.). *The Multiracial Experience:Racial Borders as the New Frontier.* Sage: Thousand Oaks.

Davis, Allison, Burleigh Gardner, and Mary Gardner. 1941. *Deep South: A Social Anthropological Study of Caste and Class.* Chicago: University of Chicago Press.

Davis, James F. 1991. *Who is Black: One Nation's Definition.* University Park, Pennsylvania: Pennsylvania State University Press.

Dollard, John. 1957. *Caste and Class in Southern Town.* Garden City, NY: Doubleday.

Drake, St. Clair and Horace Cayton. 1962. "The Measure of Man." Pp. 495-525 in S.C. Drake and H. Cayton (Eds.). *Black Metropolis: A Study of Negro Life in a Northern City (Vol 2).* New York: Harper.

Durr, Marlese and John Logan. 1997. "Racial Submarkets in Government Employment: African American Professionals in New York State." *Sociological Forum* 12(3): 353-370.

Dyson, Michael Eric. 1997. *Between God and Gangsta Rap: Bearing Witness to Black Culture.* Oxford: Oxford University Press.

Fanon, Frantz. 1967. *Black Skin White Masks.* New York: Grove Weidenfeld.

Farley, Reynolds. 1984. *Blacks and Whites: Narrowing the Gap?* Cambridge MA: Harvard University Press.

Fields, L. 1996. "Piecing Together the Puzzle: Self-Concept and Group Identity in Biracial Black/White Youth." In M.P.P. Root (Ed.), Racially Mixed People in America. Newbury Park, CA: Sage.

Franklin, John Hope. 1980. *From Slavery to Freedom (5th ed)*. New York: Knopf.

Frazier, E. Franklin. 1957. *Black Bourgeoisie*. New York: Collier Books.

Freeman, R. 1981. "Black Economic Progress after 1964: Who has Gained and Why." In Sherman Rosen (Ed.), *Studies in Labor Markets*. Chicago: University of Chicago Press.

Gibbs, Jewell Taylor. 1997. "Biracial Adolescents." In Gibbs, Jewelle Taylor and Huang, Larke-Nahme (Eds). *Children of Color: Psychological Interventions with Culturally Diverse Youth*. New York: Jossey-Bass.

Gilliam, A. and O. Gilliam. 1999. "Odyssey: Negotiating the Subjectivity of Mulata Identity in Brazil." *Latin American Perspectives* 26: 60-84.

Goering, J. M. 1971. "Changing Perceptions and Evaluations of Physical Characteristics Among Blacks." *Phylon*. 33: 231-241.

Grier, William and Price Cobbs. 1968. *Black Rage*. New York: Basic Books.

Gwaltney, John. 1980. *Drylongso: A Self Portrait of Black America*. New York: Random House.

Hall, C. 1980. *The ethnic identity of racially mixed people: A study of Black-Japanese*. Unpublished doctoral dissertation, University of California, Los Angeles.

Hall, Ronald. 1992. "Bias Among African Americans Regarding Skin Color: Implications for Social Work Practice." *Research on Social Work Practice*. 2(4): 479-486.

Hallinan, Maureen T. and Richard A. Williams. 1987. "The Stability of Students' Interracial Friendships." *American Sociological Review*. 52(October): 653-664.

Harvey, A. R. 1995. "The Issue of Skin Color in Psychotherapy with African Americans." *Families in Society: The Journal of Contemporary Human Services.* (Jan): 3-10.

Herring, Roger. 1995. "Developing Biracial ethnic Identity: A Review of the Increasing Dilemma." *Journal of Multicultural Counseling and Development* 23:29-38.

Holtzman, J. 1973. "Color Caste Change among Black College Students." *Journal of Black Studies.* 4(1): 92-100.

hooks, bell. 1995. *Killing Rage: Ending Racism.* New York, NY: H. Holt and Co.

hooks, bell. 1992. *Black Looks: Race and Representation.* New York: South End Press.

Hughes, M. and B. R. Hertel. 1990. "The Significance of Color Remains: A Study of Life Chances, Mate Selection, and Ethnic Consciousness Among Black Americans." *Social Forces.* 68: 1105-1120.

Hunter, Margaret L. 1998. "Colorstruck: Skin Color Stratification in the Lives of African-American Women." *Sociological Inquiry.* 68(4): 517-535.

Johnson R.C. and C.J. Nagoshi, 1986. "The Adjustment of Off-spring Within Group and Interracial/Intercultural Marriages: A Comparison of Personality Factor Scores." *Journal of Marriage and the Family* 48: 279-284.

Keith, Verna and Cedric Herring. 1991. "Skin Tone Stratification in the Black Community." *American Journal of Sociology.* 97(3): 760-778.

Kerwin, Christine, Joseph G. Ponterotto, Barbara L. Jackson, and Abigail Harris. 1993. "Racial Identity in Biracial Children: A Qualitative Investigation." *Journal of Counseling Psychology.* 40(2):221-231.

Kich, G. K. 1992. "The Developmental Process of Asserting a Biracial, Bicultural Identity." In Maria Root (Ed.), *Racially Mixed People in America*. Beverly Hills, CA: Sage.

King, Rebecca and Kimberly DaCosta. 1996. "Changing Face, Changing Race: The Remaking of Race in the Japanese American and African American Communities." In Maria Root (Ed.), *Racially Mixed People in America*. Newbury Park, CA: Sage.

Korgen, Kathleen. 1998. *From Black to Biracial*. New York: Praeger.

Landry, Bart. 1987. *The New Black Middle Class*. Berkeley: University of California Press.

Miller, Robin L. 1992. "The Human Ecology of Multiracial Identity." In Maria Root (Ed.), *Racially Mixed People in America*. Newbury Park, CA: Sage.

Myrdal, Gunnar. 1944. *An American Dilemma: The Negro Problem and Modern Democracy*. New York: Transaction Publishers.

Neal, A. M. and M. L. Wilson. 1989. "The Role of Skin Color Features in the Black Community: Implications for Black Women and Therapy." *Clinical Psychology Review* 9:323-333.

Okazawa-Rey, M, T Robinson, and J. V. Ward. 1986. "Black Women and the Politics of Skin Color and Hair." *Women's Studies Quarterly* 12(1&2): 13-14.

Porter, C. P. 1991. "Social Reasons for Skin Tone Preferences of Black School-Aged Children." *American Journal of Orthopsychiatry* 61: 149-154.

Poston, W. Carlos. 1990. "The Biracial Identity Development Model: A Needed Addition." *Journal of Counseling and Development*. 69(2):152-155.

Rockquemore, Kerry Ann. 1999. "Between Black and White: Exploring the Biracial Experience." *Race and Society*. 1(2): 197-212.

Rockquemore, Kerry Ann and David L. Brunsma. 2001. *Beyond Black: Biracial Identity in America*. Thousand Oaks, CA: Sage.

Root, Maria. 1998. "Experiences and Processes Affecting Racial Identity Development: Preliminary Results from the Biracial Sibling Project." *Cultural Diversity and Mental Health* 4(3):237-247.

Root, Maria. 1996. "The Multiracial Experience: Racial Borders as Significant Frontier in Race Relations." In Maria Root (Ed.). *The Multiracial Experience: Racial Borders as the New Frontier.* Thousand Oaks: Sage.

Root, Maria. 1990. "Resolving 'other' Status: Identity Development of Biracial Individuals." *Women and Therapy* 9: 185-205

Rose, Tricia. 1994. *Black Noise: Rap Music and Black Culture in Contemporary America.* Middletown, CT: Wesleyan University Press.

Russell, Kathy, Midge Wilson and Ronald Hall. 1992. *The Color Complex: The Politics of Skin Color Among African Americans.* New York: Anchor.

Smith, W.D. 1979. "The Black Self-Concept: Some Historical and Theoretical Reflections." Pp. 149-159 in W.D. Smith, K.H. Burlew, M.H. Mosely, and W. M. Whitney (eds.) *Reflections on Black Psychology.*

Spencer, Jon Michael. 1997. *The New Colored People: The Mixed-Race Movement in America.* New York: New York University Press.

Spencer, Rainier. 1999. Spurious Issues: Race and Multicultural Politics in the United States. Boulder, CO: Westview Press.

Stephen, Cookie W. 1992. "Mixed-Heritage Individuals: Ethnic Identity and Trait Characteristics." In Maria Root (Ed.), *Racially Mixed People in America.* Beverly Hills, CA: Sage.

Stone, Gregory. 1962. "Appearance and the Self." In A. M. Rose (Ed.), Human Behavior and Social Processes. Boston: Houghton Mifflin.

Storrs, D. 1999. "Whiteness as Stigma: Essentialist Identity Work by Mixed-Race Women." *Symbolic Interaction* 22: 187-212.

Swann, W. B. Jr. 1987. "Identity Negotiation: Where Two Roads Meet." *Journal of Personality and Social Psychology* 53: 1038-1051.

Tizard, Barbara and Ann Phoenix. 1995. "The Identity of Mixed Parentage Adolescents." *Journal of Child Psychology and Psychiatry* 36(8): 1399-1410.

Udry, Richard, K. Baumann and C. Chase. 1971. "Skin Color and Mate Selection." *American Journal of Sociology* 76(4): 722-733.

Wardle, Francis. 1992. *Biracial Identity: An Ecological and Developmental Model*. Denver, CO: Center for the Study of Biracial Children.

Wardle, Francis. 1987. "Are We Sensitive to Interracial Children's Special Identity Needs?" *Young Children* 43:53-59.

Williams, Theresa K. 1996. "Race as Process: Reassessing the 'What Are You?' Encounters of Biracial Individuals." In Maria Root (Ed.), *Racially Mixed People in America*. Newbury Park: Sage.

Zuberi, Tukufu. 2001. *Thicker Than Blood: How Racial Statistics Lie*. Minneapolis MN: University of Minnesota Press.

# Chapter 7

# *Skin Tone, Class, and Racial Attitudes Among African Americans*

**Phillip J. Bowman**
University of Illinois at Chicago
**Ray Muhammad**
Northwestern University
and
**Mosi Ifatunji**
University of Illinois at Chicago

As we begin the 21st century, the relationship between skin tone, socioeconomic status and racial attitudes among African Americans remains a complex and controversial issue (e.g., Allen, Telles, and Hunter, 2000; Hill, 2000; and Hunter, 2002). Despite the popularity of "color-blind" rhetoric, what W.E.B Du Bois observed as the significance of the color line during the past century appears to be equally true for the 21st century (Massey and Denton, 1993; and Zuberi, 2001). Driven by new global arrangements, the "color line" continues to evolve with shifting relationships across western and non-western nations as well as across and within changing racial or ethnic categories at the national level (e.g., Cornell and Hartman, 1998; Hollinger, 2000; Jackson, 2000; Omi and Winant, 1994; and Reid, 2002). Historically, the "one drop rule" has made gradations in skin tone less a demarcation of racial stratification within the

United States than in the Caribbean, Mexico and other parts of Central and South Americas (Rodriguez and Cordero-Guzman, 1999; and Wright, 1999). However, skin tone effects have continued to operate in the socioeconomic status, quality of life and social relationships among African Americans in the U.S. despite shifting systems of racial stratification.

Researchers such as Rodriquez and Cordero-Guzman (1999) show how European colonizers often designed elaborate color-caste systems that legally sanctioned differential opportunity based on multiple skin tone gradations from white to black (i.e., White vs. Mestizo, Sambo, Mulatto, Quadroon, and Black). In contrast, English settlers in the United States institutionalized a White-Black caste system based on the one drop rule that defined a person as "Black" if they had one drop of African blood (e.g., Omni and Winant, 1994; Wright, 1999; and Zuberi, 2001). This unique White-Black system was enforced throughout the U.S. (with the possible exception of Louisiana and a few other isolated places with strong Spanish and/or French colonial legacies) and afforded those of African ancestry with lighter skin color less formal privileges than their counterparts in other parts of the New World. However, despite the pivotal force of the one drop rule in the U.S., skin tone has been used both formally and informally to demarcate African Americans throughout the nation's history.

It is important to highlight historical trends in skin tone considerations within official racial categories in the U.S. decennial census especially with the new mixed-race categories in the 2000 census (e.g., Anderson and Fineberg, 1999; Rodriguez and Cordero-Guzman, 1999; and Zuberi, 2001). Skin tone-related racial categories were added to the U.S. census for the first time in 1870. These categories replaced the original Constitutional "Enumeration" which was only concerned with slave status–slave or free. At the founding of the U.S., the Constitution mandated an Enumeration "by adding the whole Number of Free Persons, including those bound to service for a Term of Years, and excluding Indians not taxed, three-fifths of all other Persons." A set of more explicit skin tone-related categories were officially utilized between 1870 and 1890 in an attempt to gather information about "the new free man of color." Based on interviewer observation rather than self-reports, those with three-fourths African descent were classified as "Black." Those with three-eighths to one-half African ancestry were designated as "Mulatto." Those with one-fourth to three-eighths African heritage were called "quadroon." And those with one-eighth or less African ancestry were known as "octoroon." The mixed-race categories were dropped in 1900, but the Mulatto category was re-introduced in the 1910 and 1920 census counts. Hence, from 1930 to the 2000 Census, any offspring of Native American Indians, Europeans or Asians with detectable African ancestry would be counted simply as Negro, Black or African American.

Even with the one drop rule in the U.S., residuals of earlier mixed-race categories based on skin tone can still be observed in the tendency for African Americans with darker skin color (phenotypically more African) to receive less privilege and face more oppression than those with lighter skin color (phenotypically more racially mixed). Indeed, there is growing evidence that skin tone (dark vs. light) effects on socioeconomic status continue to operate in the U.S. among both African Americans and Latinos (e.g., Allen, Telles, and Hunter, 2000; Arce, 1987; Hughes and Hertel, 1990; and Keith and Herring, 1991). However, the specific mechanisms for these continuing skin tone effects remain unclear. In addition to formal mixed race demarcations, informal familial and social processes may have initially provided privileges to those with lighter over darker skin tone (e.g., mixed race children being provided freedom during slavery, or passing for White, or being assigned better jobs and educational opportunities). In turn, familial socioeconomic advantages among African Americans with lighter skin tone may be transferred across generations and reinforced by the socialization of related racial attitudes. A better understanding of such skin tone effects has become even more critical as the 2000 U.S. Census officially counts not only biracial but also a wide range of multi-racial identifications among African Americans and other racial/ethnic groups for the first time in history (Hollinger, 2000; and Zuberi, 2001).

## Skin Tone and Socioeconomic Attainment

A growing number of studies among African Americans has consistently found skin tone to be a significant predictor of multiple indicators of socioeconomic attainment, including education, occupational status and income (Allen, Telles, and Hunter, 2000; Keith and Herring, 1991; Hughes and Hertel, 1990; and Hill, 2000). For example, based on multivariate analysis, Keith and Herring (1991) found that skin tone was an even more powerful predictor of status attainment than traditional predictors such as parental socioeconomic status in a national sample of African Americans. Despite such persistent patterns, the legacy of the one drop rule may combine with more recent post-civil rights and post industrial changes to further moderate the magnitude of skin tone effects on socioeconomic mobility as well as race-related attitudes (Billingsley, 1992; Hill, 1997; and Morris and Herring, 1996).

In contrast to earlier periods, Blackwell (1985) and others noted how the modern civil rights movement of the 1960s and 1970s provided unprecedented opportunities for socioeconomic mobility among African Americans regardless of skin tone. Moreover, skin tone effects may be further moderated by the post-industrial dislocation of many African Americans into an unprecedented type of structural joblessness during the last quarter of the 21st century (e.g., Bowman, 1988; 1991a; 1991b; and Wilson, 1978; 1987; 1996). Hence, skin tone may not operate the same way among more affluent African Americans who benefited most from the civil rights movement as among those who continue to face persistent underclass poverty.

## Skin Tone and Race-Related Attitudes

In addition to status attainment, skin tone may also differentiate

# Skin Tone, Class, and Racial Attitudes

racial attitudes and ideology among African Americans. Historically, with deep roots in European colonization and enslavement of people of color, both elaborate color-caste categories as well as the one drop rule helped to structure systems of institutionalized racism (Drake, 1987; Ernst. 1980; Jordon, 1968; and Memmi, 1965). Indeed, these racialized social systems have been reinforced through the socialization of racist ideology and internalized racism at all levels to enable European masters to effectively control and exploit their subjects in America and other parts of the world (Fanon, 1967; Fields, 1982; Frazier, 1957; and Woodson, 1993). This literature suggests that both light skin tone and related class advantages among African Americans have historically been associated with assimilationist themes, including interracial docility, ingroup contempt, and a sense of superiority over those with darker skin and lower status.

Other studies suggest that the Black power movement of the 1960s and 1970s may have reduced, but not eliminated, the relationship between skin tone and race-related attitudes, perceptions and ideology (Hall, 1995; Hunter, 1998; 2002; and Russell, Wilson, and Hall, 1992). It is especially critical to better understand possible relationships between skin tone and a range of racial attitudes, including intergroup consciousness as well as intragroup identity (Bond and Cash, 1992; Edwards, 1972; Hughes and Hertel, 1990; and Ransford, 1970). In the context of the 21st century, it is also crucial to explore how such skin tone and racial attitude relationships might vary by economic status given the profound polarization in the class structure among African Americans since the 1970s. Hence, skin tone may have a distinct relationship to race-related attitudes among African Americans who face persistent poverty, those modestly above poverty and the more economically affluent.

## A Polarizing Class Structure: Potential Moderating Influence

As illustrated in Figure 7.1, the present study explores the potential moderating role of a polarizing class structure among African Americans

Figure 7.1

### Polarizing Class Structure as a Moderator
### of the Relationship Between Skin tone and Racial Attitudes

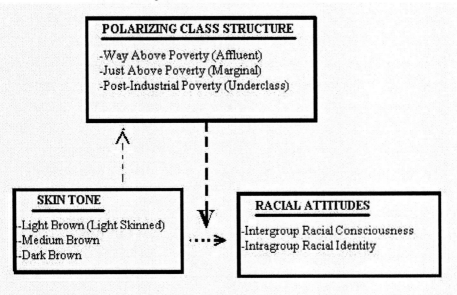

on the relationship between skin tone and racial attitudes. Since the 1970s, there has been a continuing polarization of the class structure among African Americans characterized by: (1) increasing numbers who live in families well above the poverty line, where members often have both high levels of education and high paying jobs; (2) those who live in families just above the poverty line who often have more than one member working for pay; and (3) increasing numbers who live in families below the poverty line, where members have suffer from post-industrial job displacement, labor market dislocation, chronic joblessness, and underclass stigma (e.g., Bowman, 1991a; 1991b; Farley, 2000; Jaynes and Williams, 1989; and Wilson, 1978; 1987; 1996).

Despite the fact that the White-Black income and wealth gap continues, Farley (2000: 28) noted that between the 1970s and 1990s there had been a clear "increase in both the number of Black millionaires as well as persistent Black poverty." This more polarized class structure among African Americans continues to be forged by two concurrent sets of forces–post-civil rights opportunities and post-industrial economic dislocation. Driven by the racial unrest and collective action struggles of the 1960s, much has been written about the expanded civil rights opportunities that provided significant numbers of African Americans unprecedented access to higher education, high status jobs and a family economic status well above the poverty line (e.g., Bowman, 1991a; Collins, 1998; Landry, 1987; Morris and Herring, 1996; Pattillo-McCoy, 1999; and Wilson, 1978). On the other end of the new class structure, a significant number of African Americans suffer disproportionately from global economic restructuring that has continued to dislocate families into persistent, post-industrial poverty from the 1970s to the present (Billingsley, 1992; Bowman, 1991b; 1988; Bowman and Forman, 1997; and Wilson, 1987; 1996).

African Americans continue to be at alarming risk for post industrial poverty for two major reasons: (1) the historical tracking of African American males into the most vulnerable manufacturing jobs which continue to be eliminated by automation, global restructuring, and deindustrialization, and (b) systematic race-related barriers including racial discrimination, metropolitan spatial isolation from expanding labor markets and poor quality urban schools–all of which exacerbate their chronic joblessness and obsolescence within the post industrial economy (Bowman, 1988; 1991b; Massey and Denton, 1993; Jaynes and Williams, 1989; and Wilson, 1987; 1996). In a review of related literature, Bowman (1988) noted that the impact of post industrial economic restructuring tends to ripple within the African American family from "jobless fathers," to "unmarried mothers" to "children in poverty" all of whom must struggle to maintain a livelihood in stressful urban ecologies.

After declining from 1939 to 1973, African American family poverty rates began to rise, especially in northern and western urban areas which were hardest hit by post industrial economic restructuring. Between 1970 and 1985, chronic poverty among African American families escalated dramatically along with the number of jobless fathers and unmarried mothers. By 1985, 44 percent of Black children lived in poor households compared to only 16 percent of White children. A full 75 percent of these Black children in poverty lived in female headed households where their fathers were absent (compared to only 42 percent for Whites). By March 1995, Current Population Survey data revealed two-parent households accounted for only 12.9% of all African American families with children in poverty while single-parent households represented a full 87.1% (U.S. Bureau of the Census, 1996).[1]

Perhaps the most critical findings in research on race and poverty has been that African American families not only have a higher rate of poverty, but also remain in poverty for longer periods than White families who increasingly escape poverty through the employment of both mothers and fathers (Bowman, 1991b; Jaynes and Williams, 1989; and Wilson, 1987; 1996). Unfortunately, existing welfare reform provisions focus more on moving unmarried, unskilled and often vulnerable mothers from welfare to work than on the systematic reduction of African American family poverty by removing post industrial employment barriers faced by both mothers and fathers–married and non-custodial (e.g., Bowman, 1988; Bowman and Forman, 1997; Siefert, Bowman, Heflin, Bowman, and Williams, 2000; and Tucker and Mitchell-Kernan, 1995).

## Research Questions and Methods

Guided by the related literature, the present study focuses on four central questions to explore the complex relationship between skin tone, class and racial attitudes among African Americans. Particular emphasis is placed on the potential moderating role of the polarizing class structure among African Americans on the relationship between skin tone and a range of racial attitudes:

(1) Is there a relationship between African Americans' skin tone and their location in the polarizing class structure–post industrial poverty, just above poverty, and way above poverty?

(2) Are there substantial numbers of African Americans with different skin tones within each of the three major strata of the new class structure–post industrial poverty, just above poverty, and way above poverty?

(3) Does the relationship between African Americans' skin tone and various intergroup racial attitudes–racial consciousness and affinity–depend on their location in the three distinct class structure categories?

(4) Does the relationship between African Americans' skin tone and various intragroup racial/ethnic attitudes–common fate, subethnic closeness or stereotypes–differ across the three class structure locations?

The data analyzed to explore these central research questions were collected from a national cross-sectional sample of the African American adult population living in the continental United States. Details of the methods for this study can be found in several methodological publications (Bowman, 1983; Caldwell, Jackson, Tucker, and Bowman, 1999; Jackson, 1991; and Jackson, Tucker, and Bowman, 1982).

Based on their observations, all interviewers were asked to rate each respondent's complexion on a five point scale immediately following the interview. The respondent's skin color is coded as: (1) very dark brown; (2) dark brown; (3) medium brown; (4) light brown (light skinned); or (5) very light brown (very light skinned). Based on the interviewer observations, 8.5% were rated as very dark brown, 29.9% as dark brown, 44.6% as medium brown, 14.4% as light brown, and only 2.6% as very light brown.

To tap the complexity of racial attitudes among African Americans, two sets of intragroup racial attitude items were selected as indicators of: (1) intergroup consciousness or attitudes about the nature and causes of White-Black inequalities as well as related collective action strategies, and

(2) intragroup affinity or feelings of closeness to Blacks outside the U.S. as well as other racial and ethnic groups within the U.S. In addition, three sets of intergroup racial attitude items were selected to assess: (1) a common fate belief that one's life chances are tied to what happens to other Blacks; (2) subethnic identity including the extent to which one feels a closeness toward or feels alienated from a range of African American subgroups; and (3) subethnic stereotypes including the extent to which one endorses a range of positive and negative stereotypical beliefs about African Americans in general.

## National Findings
### Skin Tone and Location in the Class Structure

Is there a relationship between African Americans' skin tone and their location in the polarizing class structure–post industrial poverty, just above poverty, and way above poverty? To explore this question, Figure 7.2 presents findings on the proportion of African Americans with different

Figure 7.2: Relationship Between Skin Tone and Class Structure Location

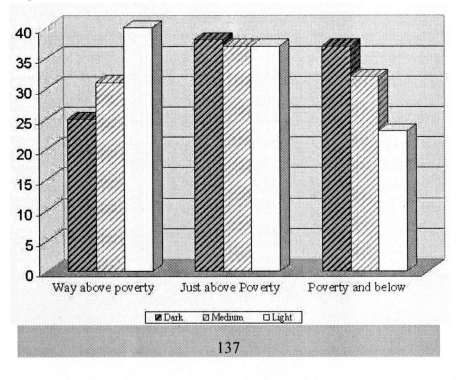

skin tones who were in post industrial poverty, just above poverty and way above poverty. These findings reveal a relationship where the proportions of those with the darkest skin tone were most likely to be in post industrial poverty while those with lightest skin tone were most likely to be way above poverty. For example, 37% of those with dark skin tone were in post-industrial poverty compared to only 23% of those with light skin tone. By contrast, a full 40% of those with light skin tone were located way above poverty compared to 31% with medium skin tone and only 25% of those with dark skin tone.

Are there substantial numbers of African Americans with different skin tones within each of the three major strata of the new class structure–post industrial poverty, just above poverty, and way above poverty? Despite the statistically significant skin tone and class structure relationship, substantial wide skin tone variability remains within each of the three class structure contexts. As illustrated in Figure 7.2, substantial numbers of African Americans with different skin tones can be found among those in post industrial poverty, just above poverty and as well as those way above poverty. Hence, in this national sample, there are substantial numbers of African Americans with dark skin tone who are way above poverty and substantial numbers with light skin in post industrial poverty. This skin tone variability within each of the three class categories provides an opportunity to explore the moderating impact of class structure on the relationship between skin tone and racial attitudes as well as other outcomes. As suggested by Babbie (1991) and others, such analysis of class structure as a moderator variable can help: (1) to specify more clearly class conditions under which skin tone may have unique effects on racial attitudes; and (2) to clarify the manner in which class structure might mediate skin tone effects on race-related attitudes.

## Skin Tone and Intergroup Racial Attitudes

Does the relationship between African Americans' skin tone and various intergroup racial attitudes–racial consciousness and affinity–depend on their location in the class structure? To address this question, Tables 7.1-7.4 present findings on the relationship between skin tone and the selected intergroup racial attitudes. First, relevant findings are presented for the total sample and then under the three class structure conditions–post industrial poverty, just above poverty, and way above poverty. Overall, African Americans with different skin tones were strikingly similar on the various intergroup attitude measures of both racial/ethnic consciousness and affinity–regardless of class structure location. However, some skin tone differences did emerge on specific intergroup consciousness and affinity measures under particular class structure conditions.

Tables 7.1 shows findings on intergroup consciousness that reveal statistically significant differences on both beliefs about Whites' orientation toward Blacks and system blame beliefs about the causes of White-Black inequality. Specifically, to tap beliefs about Whites' orientation, respondents were asked: "On the whole, do you think most White people want to see Blacks get a better break, or do they want to keep Blacks down or don't they care one way or the other?" Only in the post industrial poverty condition, were African Americans with darker skin tone significantly more likely (49%) than those with either medium (28%) or light (27%) skin tones to believe that Whites want to keep Blacks down. Among those way above poverty, a similar trend emerged where African Americans with dark skin (34%) were more likely than those with light skin (20%) to perceive that Whites want to keep Blacks down rather than see them get a better break. By contrast, among those just above poverty, the opposite trend emerged–African Americans with lighter (46%) rather than darker (33%) skin tone were the most likely to perceive that Whites want to keep Blacks down.

As shown in Table 7.2, to tap system blame beliefs respondents were asked: "In the United States, if Blacks don't do well in life, it is because: (a) they are kept back because of their race, or (b) they do not

**Table 7.1: Distribution of Intergroup Racial Attitudes by Skin Tone and Poverty Status**

| Table 7.1 | Total sample | | | Poverty and below | | | Just above poverty | | | Way above poverty | | |
|---|---|---|---|---|---|---|---|---|---|---|---|---|
| | Dark | Medium | Light | Dark | Medium | Light | Dark | Medium | Light | Dark | Medium | Light |
| **How true do you think each of these words is in describing most black people?** | | | | | | | | | | | | |
| Are ashamed of selves | 6 | 6 | 5 | 9 | 8 | 12 | 3 | 5 | 4 | 7 | 5 | 3 |
| Neglect their families | 11 | 10 | 9 | 15 | 12 | 15 | 10 | 11 | 12 | 8 | 7 | 4 |
| Are lazy | 16 | 12 | 10 | 21 | 16 | 15 | 14 | 14 | 12 | 10 | 7 | 7 |
| Give up easily | 12 | 10 | 12 | 15 | 12 | 16 | 12 | 10 | 12 | 10 | 8 | 7 |
| Are selfish | 13 | 11 | 10 | 15 | 14 | 13 | 12 | 8 | 10 | 11 | 9 | 5 |
| Are weak | 13 | 10 | 10 | 17 | 10 | 17 | 13 | 10 | 9 | 10 | 8 | 8 |
| Are lying or trifling | 13 | 11 | 9 | 16 | 14 | 12 | 13 | 11 | 10 | 8 | 8 | 7 |
| **Do most white people want to see blacks get a break or keep them down?** | | | | | | | | | | | | |
| Keep Blacks down | 39 | 38 | 39 | 49 | 28 | 27 | 33 | 41 | 46 | 34 | 32 | 20 |
| Give Blacks a better break | 23 | 20 | 20 | 51 | 72 | 73 | 67 | 59 | 54 | 66 | 68 | 80 |

**Table 7.2: Distribution of Intergroup Racial Attitudes by Skin Tone and Poverty Status**

| Table 7.2 | Total sample | | | Poverty and below | | | Just above poverty | | | Way above poverty | | |
|---|---|---|---|---|---|---|---|---|---|---|---|---|
| | Dark | Med. | Light | Dark | Med. | Light | Dark | Med. | Light | Dark | Med. | Light |
| In the United States, if black people don't do well in life, it is because . . . | | | | | | | | | | | | |
| System keeps Blacks back | 55 | 51 | 53 | 55 | 52 | 61 | 61 | 51 | 54 | 56 | 54 | 56 |
| Blacks don't work hard | 40 | 44 | 42 | 55 | 42 | 39 | 39 | 49 | 46 | 44 | 46 | 44 |
| To have power and improve their position in the United States . . . | | | | | | | | | | | | |
| Work as a group | 88 | 88 | 87 | 90 | 89 | 87 | 92 | 91 | 85 | 91 | 89 | 93 |
| Get ahead individually | 18 | 18 | 11 | 10 | 11 | 13 | 8 | 9 | 15 | 8 | 11 | 7 |
| Indicate whether you feel (very) close to . . . | | | | | | | | | | | | |
| Blacks in Africa | 60 | 53 | 51 | 62 | 55 | 51 | 60 | 57 | 55 | 59 | 51 | 47 |
| West Indians | 47 | 40 | 42 | 45 | 38 | 42 | 48 | 41 | 45 | 52 | 41 | 41 |
| American Indians | 41 | 38 | 44 | 41 | 35 | 33 | 41 | 39 | 50 | 46 | 41 | 37 |
| Spanish-speaking Americans | 34 | 33 | 34 | 36 | 27 | 25 | 31 | 39 | 35 | 35 | 37 | 34 |
| Asian Americans | 22 | 22 | 22 | 25 | 26 | 16 | 19 | 22 | 28 | 24 | 22 | 16 |

work hard enough to get ahead." Only in the just above poverty condition were African Americans with dark skin tone significantly more likely (61%) than those with either medium (51%) or light skin (54% ) to blame the system, rather than Black deficits, for racial inequalities. By contrast, under post industrial poverty, there is a greater tendency for those with lighter (61%) rather than darker (55%) skin tone to endorse such system blame beliefs. Among African Americans way above poverty, slightly over half blamed the system rather than individual deficits, regardless of skin tone. Moreover, regardless of skin tone, the great majority of African Americans (85%-93%) endorsed collective action over individual mobility strategies to cope with racial inequalities when asked: "To improve their condition the U.S.: (a) Black people should work together as a group, or (b) each Black person should work to get ahead on his or her own."

Table 7.2 also presents findings on the relationship between skin tone and intergroup affinity–or feelings of closeness to Black groups outside the U.S. (Africa and West Indies) as well as other non-White groups in the U.S. (American Indians, Spanish-Speaking Americans, and Asian Americans). Skin tone differentiated feelings of closeness with Blacks in Africa most clearly for those way above poverty–although a similar trend emerged for those just above and in post industrial poverty. African Americans with darker skin were slightly more likely (55%) than those with light (47%) skin tone to feel either "very or fairly" close in their ideas and feelings about things to Blacks in Africa. Among African Americans way above poverty, there is also a similar tendency for those with darker skin (59%) to feel closer to West Indians than those with either medium (51%) or lighter (47%) skin tone. No significant relationship emerged between skin tone and feelings of closeness to American Indians, Spanish-Speaking Americans or Asian Americans. However, under the just above poverty condition, a general tendency for African Americans with darker skin tone to feel closer to other racial/ethnic groups of color appears to reverse. Only in this "in between" class category did those with darker skin feel less close to other groups of color than those with lighter skin tone.

**Skin Tone and Intragroup Racial Attitudes**

Does the location of African Americans in the polarizing class structure moderate the relationship between their skin tone and various intragroup racial or ethnic attitudes? To address this question, Tables 7.3 and 7.4 present findings on the relationship between skin tone and the selected intragroup racial attitudes under each of the three class structure conditions–post industrial poverty, just above poverty and way above poverty. Under each class structure condition, African Americans with different skin tones are compared on several intragroup attitudes–common fate beliefs, subethnic closeness (identity and alienation) and subethnic stereotypes (positive and negative). Overall, regardless of class structure, African Americans with different skin tones were very similar on most of the measures of intragroup racial or ethnic attitudes. However, class structure did appear to moderate the relationship of skin tone to common fate beliefs, closeness to "Black people who rioted," and positive the subethnic stereotype that "most Blacks do for others."

Among African Americans just above poverty, those with darker skin were significantly more likely to endorse the common fate belief that their "chances in life depend on what happens to Black people as a group" rather than on what they do themselves. Such common fate beliefs were expressed by 45% with dark skin, 36% with medium brown skin, and 32% with light skin tone. A similar trend emerged for those way above poverty, but the pattern among those in post industrial poverty appear more complex. Among these poorest respondents, those with the lightest and darkest skin tone were equally likely to express common fate beliefs (46% and 45% respectively) while those with medium skin tone perceived less common fate (33%).

African Americans with different skin tones were extremely similar in their subethnic closeness or tendency to feel "most close to" certain

**Table 7.3: Distribution of Intergroup Racial Attitudes by Skin Tone and Poverty Status**

| Table 7.3 | Total sample | | | Poverty and below | | | Just above poverty | | | Way above poverty | | |
|---|---|---|---|---|---|---|---|---|---|---|---|---|
| | Dark | Medium | Light | Dark | Medium | Light | Dark | Medium | Light | Dark | Medium | Light |
| Do your chances in life depend more on what happens to black people as a group, or does it depend more on what you do yourself? | | | | | | | | | | | | |
| What happens to Blacks | 44 | 36 | 35 | 46 | 33 | 45* | 45 | 36 | 32* | 40 | 35 | 35 |
| What you do yourself | 56 | 64 | 65 | 54 | 67 | 55 | 55 | 69 | 68 | 60 | 65 | 65 |
| For each group, indicate whether you feel (very) close to them in your ideas and feelings about things. | | | | | | | | | | | | |
| Poor Blacks | 29 | 27 | 28 | 32 | 33 | 29 | 33 | 28 | 35 | 22 | 21 | 23 |
| Working class Blacks | 13 | 15 | 19 | 10 | 89 | 12 | 15 | 17 | 15 | 17 | 21 | 25 |
| Middle class Blacks | 4 | 6 | 4 | 3 | 3 | 1 | 3 | 5 | 2 | 9 | 10 | 8 |
| Young Blacks | 12 | 11 | 13 | 15 | 10 | 13 | 10 | 11 | 12 | 12 | 12 | 12 |
| Older Blacks | 14 | 15 | 10 | 18 | 17 | 16 | 14 | 15 | 11 | 8 | 11 | 9 |
| Religious Blacks | 21 | 21 | 20 | 15 | 22 | 20 | 21 | 21 | 21 | 23 | 19 | 18 |

**Table 7.4: Distribution of Intergroup Racial Attitudes by Skin Tone and Poverty Status**

| Table 7.4 | Total sample | | | Poverty and below | | | Just above poverty | | | Way above poverty | | |
|---|---|---|---|---|---|---|---|---|---|---|---|---|
| | Dark | Medium | Light | Dark | Medium | Light | Dark | Medium | Light | Dark | Medium | Light |
| For each group, indicate whether you do not feel close(at all) to them in your ideas and feelings about things. | | | | | | | | | | | | |
| Blacks against the law | 41 | 42 | 46 | 40 | 39 | 38 | 41 | 42 | 50 | 50 | 50 | 52 |
| Blacks who rioted | 30 | 30 | 21 | 29 | 31 | 26 | 36 | 34 | 19 | 24 | 22 | 18 |
| Black elected officials | 8 | 9 | 9 | 8 | 9 | 9 | 7 | 9 | 14 | 11 | 7 | 7 |
| Black professionals | 4 | 4 | 3 | 4 | 5 | 4 | 4 | 3 | 4 | 6 | 5 | 2 |
| How true do you think each of these words is in describing most black people? | | | | | | | | | | | | |
| Are proud of selves | 56 | 54 | 56 | 59 | 60 | 59 | 59 | 52 | 57 | 49 | 52 | 43 |
| Love their families | 65 | 68 | 66 | 69 | 66 | 70 | 65 | 68 | 67 | 62 | 68 | 65 |
| Are hard working | 57 | 56 | 55 | 62 | 63 | 62 | 57 | 51 | 60 | 57 | 53 | 45 |
| Keep trying | 57 | 56 | 57 | 64 | 58 | 59 | 54 | 55 | 54 | 51 | 53 | 60 |
| Do for others | 30 | 28 | 25 | 39 | 28 | 33 | 25 | 27 | 23 | 28 | 31 | 18 |
| Are strong | 51 | 51 | 51 | 49 | 52 | 58 | 53 | 47 | 50 | 52 | 52 | 49 |
| Are honest | 24 | 20 | 23 | 27 | 18 | 20 | 23 | 20 | 23 | 21 | 22 | 21 |

subgroups of Black people (identity) and "least close to" to other subgroups (alienation). Regardless of class, African Americans with different skin tones identified most closely with poor Blacks, religious Blacks, older Blacks, and young Blacks. Similarly, regardless of class, those with different skin tones also felt alienated from or least close to Black people "who have make it by getting around the law" or "who rioted in the streets." However, among those just above poverty, it is interesting to note that only 19% with light skin felt least close to Black people who rioted compared to 30% with medium and 36% with dark skin tone.

With respect to subethnic stereotypes, African Americans with different skin tones were also very similar in their tendency to endorse positive stereotypes about their own group while rejecting negative stereotypes. To tap stereotypical beliefs, all respondents were asked to identify positive and negative traits that they believed were "very" true for "most" Black people: "Many different words have been used to describe Black people in general. Some of these words describe good points and some of these words describe bad points. How true do you think each of these words is in describing most Black people?" Only in the way above poverty condition were African Americans with light skin significantly less likely (18%) to believe that "most Black people do for others" compared to those with medium (31%) or dark (28%) skin tone. Regardless of skin tone or class, over half of all African Americans endorsed the positive stereotypes that (it is "very" true that "most") Black people "love their families," "are hard working," "keep trying," are proud of themselves" and "are strong." Moreover, regardless of skin tone and class, well over 80% of Black people rejected the negative subethnic stereotypes that Black people "are ashamed of themselves," "neglect their families," "are selfish," "are lying or trifling," "give up easily," "are weak," or "are lazy."

## Summary and Conclusions

This study supports the importance of national data analysis in providing unique insight into the complex relationship between skin tone, socioeconomic status and racial attitudes among African Americans. First, findings reveal a clear relationship between African Americans' skin tone and their location in the polarizing class structure–post industrial poverty, just above poverty, and way above poverty. These findings extend past research that shows consistent relationships between skin tone and other measures of socioeconomic attainment such as education, occupational status and personal income (Allen, Telles, and Hunter, 2000; Keith and Herring, 1991; Hughes and Hertel, 1990; and Hill, 2000). Hence, African Americans' skin tone is not only related to traditional measures of socioeconomic attainment, but it also differentiates their location in a polarizing class structure that continues to widen as we move further into the 21st century (e.g., Farley, 2000; Jaynes and Williams, 1989; and Wilson, 1978; 1987).

Going beyond past research, this study also highlights the substantial skin tone variability among African Americans within each of the three class categories–post-industrial poverty, just above poverty, and way above poverty. Large numbers African Americans with lighter skin remain among the post-industrial poor while large numbers of those with darker skin have moved well beyond poverty. Such skin tone variability within class groups may reflect residual effects of the one drop rule as well as the impact of both post-civil rights opportunities and post industrial economic dislocation–none of which is explicitly stratified by skin tone (Farley and Allen, 1987; Jackson, 2000; Jaynes and Williams, 1989; Morris and Herring, 1996; and Wilson, 1978).

Despite the skin tone variance within each class category, the relationship between skin tone and various racial attitudes was only modestly moderated by location in the class structure.

Within each class category, African Americans with different skin tones were quite similar in both their intergroup and intragroup racial attitudes. African Americans with different skin tones were strikingly similar on several measures of both intergroup consciousness and affinity–regardless of class structure location. For example, the great majority of African Americans across class categories endorsed collective action over individual mobility strategies to cope with White-Black inequalities. Such findings may reflect the powerful effects of the 1960s civil rights era on the convergence of Black consciousness and related racial attitudes among African Americans regardless of skin color (Gurin and Epps, 1974; Jackson, McCullough, Gurin, and Broman, 1991; and Morris and Herring, 1996). Regardless of class, no clear relationship emerged between skin tone and feelings of closeness to American Indians, Spanish-Speaking Americans or Asian Americans. Despite the fact that skin tone variance among African Americans may sometimes reflect a shared ancestry with these other groups of color, feelings of closeness to them may be moderated by the powerful residuals of the one drop rule and the Black consciousness movement which both accentuate African identity. This salience of African identity over all others was supported by stronger feelings of closeness toward both Blacks in Africa and West Indians, especially among African Americans with darker skin tone.

African Americans with different skin tones were also similar in their subethnic closeness–regardless of location in the class structure. Specifically, they expressed a strong sense of identity with poor Blacks, religious Blacks, older Blacks, and young Blacks–but alienation from Black people "who have made it by getting around the law" or who rioted in the streets." Regardless of class, African Americans also strongly endorsed positive stereotypes that Black people "love their families," "are hard working," "keep trying," "are proud of themselves" and "are strong." Moreover, they strongly rejected negative stereotypes that Black people "are ashamed of themselves," "neglect their families," "are selfish," "are lying or trifling," "give up easily," "are weak," or "are lazy." Regardless of skin color, these findings reflect a strong tendency among African Americans to affirm a positive ingroup cultural identity and to reject anti-

Black stereotypes which have long been endodrsed by the larger society (Katz and Braly, 1933; Brigham, 1971; Dovidio, Evans, and Tyler, 1986; Jackman and Senter, 1983; and Katz and Taylor, 1988).

A rather complex set of findings reveals that class structure does sometimes moderate the relationship between skin tone and particular race-related feelings, beliefs and perceptions. Under specific class conditions, skin tone had a unique relationship to three intergroup racial attitudes (Whites orientation beliefs, system blame beliefs, and affinity toward Blacks in Africa) as well as two intragroup racial attitudes (common fate beliefs, and positive stereotype that most Blacks "do for others"). Some of the findings reflect themes in past research, while others raise more questions than they answer and call for future inquiry. One set of findings is consistent with traditional themes that associate light skin tone and affluence with more assimilationist attitudes–and darker skin and poverty with stronger Black consciousness or identity (Fanon, 1967; Frazier, 1957; Hall, 1995; Russell, Wilson, and Hall, 1992). For example, the most affluent African Americans (way above poverty) who also had light skin tone felt least close to Blacks in Africa. Similarly, the most affluent Blacks with the lightest skin tone were least likely to endorse the positive stereotype that "Blacks do for others." Among those in extreme post industrial poverty, darker skin tone was associated with stronger racial consciousness beliefs that Whites want to keep Blacks down. Moreover, among those on the margins of poverty, darker skin tone was associated with both stronger system blame and common fate beliefs. By contrast, in this "in between" class group, African Americans' with lighter skin tone tend to blame deficits in Blacks themselves for racial inequalities, and they believe that their fate is not dependent on what happens to Blacks in general.

Several other findings are less explicable in terms of themes from past research and raise questions for future research. For example, findings on racial consciousness reveal that African Americans with light rather than dark skin tone are more conscious of White opposition to Black progress only when they are just above poverty (caught between the polarizing post industrial poor and more affluent). Among the post industrial poor, why were both lightest and darkest skin tones associated with stronger common fate beliefs than medium skin tone? Why is system blame strongest among darker skin Blacks just above poverty, but strongest for lighter skin Blacks caught in more extreme post industrial poverty?

In conclusion, this study provides unique insight into the complex relationship between skin tone, class and racial attitudes as we have moved into the 21st century. Generally, it appears that African American's skin tone has a clearer relationship to their position in the polarizing class structure than to their racial attitudes. Future inquiry must better clarify mechanisms such as race-related socialization through which skin tone might differentiate class outcomes as well as racial attitudes (Bowman and Howard, 1985). Race-related socialization may not only be a direct source of racial attitudes, but may also mediate the relationships between both skin tone and class on proactive racial attitudes. A focus on race-related socialization may help to explain how color and class lines interact to promote progressive racial attitudes and collective action strategies.

Although we found that class sometimes moderated the relationship between skin tone and racial attitudes, future research should also explore possible mediating relationships. For example, rather than a moderating role, class structure may actually mediate the relationship between skin tone and class structure. That is, skin tone may have direct effects on class structure, which in turn, affects racial attitudes.

Historically, those with light skin tone may have been provided class advantages over those with darker skin, and these advantages may continue to be transferred to new generations. As suggested in the present study, these historical skin tone disparities may increasingly manifest themselves in a polarizing class structure. In turn, growing disparities between the post industrial poor and the most affluent may increasingly differentiate their racial attitudes. A better understanding of such issues among African Americans is especially crucial as their class structure continues to polarize, their relationships with other racial/ethnic groups grow more complex, and post-civil rights conservatism continues to increase opposition to race-targeted public policies.

### Appendix

A national sample was drawn according to a multistage, area probability sampling procedure designed to ensure that every Black household in the United States had the same chance of being selected for an interview. Specialized screening techniques were developed to produce a sample that more accurately represented all noninstitutionalized Black adults than in past national studies. Highly trained interviewers, with the same racial background as respondents, completed 2,107 face-to-face interviews during 1979-1980 for a response rate of 67.1%. The majority of the sample resided in the south (53%) followed by the north central (22%), northeast (19%), and western (6%) regions. Twenty percent lived in rural areas while a full 80% were urban residents. The respondents ranged in age form 18 to 101 years old, 1,310 were females and 797 were males.

### Measures

Data were collected using a carefully designed, two-hour interview schedule that provided a wide range of measures in several substantive areas including interviewer observations and a wide range of self-report indicators of socioeconomic status and racial attitudes. Special focus group techniques and extensive pre-testing increased the cultural sensitivity and quality of each measure. The specific independent, moderator and dependent variables used in this investigation are operationalized below.

*Moderator Variable*

*Class Structure Location*: This three category measure of class structure distinguishes between African Americans who are in post industrial poverty, just above poverty and way above poverty. As noted earlier, these three levels reflect a polarizing trend where the gap between the upper more and lower strata has continued to expand over the past 25 years (e.g., Farley, 2000; Wilson, 1978). Rather than family income, these three class categories were derived from a more detailed ratio of total family income to a poverty need standard (equated to family size and composition). The specific income-to-needs ratio used to develop this class structure classification was the Panel Study for Income Dynamics' food costs.

*Dependent Variables*
The specific measures in the present study focus on both "intergroup" and "intragroup" feelings, beliefs or perceptions (Gurin and Epps, 1974; Jackson , 2001; Jackson, McCullough, Gurin, and Broman, 1991). These measures are discussed in greater detail along with the specific empirical findings from the statistical analysis of national data to explore the central research questions.

## Endnote

1. African American single mother households represent 82.2% of all African American families with children in poverty, single father households represent 4.9%.

## References

Allen, W., Edward Telles, and Margaret Hunter. 2000. "Skin color, income and education: A comparison of African Americans and Mexican Americans." *National Journal of Sociology* 12:129-180.

Anderson, Margo J. and Stephen E. Fienberg, S.E. 1999. *Who Counts? The Politics of Census-Taking in Contemporary America.* NY: Russell Sage Foundation.

Arce, Carlos, Edward Murguia, and W.P. Frisbie. 1987. "Phenotype and Life Chances among Chicanos." *Hispanic Journal of Behavioral Sciences* 9:19-32.

Billingsley, Andrew. 1968. *Black Families in White America*. Englewood Cliffs, NJ: Prentice Hall.

Billingsley, Andrew. 1992. *Climbing Jacobs Ladder: The Enduring Legacy of African American Families*. NY: Simon and Schuster.

Blackwell, James E. 1991. *The Black Community: Diversity and Unity*. New York: Harper Collins.

Bond, Selena and Thomas Cash. 1992. Black Beauty: Skin Color and Body Images among African American College Women. *Journal of Applied Social Psychology* 22:874-88.

Bowman, Phillip J. 1983. "Significant Involvement and Functional Relevance: Challenges to Survey Research." *Social Work Research* 19: 21-26.

Bowman, Phillip .J. 1988. "Post-Industrial Displacement and Family Role Strains: Challenges to the Black Family." Pp. 75-99 in *Families in Distress*. P. Voydanoff and L.C. Majka Eds. Beverly Hills, CA: Sage Publications.

Bowman, Phillip .J. 1991a. "Work Life." Pp. 124-55 in *Life in Black America*. J.S. Jackson Ed. Newbury Park, CA: Sage Publications.

Bowman, Phillip .J. 1991b. "Joblessness ." Pp. 156-78 in *Life in Black America*. J.S. Jackson Ed. Newbury Park, CA: Sage Publications.

Bowman, Phillip .J., and Tyrone Forman. 1997. "Instrumental and Expressive Family Roles among African American Fathers." Pp. in *Family Life in Black America*. R.J. Taylor, J. S. Jackson and L.M. Chatters Eds. Thousand Oaks, CA: Sage

Bowman, Phillip J. and Cleopatra S. Howard. 1985. "Race-Related Socialization, Motivation and Academic Achievement: A Study of Black Youth in Three Generation Families." *Journal of the American Academy of Child Psychiatry* 24:134-141.

Brigham, J.C. 1971. "Ethnic Stereotypes." *Psychological Bulletin* 76: 15-38.

Caldwell, Cleopatra Howard, James S. Jackson, M. Belinda Tucker, and Phillip J. Bowman. 1999. "Culturally Competent Research Methods in African American Communities." Pp. in *Advances in African American psychology: Theory, paradigms and reviews.* R.L. Jones Ed. Berkeley: Cobbs and Henry.

Collins, Sharon. 1998. *Black Corporate Executives: The Making and Breaking of a Black Middle Class.* Philadelphia: Temple University Press.

Cornell, S. and Hartman, D. 1998. *Ethnicity and Race: Making Identities in a Changing World.* Thousand Oaks, CA: Pine Press.

Dovidio, J.F., Evans, N., and Tyler, R.B. 1986. Racial stereotypes: The contents of their cognitive representations. *Journal of Experimental Psychology*, 22, 22-37.

Drake, St. Clair. 1987. *Black Folk Here and There.* University of California Press.

Edwards, Ozzie L. 1972. Skin color as a variable in racial attitudes of Black urbanites. *Journal of Black Studies* 3:473-83.

Ernst, K. 1980. Racialism, racialist ideology, and colonialism: Past and resent. In *Sociological Theories: Race and Colonialism.* United Kingdom: UNESCO.

Fanon, Franz. 1967. *Black Skin White Masks.* NY: Grove Weidenfeld.

Farley, Reynolds. 2000. Demographic, Economic, and Social Trends in a Multicultural America." In J.S. Jackson Ed., *New Directions: African Americans in a Diversifying Nation.* Washington, DC: National Policy Association.

Fields, Barbara. 1982. Ideology and race in American history pp. 49-55. In M. Kousser et. al. Eds., *Region, Race and Reconstruction.* NY: Oxford University Press.

Frazier, E. Franklin. 1957. *Black Bourgeoisie.* New York: Collier Books.

Gurin, Patricia and Edgar Epps. 1974. *Black Consciousness, Identity and Achievement*. NY: John Wiley.

Hall, Ronald. 1995. The Bleaching Syndrome: African Americans': Response to Cultural Domination vis-à-vis Skin Color." *Journal of Black Studies* 26:172-84.

Hill, Mark E. 2000. Color differences in the socioeconomic status of African American men: Results of a longitudinal study. *Social Forces*, 78, 1437-60.

Hollinger, D. 2000. The Ethno-Racial Pentagon." Pp. 197-210 in *Race and Ethnicity in the United States: Issues and Debates*.S. Steinberg Ed. Malden, MA: Blackwell.

Hughes, Michael and Bradley Hertel. 1990. "The Significance of Color Remains: Study of Life Chances, Mate Selection, and Ethnic Consciousness among Black Americans." *Social Forces* 68:1105-20.

Hunter, Margaret L. 2002. "'If You're Light You're Alright': Light Skin Color as Social Capital for Women of Color." *Gender and Society* 16: 171-189.

Hunter, Margaret L. 1998. "Colorstruck: Skin Color Stratification in the Lives of African American Women." *Sociological Inquiry* 68: 517-535.

Jackman, Mary and M. Senter. 1983. Different therefore unequal: Beliefs about trait differences between groups of unequal status. *Research in Social Stratification and Mobility*, 2, 309-36.

Jackson, James S. 1991. *Life in Black America*. Newbury Park, CA: Sage.

Jackson, James S. 2000. *New Directions: African Americans in a Diversifying Nation*. Washington,DC: National Policy Association.

Jackson, James S., Wayne McCullough, Gerald Gurin, and Clifford Broman. 1991. "Race Identity" Pp. 235-50 in *Life in Black America*. J.S. Jackson Ed. Newbury Park, CA: Sage.

Jackson, James S., M. Belinda Tucker, and Phillip J. Bowman. 1982.

"Conceptual and Methodological Problems in Survey Research on Black Americans." In *Methodological Problems in Minority Research*. W.T. Liu Ed. Chicago: Pacific/Asian American Mental Health Center.

Jaynes, Gerald and Robin Williams. 1989. *A Common Destiny: Blacks and American Society*. Washington, DC: National Academy Press.

Jordan, W. 1968. *White over Black*. Chapel Hill: University of North Carolina Press.

Katz, D. and Braly, K. 1933. Racial stereotypes of one hundred college students. *Journal of Abnormal and Social Psychology*, Oct-Dec, 280-90.

Katz, P.A. and Taylor, D.A. 1988. *Eliminating Racism*. NY: Plenum.

Keith, Verna and Cedric Herring. 1991. "Skin Tone Stratification in the Black Community." *American Journal of Sociology* 97:760-78.

Landry, Bart. 1987. *The New Black Middle Class*. Berkeley: University of California Press.

Massey, Douglas .S. and Nancy Denton. 1993. *American Apartheid: Segregation and the Making of the Underclass*. Cambridge, MA: Harvard University Press.

Memmi, A. 1965. *The Colonizer and the Colonized*. Boston: Beacon Press.

Morris, Aldon and Cedric Herring. 1996. "The Civil Rights Movement: A Social and Political Watershed." Pp. 206-23 in *Origins and Destinies: Immigration, race, and ethnicity in America*. S. Pedraza and R.G. Rumbaut Eds. Belmont, CA: Wadsworth.

Omni, Michael. and Howard Wannant. 1994. "Contesting the Meaning of Race in the Post-Civil Rights Movement Era." Pp. 471-91. in *Origins and Destinies: Immigration, race, and ethnicity in America*. S. Pedraza and R.G. Rumbaut Eds. Belmont, CA: Wadsworth.

Patillo-McCoy, Mary. 1999. *Black Picket Fences: Privilege and Peril among the Black Middle Class*. Chicago, IL: University of Chicago

Press.

Ransford, Edward H. 1970. "Skin Color, Life Chances, and Anti-White Attitudes." *Social Problems* 18:164-78.

Reid, M.F. 2002. "Managing Urban Ethnic Conflict." In *Globalism and local democracy: Challenges and change in Europe and North America.* R. Hambleton, H. Savitch, and M. Steward Eds. United Kingdom: Palgrave.

Rodriguez, C. and H. Cordero-Guzman. 1999. "Placing Race in Context." Pp. 57-63. In *Rethinking the Color Line: Readings in Race and Ethnicity.* G.A. Gallagher Ed. Mountain View, CA: Mayfield.

Russell, Kathy, Midge Wilson, and Ronald Hall. 1992. *The Color Complex: The Politics of Skin Color Among African Americans.* New York: Harcourt, Brace Jovanovich.

Siefert, K., Bowman, P.J., Heflin, C.M., Danziger, S. and Williams, D. 2000. Social and environmental predictors of maternal depression in current and recent welfare recipients. American Journal of Orthopsychiatry, 70 4, 510-22.

Tucker, M.Belinda and Mitchell-Kernan, C. 1995. *The Decline in Marriage Among African Americans.* NY: Russell Sage Foundation.

Wilson, William Julius. 1978. *The Declining Significance of Race.* Chicago: University of Chicago Press.

Wilson, William Julius. 1987. *The Truly Disadvantaged*: The inner city, the underclass, and public policy. Chicago: University of Chicago Press.

Wilson, William Julius. 1996. *When Work Disapears.* Chicago: University of Chicago Press.

Woodson, CarterG. 1993. *Miseducation of the Negro.* Trenton, NJ: African World Press.

Wright, L. 1999. One drop of blood pp. 46-56. In *Rethinking the Color Line: Readings in Race and Ethnicity.* G.A. Gallagher Ed.

Mountain View, CA: Mayfield.

Zuberi, Takufu. 2001. *Thicker Than Blood: How Racial Statistics Lie.* Minneapolis MN: University of Minnesota Press.

# Chapter 8

# *Toward a Critical Demography of Neo-Mulattoes:*
## *Structural Change and Diversity Within the Black Population*

**Hayward Derrick Horton**

State University of New York at Albany

and

**Lori Latrice Sykes**

State University of New York at Albany

There has been an explosion of research on the mixed-race or biracial population in the United States (Allen et al., 2000; Hunter, 2002; Thompson and Keith, 2001). The impetus for the renewed interest can be attributed to related issues. First, the political debates surrounding the mixed-race population, which ultimately led to historic changes being made to Census 2000 is one explanation. Another plausible explanation is the increase in the influence of White women, specifically White women who have mixed-race children. They are leading the charge by resisting efforts to place their children in the Black category. In some regards, they are also in a fight for their own identities (Horton, forthcoming). For whatever the reason, sociologists are again directing their attention to the social construction of race as it applies to a population unwilling to identify with conventional monolithic notions about race and racial identity.

# Critical Demography of Neo-Mulattoes

Most sociological studies concerning the mixed-race population are micro-level or medial level at best (Bratter, 2000; Goldstein, 2000; St. Jean, 1998). The over-reliance on micro-level or medial level analyses can be attributed to the misidentification of racism as "a prejudice, ignorance, or a disease that afflicts some individuals and causes them to discriminate against others just because of the way they look" (Bonilla-Silva, 2001:21). Instead, racism is a multi-level and multi-dimensional system of dominant group oppression which scapegoats the race of one or more subordinate groups (Blauner, 1972; Feagin and Vera, 1995; Bonilla-Silva, 1997; Horton, forthcoming). The argument raised here is that the mixed-race population, specifically the neo-Mulatto population is *best* understood in the context of changes in the social structure relative to racism. The purpose of this chapter is to articulate the nature of this population and to suggest potential issues for future research.

## A Critical Demography of Miscegenation in the U.S.

Any discussion of mixed-race populations in the U.S. must begin with the origins in slavery and racial oppression, specifically with a discussion about the dehumanizing control of Black reproduction. One of the most powerful works on this subject is Dorothy Roberts' *Killing the Black Body*. Roberts (1997) observes that Black reproduction sustained slavery, which gave slave owners an economic incentive to control the reproductive lives of Blacks in general and the reproductive lives of Black women in particular. Black children, from the moment of conception, belonged to the slave owner. This practice marked Black women as objects incapable of making decisions about reproduction. The control of Black reproduction was sustained by the dehumanization of people of African descent and by the control of Black women's reproduction, notes Roberts (1997).

Higginbotham (1996) identifies four stages of development in the process that led to the precept of Black inferiority, particularly in the

American legal system. The first stage occurred between 1619 and 1662 where Black inferiority was presumed but not well defined. Higginbotham calls this the laissez-faire stage of Black inferiority development. In the earliest stages, the dehumanization of Blacks was accomplished by first establishing White superiority; establishing Black inferiority; enforcing White superiority and Black inferiority publicly; and enforcing White superiority and Black inferiority through theology (Higginbotham, 1996; Kennedy, 1997).

In the second stage, occurring between 1662 and the 1830s, the legal process defined and enforced the precept of Black inferiority. During this period, the rationale for slavery was formed and based on the notion of Black inferiority and White superiority. Legislatures, as in the case of Virginia, defined the parameters of Black-White relations and controlled the behaviors of slaves and individuals interacting with slaves. Slave codes and the existence of separate judicial systems for slaves, provide the best illustrations of the dehumanization of Blacks during this period. The codes and separate judicial system were expressions of the inferior status of Blacks (Franklin and Schweninger, 1999; Higginbotham, 1977).

The third stage, lasting from the 1830s to the end of the Civil War, can be best characterized as the period when the legal process endeavored to defend and protect the failing institution of slavery. During the final stage which began during Reconstruction, the legal system tried to distance its self from the doctrine of inferiority, although unsuccessfully.

The rape and sexual exploitation of Black women by White men is evidence of the dehumanizing control of Black reproduction. Slave women were not protected by criminal law during antebellum America, and as a result, slave women were vulnerable to sexual abuse (Johnson and Smith, 1998; Robinson, 2001). Roberts (1997) notes that the sexual exploitation of slaves was reinforced by the legal system by virtue of failing to recognize the rape of slave women as a crime, although the rape of a slave woman was grounds for a divorce. Additionally, the fact that any child that was a product of slave rape also became a slave held to reinforce the rape and sexual exploitation of Black women by White men (Higginbotham, 1978). One court wrote that promiscuity was at the core of Black sexuality and as such was not relevant to the laws that dictated sexual intercourse among Whites. Therefore, the court held, the sexuality of slaves were to be left up to the slave owners to regulate. Similar crimes against White women were considered capital offenses (Roberts, 1997). Although less common, White women sexually exploited Black men as well.

As the dehumanization of Black reproduction progressed, the number of mixed-raced individuals increased, most of whom were the product of non-consensual sexual relationships between White slave owners and their Black slaves (Frazier, 1957). During the enslavement period, the Mulatto population was used to control the slaves via divide-and-conquer tactics (Jones, 1994; Hunter, 2002). Mulatto slaves were encouraged to feel superior to other slaves. Slave owners saw this division as a means for defusing alliances (Berlin, 1976). Also, greater economic value was assigned to Mulatto slaves (Myrdal, 1944), and slave owners preferred light-skinned Blacks for personal service (Keith and Herring, 1991).

Keith and Herring (1991) say that the kinship bonds between Mulatto children and their White fathers became an underlying reason for the extension of privileges to lighter skinned Blacks. Field hands performed more physically demanding tasks and were disproportionately of pure African ancestry. House servants, on the other hand, were dispropor-tionately Mulatto offspring–the children of White males and slave women. House servants performed, in contrast, more socially desirable service positions. House servants also received other advantages such as better food, clothing, and the occasional ability to learn to read and write (Franklin, 1980).

The Mulatto population held other advantages over other Black slaves. The Mulatto population was also more likely to be freed relative to other slaves (Gooding-Williams, 1998; Horowitz, 1973). In 1850, about 10%-15% of the total Black population was Mulatto. Mulattoes comprised 37% of all free Blacks and 8% of all slaves (Keith and Herring, 1991). The over-representation of Mulattoes among the free population was attributable to White masters who emancipated their slave children and to free children who were born to White women and fathered by Black men (Spickard, 1989). Mulattoes not only had occupational and educational advantages, but many also had a subsistence wage and land (Keith and Smith, 1995). Not surprisingly, the Mulatto population historically was disproportionately found among the Black leadership class (Landry, 1987), including Benjamin Banneker and Frederick Douglass.

**The Neo-Mulatto Population in Contemporary America**

Neo-Mulattoes represent the most visible remnants of the system of slavery (Jones, 1994). Figures 8.1 through 8.3 illustrate the percentage of the population that is "Black," "White," and both "Black and White."

**Figure 8.1     Percentage of Population
That is Black/African American (Only)**

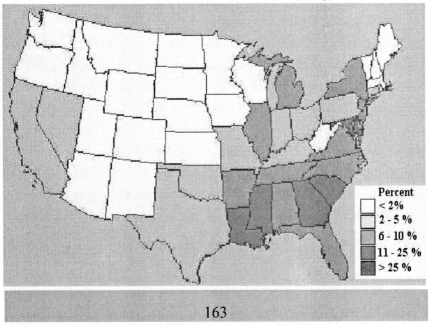

Percent
< 2%
2 - 5 %
6 - 10 %
11 - 25 %
> 25 %

# Critical Demography of Neo-Mulattoes

According to Census 2000, 2.4% of the population is identified with more than one race. Most of the individuals that identified with more than one race identified themselves with the Black and White combination. Horton (forthcoming) argues that most studies on race and ethnicity have failed to

**Figure 8.2    Percentage of the Population
That is White (Only)**

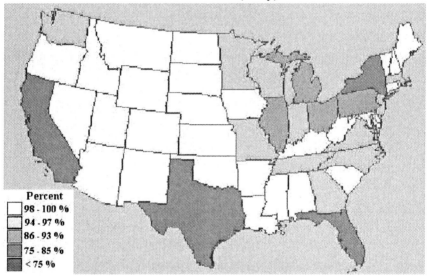

address the issue of the rising population of neo-Mulattoes. Specifically, demographers have also failed to address the efforts on the part of neo-Mulattoes to be designated as a unique racial group. Horton argues that the biracial population attributes the politically contested changes to the measurement of race on the U.S. census. The "biracial" population was not just embracing identity. Instead, this population was attempting to put distance between themselves and their Black identity. Thus, the term "neo-Mulatto" is more appropriate. The issues are far reaching and extend beyond individual level identity. Rather, the issues emerge in various social and institutional settings as evidenced by the changes to the most recent census.

The neo-Mulatto population must be placed in the appropriate historical and social context. In order to understand the emergence of this

**Figure 8.3    Percentage of the Population
That is Both White and Black**

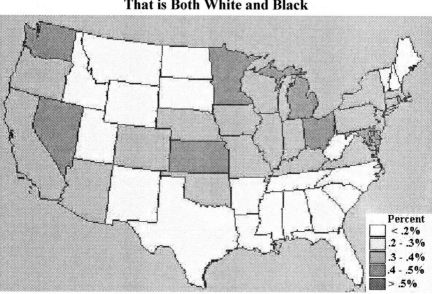

population onto the political and academic radar, we must examine the population and structural changes that have occurred over time.

Historically, a Black man could be lynched based on allegations that he may have looked in the direction of a White woman (Franklin, 1994). Spickard (1989) notes that the prohibition on interracial liaisons would become one of the main pillars of the American racial system and social structure. Just as residential segregation has increased in America since the Civil War (Massey and Denton, 1993), Spickard (1989) observes that there was proportionately more interracial mating during the colonial era than at any point in American history.

So what accounts for the change in the nation's willingness to tolerate relationships between Black males and White females? Some scholars argue that the liberalization of White attitudes about interracial marriage softened over time, particularly in the post-civil rights era (Massey and Denton, 1993). Access to structural power and influence for Black males in American society has not changed. The evidence to support consistent devaluing of Black males in American society is well-documented. Black males have higher death rates (Williams and Collins, 1995), higher unemployment rates, and lower levels of education than White males, Black females and White females (Harrison and Bennett, 1995).

What has changed is the role of White women in American society as expressed in their increased power and influence in various social and institutional settings (McLanahan and Casper, 1995). The influx of White women into the labor force since the mid-1970s was exceeded only by the civil rights movement in its impact on this society (Horton, forthcoming). Moreover, White women have been the primary beneficiaries of civil rights legislation and affirmative action policies. Also, White women have gained significant economic and political power as a group (Center for Women in Government, 2001). One latent function of this change in White womenís roles has been a de-valuation of White women as sex objects (Horton, forthcoming). Consequently, White women are no longer *the* primary symbol of the White manís power (Horton, forthcoming). Therefore, it can be shown that racism has not declined necessarily but that the relationship between White males and White females has changed dramatically. Black men are engaging in unions with White women at a time when White women are no longer the prized possessions of White men (Spikard, 1989; Horton, forthcoming). Hence more often than not, neo-Mulattoes are the products of White mothers and Black fathers.

Neo-Mulattoes because of their positionñsituated between Whites and Blacksñare indicative of the transformation in the social structure and an *evolution* in racism. Neo-Mulattoes fare better than Blacks but not as well as Whites. Many neo-Mulattoes fulfill the roles once held by other ethnic groups as middlemen minorities. In other words, the neo-Mulatto population serves as a buffer between Whites and Blacks. As such, this population has access to "whitespace" but is at the same time not immune from experiences associated with racism. Thus, while neo-Mulattoes may experience racism in more subtle forms, the experiences of this population may forecast what is to come for the general Black population.

**Implications for Public Policy**

Given the historical and contemporary position of Mulattoes and neo-Mulattoes on the Black-White continuum, it is not surprising that this population has begun a movement to create a separate racial category (U.S. Census, 1996). Only the Black-White mix is problematic and is the impetus for self-identification. The implications for public policy are far-reaching. The public policy implications include two critical issues: challenging the meaning of *blackness* in America and the emergence of the "Trojan Horse Strategy" in American racial politics.

The children of the predominately Black male-White female unions are increasingly wanting to be designated as mixed as opposed to simply Black. This is not surprising. Mothers have the primary responsibility of passing on the cultural identity (Billingsley, 1994). Accordingly, it would follow that White mothers would want their mixed offspring to be designated as "anything but Black" due to the social disadvantages of Black status. This is supported by the fact that there does not appear to be the same level of concern in the cases when the parentage is that of White with other groups. Moreover, there is some evidence that this "anything but Black" sentiment is held with other groups as well (Horton, forthcoming). Thus, the number of mixed persons who wish not to be identified with being Black is not indicative of a more tolerant society. To the contrary, neo-Mulattoes are attempting to distance themselves from a category of people that appears to be permanently the object of racism in America (Feagin, 1995).

In short, it has been nearly four decades since the historic 1964 civil rights legislation was passed into law. Over this period, differences within the Black population have persisted in the context of social class, social isolation and social dislocation (Wilson, 1987). This is sufficient time for class differences to evolve into ethnic differences for Blacks in America (Horton, 1992). The ethnic divide within the Black population is likely to be one of the greatest challenges to both demographers and society as well. For demographers, the challenge involves rethinking the implications of segments of a population that are so different on socio-demographic indicators as to be considered separate populations altogether. For the larger society, it may mean having to deal with an increasingly disadvantaged population without the benefit of the class of individuals who have traditionally provided the leadership for both the Black underclass and society itself.

There is already evidence that in the contemporary era, self-appointed neo-Mulatto leaders are posing as Blacks while espousing anti-Black rhetoric. Shelby Steele and Ward Connelly are only two examples. The ultimate goal of this segment of the neo-Mulatto population is to abolish affirmative action through the manipulation of traditional civil rights jargon (Omi and Winant, 1994) and the formal recognition of neo-Mulattoes as a separate racial group.

## Implications for Future Research on Neo-Mulattoes

There are several implications for future research on neo-Mulattoes, which can best be understood by the critical demography paradigm. This is based on the paradigm's explanatory and predictive power, its courage to challenge the social order, and its reflective nature (Horton, 1999). Within this framework, it is possible to estimate the demography and sociology of the neo-Mulatto population, including the size, distribution, structure and change. Demographers and sociologists alike can examine the socioeconomic status of neo-Mulattoes, assessing change over time and change relative to the total Black population.

Moreover, the ability to measure change in the neo-Mulatto population's access to *whitespace* will be possible. Demographic and sociological research on the neo-Mulatto population can be used as the "canary in the coal mine" relative to the social structure–signaling what is to come for the total Black population. Finally, the critical demography paradigm can also facilitate the estimation of the social, political and economic impact of the exodus of neo-Mulattoes from the general Black population.

## Conclusions

The argument put forth in this chapter is that the neo-Mulatto population is *best* understood in the context of changes in the social structure relative to racism. The purpose of this chapter was to articulate the nature of this population and to suggest potential issues for public policy and future research. We offered a critical demography of miscegenation in the United States, which included a discussion of the origins of racial oppression as it relates to the establishment of the Mulatto class. We then discussed the neo-Mulatto population in contemporary America by demonstrating the role that this population plays in understanding the transformation in the social structure and the evolution of racism.

In this chapter, we also addressed the public policy and research implications. The public policy implications include challenging the meaning of blackness in America and a new breed of Black leadership that possesses an ideology that is contrary to the views held by the Black population as a whole. The future research implications include estimating the demography and sociology of the neo-Mulatto population and using this population to explain and predict change among the total Black population. The final research implication discussed is the impact of the social, political, economic and emotional flight of neo-Mulattoes on the total Black population.

In this chapter, we have shown that neo-Mulattoes represent an important area of research for the specialty area of race and ethnicity. Their emergence as a distinct sub-population among Blacks likewise promises to have a dramatic impact on the future of the Black community. Fortunately, the Critical Demography paradigm facilitates placing the emergence of this group in perspective relative to the social structure.

## References

Allen Walter, Edward Telles, and Margaret Hunter. 2000. "The Significance of Color for African-Americans and Mexican Americans." *National Journal of Sociology.* 12 (1):129-80.

Berlin, Ira. 1976. "The Structure of the Free Negro Caste in the Antebellum United States." *Journal of Social History.* 9(3):297-318.

Billingsley, Andrew. 1994. *Climbing Jacob's Ladder: The Enduring Legacy of African American Families.* New York: Touchstone Books.

Blauner, Robert. 1972. *Racial Oppression in America.* New York: Harper & Row, Publishers.

Bonilla-Silva, Eduardo. 1997. "Rethinking Racism: Toward a Structural Interpretation." *American Sociological Review* 62:465-480.

Bratter, Jenifer. 2000. "A Matter of Place, Region, and Race: A Spatial Discussion of Black-White Intermarriage in 1990." *Sociological Imagination.* 37(4):283-305.

Center for Women in Government. 2001. *Appointed Policy Makers in State Government. A Demographic Analysis: Gender, Race and Ethnicity Data.* State University of New York at Albany.

Feagin, Joe R. and Hernan Vera. 1995. *White Racism*: The Basics. New York: Routledge.

Franklin, John Hope. 1980. From Slavery to Freedom. New York: Knopf.

Franklin, John Hope. 1994. *From Slavery to Freedom: A History of African Americans.* 7th edition, New York: McGraw-Hill, Inc.

Franklin, John Hope and Loren Schweninger. 1999. *Runaway Slaves:*

*Rebels on the Plantation.* NY: Oxford University Press.

Frazier, E. Franklin. 1957. *The Black Bourgeoisie.* New York: Free Press.

Goldstein, Joshua R. 2000. "Kinship Networks That Cross Racial Lines: The Exception or the Rule?" *Demography.* 36(3), Aug: 399-407.

Gooding-Williams, Robert. 1998. "Race, Multiculturalism and Democracy." *Constellations.* 5(1) Mar, 18-41.

Harrison, Roderick and Claudette Bennett. 1995. Race and Ethnic Diversity. In *State of the Union. Volume 2. Social Trends.* Edited by Reynolds Farley. NY: Russell Sage Foundation. 141-210.

Higginbotham, A. Leon. 1978. *In the Matter of Color.* NY: Oxford University Press.

Higginbotham, A. Leon. 1996. *Shades of Freedom.* NY: Oxford University Press.

Hill, Patricia Collins. 1990. *Black Feminist Thought.* Boston: Unwin Hyman.

Horowitz, Donald L. 1973. "Color Differentiation in the American Systems of Slavery." *Journal of Interdisciplinary History.* 3(3): 509-541.

Horowitz, Donald. 1973. "Color Differentiation in the American Systems of Slavery." *Journal of Interdisciplinary History.* 3(3):509-541.

Horton, Hayward Derrick. 1992. "A Sociological Approach to Black Community Development: Presentation of the Black Organizational Autonomy Model." *Journal of the Community Development Society* 23:1-19.

Horton, Hayward Derrick. 1999. "Critical Demography: The Paradigm of the Future?" *Sociological Forum* 14(3)363-366.

Horton, Hayward Derrick. Forthcoming. "Rethinking the 'R' Word." *Critical Demography.* Volume 1.

Hunter, Margaret. 2002. "If You're Light You're Alright." *Gender and Society.* 16: 175-193.

Johnson, Charles and Patricia Smith. 1998. *Africans in America: America's Journey through Slavery.* NY: Harcourt Brace & Company.

Jones, Rhett S. 1994. "The End of Africanity? The Bi-Racial Assault on Blackness." *Western Journal of Black Studies* 18(4), Winter:201-210.

Keith, Verna and Cedric Herring. 1991. Skin Tone and Stratification in the Black Community. *American Journal of Sociology.* 97(3):760-778.

Kennedy, Randall. 1997. *Race, Crime and the Law*. NY: Vintage Books.

Landry, Bart. 1987. *The New Black Middle Class*. Berkeley: University of California Press.

Massey, Douglass and Nancy Denton. 1993. *American Apartheid: Segregation and the Making of the Underclass*. Cambridge, MA: Harvard University Press.

McLanahan, Sara and Lynne Casper. 1995. "Growing Diversity and Inequality in the American Family." Pp. 1-46 in *State of the Union. Volume 2. Social Trends*. Reynolds Farley (Ed.). NY: Russell Sage Foundation.

Myrdal, Gunnar. 1944. *An American Dilemma*. New York: Harper & Row.

Omi, Michael & Winant, Howard. 1994. *Racial Formation in the United States: From the 1960s to the 1990s*. Second Edition. New York: Routledge.

Riley, Nancy. 1999. "Challenging Demography: Contributions from Feminist Theory." *Sociological Forum* 14(3): 369-398.

Roberts, Dorothy. 1997. *Killing the Black Body*. NY: Vintage Books.

Robinson, Randall. 2001. *The Debt: What America Owes to Blacks*. Dutton.

Smith, Verna and Cedric Herring. 1991. "Skin Tone and Stratification in the Black Community." *American Journal of Sociology.* 97(3): 760-778.

Spickard, Paul. 1989. *Mixed Blood: Intermarriage and Ethnic Identity in 20th Century America*. Madison: University of Wisconsin Press.

St. Jean, Yanick. 1998. "Let People Speak for Themselves: Interracial

Unions and the General Social Survey." *Journal of Black Studies.* 28(3):398-414.

Sykes, Lori Latrice. 2002. "Wealth Inequalities Among and Between Asian, Black, Hispanic and White Women." *Journal of Intergroup Relations* 29(1): 3-15.

Thompson, Maxine and Verna Keith. 2001. The Blacker the Berry: Gender, Skin Tone, Self-esteem, and Self-efficacy. *Gender and Society* 15: 336-57.

U.S. Census Bureau, Census 2000 Redistricting Data (P.L. 94-171) Summary File for States, Table PL1.

U.S. Census Bureau. 1996. *Findings on Questions on Race and Hispanic Origin Tested in the 1996.* National Content Survey.

Williams, David. and Chiquita Collins. 1995. "US Socioeconomic and Racial Differences in Health." *Annual Review of Sociology.* 21:349-86.

Wilson, William Julius. 1987. *The Truly Disadvantaged: The Inner City, the Underclass, and Public Policy.* Chicago: University of Chicago Press.

# Chapter 9

## *Demystifying Color-Blind Ideology:*
### *Denying Race, Ignoring Racial Inequalities*

**Kimberly L. Ebert**
University of California, Davis

A merican society ostensibly promotes color blindness as a value that is fundamental to the organization and administration of democracy. Currently, the thought of America as a color-blind society is cited as one of the "uniquely" American characteristics that forms the foundation of our nation. This is apparent in countless Supreme Court decisions that have espoused the color-blind ideal. Despite the fact that race is embedded in American social life, "color blindness" has recently emerged as the dominant ideology of race.

In this chapter, I explore color-blind ideology, alternative beliefs about inequality that contradict the dominant color-blind ideology, and White narratives and privileges that reinforce the significance of race in persistent racial inequalities. This chapter also seeks to explore color blindness in relation to beliefs about racial inequalities. It explores the paradox between the promotion of color blindness and the charge of "reverse discrimination." These simultaneous concerns differentiate this line of work from past research and theorizing.

The belief that America is meritocratic, egalitarian, and color blind requires that we ignore current inequalities that fall primarily along racial lines. Despite the correlation of race and inequality, the color-blind ideal persistently denies the significance of race. Correspondingly, those who subscribe to the belief that America is a color-blind society eschew the idea that certain racial groups are more privileged than others. Indeed, the color-blind ideal teaches that America presents equal opportunity for all regardless of race. It suggests that the problems of entire social or racial groups result from individual deficiencies rather than privilege for one race and discrimination against others. Although this color-blind ideal is ahistorical and ignores the many dimensions of structured racism, its simplistic logic continues to persuade.

What Americans see as the color-blind ideal–an American value for which we must ceaselessly strive–is really nothing more than an ideology of racial subjugation that perpetuates long-established inequality. This chapter explores ideologies of racial domination that work to uphold, reinforce, and regulate patterns of racial inequality. Through the promotion of race-neutral ideologies, White America displays a studied ignorance of the history of racial oppression and the established social order that continues to push minorities to the fringes of American society. In doing so, the dominant group commandeers idyllic and utopian language to reinforce its dominant position.

Essential to the discussion of color-blind ideology is the inherent paradox of using race-neutral language to reinforce the racial inequalities that persist. Despite platitudes about color-blind America, Whites exhibit a "White consciousness" or an awareness of their whiteness. This is evident in charges of "reverse discrimination" in circumstances when the dominant position is questioned. Thus, color-blind ideology is a discourse that is race-neutral on the surface. Nevertheless, it acknowledges race consciousness when White privilege is threatened. It demands reference to skin color when the dominant position is endangered. Simultaneously, it requires that the existence of White privilege be denied.

The overarching goal of this chapter is to explore ideologies that work to uphold current racial inequalities. It also examines the ideologies of racial domination that reinforce and regulate patterns of racial inequality. The reason I address color-blind ideology is that, although racial inequalities are obviously present, many people deny the significance of race. They also deny that certain racial groups are more privileged than others. Further, most Americans, especially Whites, assert that America is a meritocracy and that the problems of entire social or racial groups have to do with individual deficiencies. As we will see below, such explanations are both simplistic and ahistorical. They ignore the many dimensions of structured racism.

Other authors have addressed various aspects of color-blind ideology. Eduardo Bonilla-Silva (2001) seeks to define White racism and supremacy after the civil rights movement. While he does address color blindness, he does not explicitly investigate it. Rather, for him, color blindness rests within his purpose but is not highlighted. Color-blind ideology needs to be explicitly explored as a dominant ideology in the U.S. Moreover, research must uncover its relationship to explanations of racial inequality and how the promotion of color blindness perpetuates current racial inequalities.

Charles Gallagher (2002) defines and explicitly explores this ideology and its relationship to the disguise and perpetuation of racial inequalities. Nevertheless, Gallagher's main objective is to explain color-blindness as a White pleasure. In contrast, this chapter seeks to dismantle the myth of color blindness, identify the way in which color-blind ideology perpetuates racial inequality, and reveal its role in the enhancement of White privilege.

### Declining Significance of Race?

Although William Julius Wilson's *Declining Significance of Race* (1978) is dated, his claim that race is much less important than class in determining life chances for African Americans is pervasive in the American public. Wilson argues that it would be inadequate to explain the current conditions of the Black "underclass" as resulting from traditional forms of racial segregation and discrimination. While this may be partly true, traditional forms of discrimination are still evident. Furthermore, race remains a significant–if not the most important–determinant of life chances.

Joe Feagin points out that "Blacks must be constantly aware of the repertoire of possible responses to chronic and burdensome discrimination" (1991: 115). Whites have the luxury of ignoring racial inequalities, and the privilege of denying the historical impact of constant and consistent negative acts relating to race. Indeed, current realities of racial inequality, in terms of housing, health care, wealth, income, occupational advancement, and equal opportunities, make it clear that race is obviously a major factor in everyday life. Whites are far more likely to own their own homes and to possess far more assets than African Americans and Latinos. Whites have lower rates of pregnancy-related mortality, sudden infant death syndrome, diabetes, and tuberculosis than Latinos and African Americans. In 1997, 27% of Blacks, 27% of Latinos, and 14% of Asians lived below the poverty line compared with 8.6% of Whites. Also in 1997, 22% of Blacks, 34% of Latinos, and 21% of Asians did not have private or public health care coverage compared with 15% of Whites (Gallagher, 2002: 19).

Despite the realities of racial inequalities, the dominant ideology of race in America is that of color blindness. Below, I explain this apparent paradox as a myth of color blindness.

## Color-Blind Ideology

Ideologies consist of "broad mental and moral frameworks or 'grids' that social groups use to make sense of the world, to decide what is right and wrong, true or false, important or unimportant" (Bonilla-Silva, 2001: 62). Color-blind ideology is one in which social groups believe that racism and discrimination have been replaced by equal opportunity; that one's qualifications, not one's color or ethnicity, are the method by which upward mobility is achieved.[1] Color blindness is much more general than this. Rather than merely being applicable to upward mobility, it is evident in the everydayness of life. In reality, it is a falsehood to argue that American society is color blind. The ideology does not fail to notice race; rather, it acknowledges race but ignores racial hierarchy (Gallagher, 2002). Color-blind ideology assumes a race-neutral context, and it promotes a racially assimilated society in which race is portrayed as irrelevant; thus, it serves to reinforce the current racial order.

# Demystifying Color-Blind Ideology

After the civil rights movement, mainstream social thought came to embrace the ideal of color blindness as the dominant ideology about race. The racial logic of a color-blind society especially helps the dominant group, in this case, White America, to support an ideology that appears race-neutral but maintains the current racial order and allows Whites to benefit from their own skin color. Color blindness directly relates to American beliefs in meritocracy.[2] Just as color blindness is a myth, so is the belief that America is a meritocracy. While meritocracies support the belief that individual advancement is a reflection of hard work and qualification, it makes no sense in a society where the socioeconomic position of some groups has historically been far less than that of dominant groups. In meritocracies, "… the right of the individual comes into direct conflict with the right of the disadvantaged group to advance its collective socioeconomic position" (Jackman and Muha, 1984: 760).

Critical Race Theory (CRT) questions the validity of color-blind ideology and America as a meritocracy. It began as a movement to support a new direction of racial reform opposing traditional civil rights reform. It challenges the experiences of Whites as the "normative standard" while promoting the distinct experiences of people of color and experiences of racial oppression. Critical race theorists argue that individual acts of discrimination merely reflect larger institutional and structured White hegemony (Taylor, 1998). These theorists argue that color-blind ideology is illogical in a society that has historically based stratification on ascribed statuses such as race and class. Neil Gotanda (1995) argues that the Supreme Court's promotion of the Constitution as color blind fosters White racial ideology. He asserts that the aim of this promotion is a racially assimilated society in which race has no real significance. He argues that the support of "color-blind constitutionalism" is inadequate to deal with our racially stratified society that is culturally diverse and economically divided. Kimberle Crenshaw (1997) argues that race-neutrality reinforces Whites' sense that American society is truly meritocratic. Thus, racist ideology operates in conjunction with the class components of legal ideology to reinforce the status quo, both in terms of race and class:

The danger of color blindness is that it allows us to ignore the racial construction of whiteness and reinforces its privileged and oppressive position. Thus, whiteness remains the normative standard and blackness remains different, other, and marginal. Even worse, by insisting on a rhetoric that disallows reference to race, blacks can no longer name their reality or point out racism (Taylor, 1998: 123).

Color blindness emerged with the historical transformation of racism. Bonilla-Silva (2001) says that color blindness is directly tied to this new form of racism, as Whites commonly use language that avoids race and being labeled racist. These theorists argue that the traditional focus against racism of the civil rights movement is no longer as appropriate and that racism has evolved since the 1960s. White privilege was formerly achieved through obvious, overt, and explicitly racial practices. Today, however, it is accomplished through much more institutional, subtle, and apparently nonracial means, although traditional forms of racism still exist (Feagin, 1991). Although names for this new racism differ (e.g., "competitive" [Essed, 1996], "contemporary" [Dovidio, 2001; Forman, 2001], "color-blind" [Bonilla-Silva, 2001], "symbolic" [Sears, 1988], "modern" [Kinder and Sanders, 1996], and "laissez-faire" [Bobo, Kluegel, and Smith, 1997]), the authors agree that racism has evolved since the 1960s.

Lawrence Bobo, James Kluegel, and Ryan Smith (1997) are among those who suggest that racism has evolved from Jim Crow racism before the 1960s to "laissez-faire" racism that emerged since then. Bobo (1999) argues that class or other economic orders will not replace the importance of race; instead, race will change to suit the new economic climate. This shift has seen a near disappearance of overt discrimination and beliefs in the biological inferiority of African Americans. Instead, it has been replaced by an institutionalized racism supported by a modern free market or laissez-faire racist ideology. This kind of racism involves persistent negative stereotyping of African Americans, a tendency to blame Blacks themselves for the Black-White gap in socioeconomic standing, and resistance to meaningful policy efforts to improve U.S. racist social conditions and institutions. The authors argue that the demise of Jim Crow racism came not only as a result of the civil rights movement, but also because the transformation of the social and economic order made it unnecessary. An existing color line was already so pervasive, it did not need to be strictly enforced anymore. This new ideology was needed to justify the disadvantaged socioeconomic status of African Americans. It serves to maintain the status quo. Racial inequalities currently persist through subtle means. Maintaining them relies on the use of the market and informal racial bias. They are re-created through the support of not only the dominant group, but through the consent of large numbers of the subordinate group. In other words, the dominant group actively supports strategies to maintain their economic, political, and social privilege, and a large portion of the subordinate group supports the dominant ideology as well, suggesting its hegemonic nature.

## Beliefs about Racial Inequality

Post civil rights racism is highly related to American values such as meritocracy, and individualism. It specifically translates into more individualistic interpretations of the causes of racial inequality. Both an indirect and direct result of the civil rights movement is the transformation of norms and socialization patterns that discourage obvious and overt racist behaviors and attitudes, as evident in the previous discussion regarding contemporary racism. Consequently, studies of White racial attitudes show a dramatic increase of egalitarian principles since the 1960s[3] (Bobo et al., 1997; Schuman, Steeh, Bobo, and Krysan, 1997). The same studies of White racial attitudes explain that Blacks remain structurally disadvantaged partly because of contradicting White racial attitudes. While Whites believe in equality in principle, they do not especially support the implementation of these egalitarian principles that are designed to improve the socioeconomic status of racial minorities. Therefore, there is a gap between increasingly egalitarian principles and remaining resistance to government implementation of such programs as affirmative action.

There are three types of beliefs about inequality: individualistic, structuralist, and fatalistic (Feagin, 1975). Individualistic interpretations are linked to deficiency theories of inequality. Structuralist interpretations stress racism backed by social forces, institutions, and in some cases, hegemony. Fatalistic interpretations suggest luck or chance in determining the upward mobility of the individual or social group.

Mario Barrera (1982) explores these various theories of racial inequality. Deficiency theories–including biological, cultural and social structural deficiencies–assert that there are deficiencies within individuals, cultures, or communities that lead individuals or social groups into poverty. Such theories suggest that individuals within oppressed groups tend to have characteristics different from those who are successful in the United States. These "characteristics of success" include talent, willingness to work hard, willing to develop special skills, motivated, control of sex drive, and faith in capitalism. Bias theories, on the other hand, argue that bias or prejudice plays a role in generating inequalities. These theories include human capital theories, which suggests that "rational" employers should not discriminate; rather, in their economic interest, should hire individuals based on skills and productivity. The deficiency and bias theories lack a historical perspective; rather, not everyone starts off equal in life. Structural theories argue that there is something inherent in the structure of American society that leads to inequalities, and many provide historical accounts for the causes of inequalities.

Bonilla-Silva (1996) expands on Barerra's interpretation of structural theories of racial inequalities. He argues that past and present theories of racism lack in structural orientation. He proposes an alternative explanation which he calls the "racialized social order." This formulation elaborates on the institutional, the internal colonial, and the racial formation perspectives put forth by Omi and Winant (1994). Racialized social systems refer to "societies in which economic, political, social and ideological levels are partially structured by the placement of actors in racial categories" (Bonilla-Silva 1996: 469). These categories are hierarchically organized and hegemonically dominated, that is, more by consent than through coercion. Bonilla-Silva argues that his alternative perspective is beneficial in many ways, including the fact that racial incidents are seen as "normal," or part of the racist structure. This explains both overt and covert racial behavior. He suggests that the social system should be interpreted from a non-functionalist position to understand societies structured in dominance.

Despite evidence suggesting that racial inequalities are the result of the structured racial social order, there is a dominant ideology of individualism in the United States organized around a belief in equal opportunity. The dominant ideology also asserts that an individual's outcomes depend on effort, ability, or other individual-level character traits, with egalitarianism functioning as a weaker "challenging" belief[1] (Huber and Form, 1973; and Kluegel and Smith, 1986). Furthermore, those who benefit from the current stratification system are those who most likely will support the dominant ideology. This includes believing in the American ideology of opportunity and the political mechanisms that sustain it.

Trends in racial attitudes suggest that among Whites there is not much recognition of past or present discrimination in preventing the achievement of people of color. Rather, Whites attribute disadvantage to lack of individual motivation. Blacks, on the other hand, emphasize discrimination, reporting this as the greatest cause of Black economic disadvantage. Both Blacks and Whites stress education to alleviate Black economic disadvantages. Blacks believe that unfair treatment has risen over time whereas Whites believe it has fallen (Schuman et al., 1997; and Sigelman and Welch, 1991).

Even among minority groups, there exists an agreement with dominant views on inequality that signifies its hegemonic character (Hunt 1996, 2000, and 2001). Past research indicates that Americans favor internal self-explanations (the dominant ideology of individualism), as opposed to external explanations for their personal outcomes in the domains of work and education. However, Latinos and Blacks have distinct experiences and histories that may have implications for how members of these groups perceive themselves, other groups, and American society. Matthew Hunt (1996) finds that Latinos rank highest on individualism followed by Blacks and Whites in that order. Both minority groups show a similar mean and both are much more structuralist in their beliefs than Whites. In accordance with the research of Michael Mann (1970), Lawrence Bobo (1991), and James Kluegel and Eliot Smith (1986), Blacks demonstrate the strongest group consciousness in their support for structural challenges to the dominant ideology. Nevertheless, they "stop short of denying the justice of economic inequality in principle and of dismissing the ideas that the rich and poor as individuals are deserving of their fate" (Kluegel and Smith, 1986: 290).

These contradictory, inconsistent, and fluctuating beliefs about inequality are evident among the White population and also among the beliefs of different races and ethnicities (Mann, 1970; Kluegel and Smith, 1986; Hunt 1996, 2000, and 2001). The reality of divergent trends in attitudes may reflect the hegemonic nature of racial ideology.[5] Within liberal democracies there exists a lack of consensus on system-challenging values, particularly among the working class and oppressed minority groups. This lack of consensus rests in the inconsistent explanations for the causes of poverty, namely between structuralist and individualistic explanations (Mann, 1970; and Bobo, 1991). There exists a dual belief system of low status groups, as there is an egalitarian and structuralist "social responsibility" outlook that oppressed groups are especially likely to draw upon to counter economic individualism. Even poor Blacks have much more faith in the "American Dream" than middle class Blacks (Hochschild, 1995). The American public treats the individualism explanation as a dominant ideology, where its hegemonic appearance remains because of the lack of cohesiveness among oppressed groups (Hunt, 1996).

## White Privilege

Color blindness hides white privilege behind a mask of

assumed meritocracy while rendering invisible the institutional arrangements that perpetuate racial inequality (Gallagher, 2002: 7).

They [whites] remained oblivious to the worlds within worlds that existed just beyond the edge of their awareness and yet were present in their very midst (Harris, 1997: 276).

While research maintains that Whites commonly deny white skin privilege, White identity is often constructed in opposition to other races, particularly African Americans. Whites frequently justify everyday practices of avoiding other races by using stereotypes, which Whites have arguably directly and indirectly created. At the same time and despite current realities of Whites at the pinnacle of "success," many Whites claim that their racial group has increasingly been the victim of "reverse discrimination." Moreover, many Whites claim that minority groups and immigrants have more opportunities to succeed in America than even native-born Whites themselves.

As previously noted, Whites are more individualistic in explaining current racial inequalities. As evident in racial attitude surveys and White narratives, Whites commonly deny race privilege (Gallagher, 1995, 2002; Bonilla-Silva, 2001; Feagin and Vera, 1995; Blauner, 1989; Entman and Rojecki, 2000; and Rubin, 1994). In a study of White college students, Gallagher asserts that "Many young Whites refuse to feel in any way responsible for the role Whites have played in US race relations. . . . Perhaps more troubling than their denial of U.S. racial history is White students' beliefs that they in no way benefit from their skin color" (1995: 179).

While Whites deny White privilege, they construct much of White identity in opposition to blackness. This serves to confirm the negative status of Blacks and to justify White housing preferences at a distance from African Americans. White identification with their race is a form of positive self-esteem among Americans of European origin; thus, minority race identification is associated with shame and dishonor (Bashi and McDaniel, 1997). Negative stereotypes of minorities–such as the notion that they lack intelligence; are uncivilized; lack a work ethic; take advantage of government benefits such as welfare; and are more difficult to get along with–stand in contrast to White moral norms (Farley, 1996; Meyer, 2000; Hirsch, 1996; and Rieder, 1985). Resulting from two hundred years of slavery and Jim Crow segregation, racist stereotypes are firmly rooted in Social Darwinist beliefs that African Americans are socially, biologically, and culturally inferior to Whites.

Significant to forming their identities as Americans, many immigrants, in the process of becoming "American" learn that to become fully American, they must distance themselves from African Americans, the epitome of anti-American status (Roediger 1991). Rieder connects this to his population of Jews and Italians as being "too close to their own humble beginnings to think of themselves as exploiters" (1985: 120). In other words, those close to the assimilation process argue their resistance to racial succession is not racist; rather, Blacks will soon experience this "ritual ordeal" of assimilation. Until then, their existence in one's neighborhood threatens the status, the "whiteness," of their community.

"To be fully American was to be White" (Sugrue 1996: 9). Therefore, even oppressed immigrant groups in the process of "assimilation" express opposition to living near African Americans. Among the foreign born, 37% of Latinos and 43% of Asians exclude Blacks entirely when describing their neighborhood preferences (Charles, 2000). Research on housing location preferences indicates considerable hostility toward African Americans. The preference for neighborhoods dominated by co-ethnics is strongest among Whites. Whites are also the group most likely to prefer entirely same-race neighborhoods. Results reveal persisting respondent race and nativity status differences in preferences for particular out-groups as neighbors. To privilege their position, the White working class has privileged their race over class by placing the blame for their marginalized economic positions on African Americans rather than the

White elite. The White working class, already in an economically threatened position, does not want to ostracize itself against the White elite by living next to African Americans as this threatens their social status as Whites (Meyer, 2000).

These social groups often justify their housing preferences and stereotypes of African Americans through references to the "underclass." Sugrue (1996) discusses the construction of the "underclass." He shows how Whites rationalized and justified discrimination in the workplace and in housing. The perceptions of African Americans, that is, on the street corners, jobless and hopeless, justified White actions to keep Blacks out of their neighborhoods and jobs for fear that their quality of life would suffer. However, racial isolation and segregation may cause White racist ideology, which is reinforced by Black images in segregated areas. Logan and Molotch argue that, "We must consider the stratification of places along with the stratification of individuals in order to understand the distribution of life chances" (1987: 19-20). However real and true this statement is, this argument has been manipulated to explain the existence of a "culture of poverty" or an "underclass" within the Black "ghetto[6]" (Jargowsky, 1997; Wilson, 1987). Wilson describes the underclass: "one cannot deny that there is a heterogeneous grouping of inner-city families and individuals whose behavior contrasts sharply with that of mainstream America" (1987: 7). Wilson emphasizes the role of the environment in creating this unflattering "ghetto-related behavior" (1996: 51). This is associated with "the image of poor minority families mired in endless cycles of unemployment, unwed childbearing, illiteracy, and dependency" (Massey and Denton 1993: 4). These images are perpetuated and reinforced by media images and political support of the stereotypes of racial minorities. Locating African Americans in an ahistorical context, the media perceptions that are generated reinforce the Black population as being welfare cheats, welfare queens, hanging out on street corners, out of work, and lazy, the characteristics associated with the "underclass" that was explored earlier. There has been a media barrage of Blacks as the root of all problems that has actively spread and perpetuated stereotypes of African Americans: "Media packages Blacks (and feminists secondarily) as the root cause of problems in contemporary American society [and] those who experience loss are actually encouraged to center all that is wrong with society on African Americans, particularly men" (Fine and Weis, 1998: 58). However, the adverse realities of these neighborhoods are not the result of behavioral pathologies but institutional neglect (Vanketesh, 2000). Wacquant (1994) argues that these neighborhoods are merely organized differently than others. By constantly focusing on their negative characteristics, stereotypes of the people who live in these areas will be perpetuated. Nonetheless, politicians capitalize on White discontent with changing social, cultural, racial and economic aspects that threaten the White American public, and encourage Whites to protect their neighborhoods and the American dream.[7] They encourage the economically and socially threatened working class whites to use blacks as scapegoats.

White narratives suggest that many whites do just that. Many frame their whiteness more as a liability than as an asset and claim reverse discrimination (Fine and Weiss, 1998; Omi and Winant, 1994; Rieder, 1985; Gallagher, 1995). In some studies, "a majority of the whites argued that we live in a meritocracy where nonwhites have every advantage whites do and, in some cases, more opportunity because of affirmative action" (Gallagher, 1995: 175-176). In other words, they ignore current realities of persistent racial inequalities. Rieder describes reactions to racial "succession" of the working middle class white community of Canarsie, a neighborhood in New York City. "Everything in the world of Canarsie impelled the residents to rail against people rather than slavery, labor markets, or similarly arcane forces. From where they stood, the people of Canarsie believed they were the victims" (1985: 26). The perception that whites were and are the ones who suffered and lost from racial succession is echoed elsewhere. Many whites, most notably working class men, cry "reverse discrimination." In interviews with working class men, Fine and Weiss (1998) find that they are often disgusted with "quotas," or affirmative action, and other similar policies. This notion maintains that many whites believe that they deserve economic success and government aid and others do not.

Indeed, whites are race-conscious. As evident in the construction of White identity, in processes of assimilation, and in the justification of housing patterns, whites and other races are aware of race. However, most whites proclaim to be color-blind and communicate that ideally race should not matter at all in America; "[y]et whites tend to navigate every day a 'white habitus' and seem to be rather 'color-conscious' in terms of their choice of significant other," friends, and places to live (Bonilla-Silva, 2001: 141). Whites argue it is class, not race in determining everyday choices; however, current racial realities suggest otherwise.

**Conclusions**

America is an extremely race-conscious society. While color-blind ideology has emerged dominant in post-civil rights America, persistent racial inequalities confirm that race remains extremely significant in the distribution of life chances. Color blindness is illogical in a society where socioeconomic stratification is and has historically been based on ascribed status. Racial inequalities are not only caused by traditional forms of discrimination, but also by new forms that are easily hidden and at times transparent. They are, therefore, difficult to identify. By claiming color blindness in an era of massive racial inequalities, the significance of race is ignored, the inequalities are ignored, and therefore, these inequalities will continue to persist. Furthermore, by claiming color blindness, whites deny their everyday lives that are based on race and the oppression of other races. They are able to justify housing, schooling, and work preferences through the use of stereotypes without having to admit the racial nature of these stereotypes. Moreover, because these images are based in the structure and are supported and re-created by the media, politicians, and other institutions, the stereotypes become hegemonic. That is, even oppressed social groups will freely adopt and act upon these stereotypes, and in turn, make racism much more powerful.

The fact that racial inequalities are being ignored through the promotion of color blindness is alarming. Racism remains a backdrop of those who claim or assume color blindness. However, it is at times hidden, and this is what makes it so powerful and much more difficult to overcome or to challenge. Ideally, we would not be judged on the basis of our race. In Martin Luther King's 1963 famous speech, he described his dreams of a nation where his children would "not be judged by the color of their skin but by the content of their character." Given the persistence of racism in American society, some suggest that in order to alleviate this, we must include the goal of color blindness. However, for the victims of racial oppression, both historical and present-day, specific social, economic, or legislative remedies are required.

**Future Research**

I think a major problem within the complex concepts presented in social science circles is the lack of dissemination of the ideas among the public. These are extremely important ideas that may help the public better understand the historical, political, economic, and social formation of racism and the perpetuation of massive racial inequalities throughout the U.S. Sadly, much of what is produced in the public promotes the belief that America is a color-blind meritocracy. Thus, those in dominant positions can justify their beliefs with popular literature.

I also think that there should be more qualitative research exploring color-blind ideology among not only whites, but also the entire population. Charles Gallagher has completed much research on whites and whiteness, but has yet to investigate how hegemonic color blindness is in the general U.S. public. That is, how do racial ideologies work and how are they maintained?

Furthermore, an important question to ask is, when do these ideas develop? There is little research on young people, possibly because it is difficult to obtain permission to research young people. However, exploring when these ideologies develop is important in investigating how to change these ideas. We cannot dismiss ideas and questions simply because we think there are not clear-cut answers. If we lose hope that racist ideologies can be changed into something less unfair, then we should just stop researching in general.

Future work in this area needs to acknowledge that racial inequalities exist not because of individual pathologies or deficiencies, but rather, because there are social and structural problems that require social action to counter them.

## Endnotes

[1]"Legitimizing myths" are important in understanding the dominant group's promotion of color-blind ideology. These legitimizing myths, such as the American Dream, individualism color-blind constitutionalism, equal opportunity, consist of attitudes, values, beliefs, stereotypes, and ideologies that provide moral and intellectual justification for the social practices that distribute social value within the social system (Sidanius, 1999). Feagin and Vera (1995) name this concept "sincere fictions;" that Whites develop these fictions that often hide everyday racial realities. Whites have developed these mythologies that includes a sense of White superiority and that discrimination is no longer a serious problem in the U.S.

[2]Meritocracy is the belief that "all people in the United States have equal chances to achieve success, and that inequalities in the distribution of wealth, power, and influence reflect the qualifications or merit of individuals in each stratum. Affluence is perceived to be a result of the personal qualities of intelligence, industriousness, motivation, and ambition, whereas poverty is perceived to exist because the poor lack those attributes" (Kammeyer et al. 1994: 238).

[3]Qualitative researchers, on the other hand, contend that Whites display significantly higher levels of race-based views on issues as diverse as immigration, affirmative action, welfare, crime, housing, and school integration as compared to results from survey research (Bonilla-Silva 2001).

[4]Bobo (1991) suggests that even while traditional American values include hard work and self-reliance, they also include a commitment to a certain kind of egalitarianism, or a sense of social responsibility. Bobo's research suggests that the

inconsistency in the beliefs of those of lower socioeconomic status is better understood in terms of likely underlying value priorities. Therefore, while traditional American values may tend to side with color-blind ideology, there may be room for more "just" values, such as social responsibility.

[5]Jackman and Muha (1984) argue that highly educated individuals in dominant groups are the most well trained distributors of ideologies such as meritocracy. These ideologies defend the interests of the dominant group.

[6]The definition and the existence of the word "ghetto" have been contested. Massey and Denton define ghettos as a "set of neighborhoods that are exclusively inhabited by members of one group, within which virtually all members of that group live" and that African Americans are the only population that have been ghettoized (1993: 18-19). Jargowsky (1997) refers to all high poverty neighborhoods as ghettos.

[7]There has been discussion of the 1960s race movements as changing the political landscape of racial ideology. Rieder discusses former "liberal" Italians and Jews of New York City who after experiencing the influx of minorities in their neighborhoods, became disgusted with the Democratic party, associating them with "profligacy, spinelessness, malevolence, masochism, elitism, fantasy, idealism, softness, irresponsibility, and sanctimoniousness," and associating the conservative party with "connotations of pragmatism, character, reciprocity, truthfulness, stoicism, manliness, realism, hardness, vengeance, strictness, and responsibility" (1985: 6). Sugrue (1996) discusses how working class Whites during in 1960s Detroit rallied behind racially conservative politicians who rebuked urban spending, welfare programs, and affirmative action.

## References

Barrera, Mario. 1982. *Race and Class in the Southwest*. South Bend, IN: University of Notre Dame Press.

Bashi, Vilna and Antionio McDaniel. 1997. "A Theory of Immigration and Racial Stratification." *Journal of Black Studies*. 27 (5):668-682.

Blauner, Robert. 1989. *Black Lives, White Lives*. Berkeley, CA: University of California Press.

Bobo, Lawrence. 1999. "Prejudice as Group Position: Microfoundations of a Sociological Approach to Racism and Race Relations." *Journal of Social Issues* 55(3):445-472.

Bobo, Lawrence. 1991. "Social Responsibility, Individualism, and Redistributive Policies." *Sociological* Forum. 6(1):71-92.

Bobo, Lawerence, James Kluegel and Ryan Smith. 1997. "Laissez-Faire Racism: The Crystallization of a Kinder, Gentler, Antiblack Ideology." Pp. 15-42 in *Racial Attitudes in the 1990s: Continuity and Change*, edited by Steven A. Tuch and Jack Martin. Westport, CT: Praeger.

Bonilla-Silva, Eduardo. 2001. *White Supremacy and Racism in the Post-Civil Rights Era*. Boulder, CO: Lynne Rienner Publishers.

Bonilla-Silva, Eduardo. 1996. "Rethinking Racism: Toward a Structural Interpretation." *American Sociological Review* 62: 465-480.

Charles, Camille Zubrinsky. 2000. "Neighborhood Racial-Composition Preferences: Evidence from a Multiethnic Metropolis." *Social Problems*. 47:379-407.

Crenshaw, Kimberle W. 1997. "Color-blind Dreams and Racial Nightmares: Reconfiguring Racism in the Post-Civil Rights Era." Pp. 97-168 in *Birth in a Nation'hood* edited by Toni Morrison and Claudia Lacour. New York, NY: Pantheon Books.

Dovidio, John F. 2001. "On the Nature of Contemporary Prejudice: The Third Wave". *Journal of Social Issues* 57(4):829-849.

Entman, Robert and Andrew Rojecki. 2000. "White Racial Attitudes in the Heartland." Pg. 16-45 in *The Black Image in the White Mind: Media and Race in America*. Chicago, IL: University of Chicago Press.

Essed, Philomena. 1996. *Diversity: Gender, Color, and Culture*. Amherst, MA: University of Massachusetts Press.

Farley, Reynolds. 1996. *The New American Reality: Who We Are, How We Got Here, Where We Are Going*. New York: Russell Sage Foundation.

Feagin, Joe R. 1991. "The Continuing Significance of Race: Antiblack Discrimination in Public Places." *American Sociological Review*

56:101-116.

Feagin, Joe R. 1975. *Subordinating the Poor*. Englewood Cliffs, NJ: Prentice Hall.

Feagin, Joe R. and Hernan Vera. 1995. *White Racism: The Basics*. New York: Routledge.

Fine, Michelle and Lois Weiss. 1998. *The Unknown City: The Lives of Poor and Working Class Young Adults*. Boston: Beacon Press.

Forman, Tyrone. 2001. "Social Determinants of White Youths' Racial Attitudes: Evidence from a National Survey." *Sociological Studies of Children and Youth*. 8:173-207.

Gallagher, Charles A. 2002. "Color-blind Pleasures: The Social and Political Functions of Erasing the Color Line In *Post Race America. Forthcoming The Power of Pleasure*, edited by Laurie Essig and Sarah Chinn, New York, NY: Routledge Press.

Gallagher, Charles A. 1995. "White Construction in the University." *Socialist Review*. 24 (1&2): 165-187.

Gotanda, Neil. 1995. "A Critique of 'Our Constitution Is Color-Blind.'" *Critical Race Theory: The Key Writings that Formed the Movement*. Edited by Kimberle Crenshaw, Neil Gotanda, Gary Peller, and Kendall Thomas. New York, NY: The New Press.

Harris, Cheryl I. 1997. "Whiteness as Property." In *Critical Race Theory and Legal Doctrine*. Neil Gotanda, Gary Peller, and Kendall Thomas, eds. NY, NY: The New Press.

Hirsch, Arnold. 1998. *The Making of the Second Ghetto: Race and Housing in Chicago 1940-1960*. Chicago: The University of Chicago Press.

Hochschild, Jennifer. 1995. "'Succeeding More' and 'Under the Spell': Affluent and Poor Blacks' Beliefs about the American Dream." Pg. 72-88 in *Facing Up to the American Dream*. Princeton, NJ: Princeton University Press.

Huber, Joan and William Form. 1973. *Income and Ideology*. New York: Free Press.

Hunt, Matthew O. 2001. "Self-Evaluation and Stratification Beliefs." Pp. 330-350 in *Extending Self-Esteem Theory and Research: Sociological and Psychological Currents*, edited by Timothy J. Owens, Sheldon Struker, and Norman Goodman. New York, NY: Cambridge University Press.

Hunt, Matthew O. 2000. "Status, Religion, and the 'Belief in a Just World': Comparing African Americans, Latinos, and Whites." *Social Science Quarterly.* 81(1):325-343

Hunt, Matthew O. 1996. "The Individual, Society, or Both? A Comparison of Black, Latino, and White Beliefs about the Causes of Poverty." *Social Forces.* 75(1):293-322.

Jackman, Mary R. and Michael J. Muha. 1984. "Education and Intergroup Attitudes: Moral Enlightenment, Superficial Democratic Commitment, or Ideological Refinement?" *American Sociological Review.* 49(6):751-769.

Jargowsky, Paul A. 1997. *Poverty and Place: Ghettos, Barrios, and the American City.* New York: Russell Sage Foundation.

Kammeyer, Kenneth C. W., George Ritzer, and Norman R. Yetman. 1994. *Sociology: Experiencing Changing Societies.* Boston: Allyn and Bacon.

Kinder, Donald and Lynn Sanders. 1996. "Subtle Prejudice for Modern Times." Pp. 92-127 in Divided by Color: *Racial Politics and Democratic Ideals.* Chicago, IL: University of Chicago Press.

Kluegel, James R. and Eliot R. Smith. 1986. *Beliefs about Inequality: Americans' Views of What Is and What Ought to Be.* New York: Aldine De Gruyter.

Logan, John R. and Harvey L. Molotch. 1987. *Urban Fortunes: The Political Economy of Place.* Berkely, CA: University of California Press.

Mann, Michael. 1970. "The Social Cohesion of Liberal Democracy." *American Sociological Review* 35(3): 423-439.

Massey, Douglas and Nancy Denton. 1993. *American Apartheid:*

*Segregation and the Making of the Underclass*. Cambridge, MA: Harvard University Press.

Meyer, Stephen Grant. 2000. *As Long as They Don't Move Next Door: Segregation and Racial Conflict in American Neighborhoods*. Lanham, MD: Rowman & Littlefield Publishers, Inc.

Omi, Michael and Howard Winant. 1994. *Racial Formation in the United States: From the1960s to the 1990s*. New York: Routledge.

Rieder, Jonathan. 1985. *Canarsie: The Jews and Italians of Brooklyn against Liberalism*. Cambridge, MA: Harvard University Press.

Roediger, David R. 1991. *The Wages of Whiteness: Race and the Making of the American Working Class*. New York: Verso.

Rubin, Lillian. 1994. *Families on the Fault Line*. New York, NY: Harper Collins.

Schuman, Howard, Charlotte Steeh, Lawrence Bobo, and Maria Krysan. 1997. *Racial Attitudes in America*. Cambridge, MA: Harvard University Press.

Sears, David. 1988. "Symbolic Racism." Pp. 53-84 in *Eliminating Racism: Profiles in Controversy*, edited by Phylis Katz and Dalmas Taylor. New York, NY: Plenum.

Sidanius, Jim. 1999. *Social Dominance*. New York, NY: Cambridge University Press.

Sigelman, Lee and Susan Welch. 1991. "Blacks' Perceptions of Racial Inequality." Pg. 47-66 in *Black Americans' Views of Racial Inequality*. New York, NY: Cambridge University Press.

Sugrue, Thomas J. 1996. *The Origins of the Urban Crisis: Race and Inequality in Postwar Detroit*. Princeton, N.J.: Princeton University Press.

Taylor, Edward. 1998. "A Primer on Critical Race Theory." *The Journal of Blacks in Higher Education* . 19:122-124.

Vanketesh, Sudhir. 2000. *American Project*. Cambridge, MA: Harvard University Press.

Wacquant, Loic. "The New Urban Color Line: The State and Fate of the Ghetto in Postfordist America." Pp. 231-276 in *Social Theory and the Politics of Identity*. Edited by Craig J. Calhoun. Oxford and Cambridge: Basil Blackwell, 1994.

Wilson, William Julius. 1996. *When Work Disappears: The World of the New Urban Poor*. New York: Vintage Books.

Wilson, William Julius. 1987. *The Truly Disadvantaged: The Inner City, the Underclass, and Public Policy*. Chicago: The University of Chicago Press.

Wilson, William Julius. 1978. *Declining Significance of Race: Blacks and Changing American Institutions*. Chicago: University of Chicago Press.

# Chapter 10

# *Race South of the Equator:*
## *Reexamining the Intersection of Color and Class in Brazil\**

### Vânia Penha-Lopes
Bloomfield College

Myths, perhaps because they may fulfill societal wishes, die hard. Take, for example, the image of Brazil as a racial democracy. Since formulated and promoted by the Brazilian elite at the turn of the 20th century, it was widely endorsed, by lay people and even by such social critics as E. Franklin Frazier, who, after a five-month visit in the early 1940s, naively declared, "Brazil has no race problem" (1992). The view of Brazil as a paradise for people of African descent spread throughout the 20th century despite numerous studies and personal testimonies attesting to the contrary, and the fact that Afro-Brazilian have lagged behind Whites in every significant social indicator. For example, just as it was true four decades ago (Silva, 1985), recent data show that Brazilian Blacks and Mulattoes continue to be much more likely than Whites to be unemployed, to earn lower wages, and, consequently, to be poor (DIEESE, 2000). Moreover, according to the 2000 Brazilian census, education pays off significantly better for Whites, who experience an increase in wages twice as large as do Blacks and Mulattoes for each additional year of schooling (IBGE, 2002a:1). Furthermore, while living conditions in general improved in the last decade of the last century, racial inequalities remained unchanged (Farid, 2001:1), so that Brazil is ranked 63rd in the world in terms of the quality of life of its general population, but 120th in the world regarding its Black population alone (Ramalho et al., 1998:2).

Indeed, the persistence of glaring socioeconomic inequalities by race, together with decades of Black activism and a slow governmental awareness of racial problems, seem finally to corrode the foundation of Brazil's image of racial harmony. To wit, "from 1995 onward, . . . full citizenship of the Black population has become a government goal with the recognition of the mechanisms of unequal development to which this segment of society has been submitted" (Pereira, n.d.:1). This is no small feat: as late as 1969, the federal government found it necessary to pass a law deeming subversive any mention of racial discrimination in the nation, quite an irony in a purportedly discrimination-free society (Fontaine, 1985:3; Gilliam, 1992:180; 181). Since the mid-1990s, the federal government has been actively formulating a "policy of affirmative action" which includes proposals for increasing the representation of Black students at universities and eliminating racial discrimination on the job market (Ramalho et al., 1998). In July of 2002, the Ministries of Science and Technology, Justice, Culture, and Foreign Affairs announced the release of scholarship funds for 20 Afro-Brazilians to prepare for a career in diplomacy, thus taking steps finally to break the racial barrier for which the Brazilian foreign service is known (Fundação Cultural Palmares, 2002).

In about a century, then, Brazil has undergone a major shift concerning its conception of race: from promoting the myth of racial democracy, in which class is believed to matter more than race, due to the perception that "money whitens," to the acknowledgment of deep-seated racism and serious racial inequality, and the consequent development of affirmative action policies. That sounds like the reverse trajectory race has taken in the United States according to William Julius Wilson (1980:3): from the initial supremacy of racial-caste oppression on to class conflict amid continuing racial oppression to, for the past forty years, a "progressive transition from racial inequalities to class inequalities."

In this chapter, I apply to the Brazilian situation Wilson's now-classic argument that social class becomes paramount for the status of African Americans only after affirmative action policies are implemented, i.e., after Blacks can take advantage of educational opportunities and gain access to better-paying jobs. In order to develop my argument, I start by providing an overview of the myth of racial democracy and Brazil's fluid racial classification. I then review Wilson's thesis, drawing comparisons with the Brazilian situation. Next, using educational attainment, income, unemployment rates, and other social indicators based on data from the 2000 Brazilian Census, the 1999 National Household Survey (Pesquisa Nacional por Amostra de Domicílios–PNAD), and the 2000 Survey of Employment and Unemployment (Pesquisa de Emprego e Desemprego–PED), I show that race continues to seriously affect life chances in Brazil, which renders governmental intervention necessary.

### The Birth and Death of the Myth of Racial Democracy

In May of 2002, U.S. president George W. Bush was quoted in the German newspaper *Der Spiegel* as showing ignorance about the existence of Blacks in Brazil during a conversation with Fernando Henrique Cardoso, then the Brazilian president. Bush was saved by national security adviser Condoleeza Rice, who informed him that Brazil probably had more Blacks than the United States. Fernando Henrique, himself a sociologist famous for his work on racism and on economic development, ironically concluded that, "regarding Latin America, Bush was still in his 'learning phase'" (*Der Spiegel*, 2002).

While one could argue that Bush should have done his homework, his lack of knowledge of the racial composition of Brazil is not that surprising if one admits that Brazil has done a rather good job at camouflaging it. After all, according to official statistics, the Black population steadily dwindled from a high of over half of all Brazilians in the 1870s to just one-tenth of the population in 1950 (Degler, 1971). At present, as Table 10.1 shows, the official proportion of Brazilian Blacks is a meager 6 percent; Mulattoes constitute 39 percent, and Whites, fully 53 percent of the total population (IBGE, 2002b: Table 1.1.1). Rapid and intensive miscegenation, even coupled by high Black mortality rates, would most likely not have accounted for such a dramatic decline in the Black population. Rather, given that the Brazilian Institute for Geography and Statistics (IBGE, 2002c) catalogs "color" or "race" as subjective responses to four closed-ended options (i.e., White, Black, Yellow, Mulatto, or Indigenous)[1], it is clear that a large proportion of the population has routinely opted out of being Black.

**Table 10.1**
Resident Population, by Color or Race, by the Great Regions

| Great Regions | Total | White | Black | Yellow | Mulatto | Indigenous |
|---|---|---|---|---|---|---|
| Brazil | 169,799,170 | 53.4% | 6.1% | .5% | 38.9% | .4% |
| North | 12,900,704 | 29.3 | 5.0 | .2 | 62.7 | 1.6 |
| Northeast | 47,741,711 | 31.9 | 7.5 | .1 | 59.3 | .3 |
| Southeast | 72,412,411 | 62.0 | 6.5 | .8 | 29.8 | .2 |
| South | 25,107,616 | 83.9 | 3.8 | .5 | 11.2 | .2 |
| Center-West | 11,636,728 | 48.8 | 4.3 | .5 | 44.8 | 1.1 |

*Source:* Instituto Brasileiro de Geografia e Estatística (IBGE, 2002b), Censo Demográfico 2000.

Elsewhere (Penha-Lopes, 1996; 1997) I discuss in detail the whitening ideology in Brazil. Here, suffice it to say that it was a state-endorsed "solution" for Brazil's deep inferiority complex regarding its African past and widespread miscegenation, a complex which had been created by the pseudo-scientific racial theories of the nineteenth century. That ideology inspired the immigration of millions of Europeans to Brazil, who were given preference over Blacks both in farming and in the country's incipient industrialization (Pereira, n.d.:2). The plan was relatively simple: to infuse the country with as many Whites as possible and to promote amalgamation as the process which would allow the best of each race to emerge (Freyre, 1946), even if White was ultimately the "superior" race (Skidmore, 1993). In other words, if at the turn of the century the Brazilian elite saw the country's racially mixed reality as a disgrace, by 1920 it considered it an asset. Racial democracy, then, is the harmonious coexistence of different races on the road to whitening. As Hasenbalg (1985:25) concluded, "The implicit corollary of this idea is the absence of racial prejudice and discrimination and, consequently, the existence of equal economic and social opportunities for Whites and Blacks."

Only racism has never been absent; for the most part, however, it has been so subtle that foreigners such as Americans used to blatant racist orgies like lynchings might miss it. For example, the criterion of "good appearance" on job advertisements has long been understood as a metaphor for whiteness. That has prevented Blacks from obtaining, in particular, jobs that require direct contact with the public, such as receptionists, secretaries, and bank tellers. That deeply ingrained practice was finally attacked in 1997, when Maninha, a congresswoman from Brasília, authored Law 1740, which "forbids the use of [that] or a similar expression on job announcements" (Ramalho et al.1998:21; my translation).

Brazil may have never met Jim Crow in the flesh, but it is not immune to violence against Blacks. The stereotype of Blacks as criminals led to, in the beginning of last century, the persecution of all popular Afro-Brazilian manifestations, including samba and Afro-Brazilian religions, and culminated with the summary execution of seven street boys on the streets of Rio de Janeiro by the police in 1993 (Penha-Lopes, 1997).

Curiously, the Brazilian elite so conceived of racial democracy as a sign of peaceful race relations that it became an issue of national security to question it. As such, in the 1960s, the military dictatorship expelled university professors (including Brazil's penultimate president, Fernando Henrique Cardoso) and "identified studies and reports on racial discrimination in that country as subversive" (Fontaine, 1985:2). The "prejudice of not having prejudice" peaked when the Brazilian Census Commission voted to exclude race or color from the 1970 census, with the excuse that it was impossible to collect meaningful data on race (Skidmore, 1985:17). While it is a fact that the hundreds of racial categories collected by the 1950 Census were much too confusing (Penha-Lopes, 1996), it is doubtful that having no data at all was an appropriate alternative. Given the political climate at the time, such a move seemed to be masking ulterior motives: "Without data, of course, discussion would continue being reduced to the anecdotal level. That is where defenders of Brazil's racial myth have always preferred to operate, dwelling on examples of famous Brazilians whose physical features bore little relation to their station in life" (Skidmore, 1985:17).

Only in the late 1970s, when the military dictatorship launched the "democratic opening" of the country, did suppression of attacks on the myth start to die out. Since then, in 1978, 2,000 Blacks protested against racial discrimination in the city of São Paulo (Mitchell, 1985:96); the following year, "the first National Congress of the MNU [Movimento Negro Unificado–Unified Black Movement] was held in the municipality of Caxias, Rio de Janeiro, with militant representatives from the states of São Paulo, Minas Gerais, Bahia, Rio Grande do Sul, and Rio de Janeiro"

(Gonzales, 1985:128).

The beginning of the end of the myth of racial democracy can be traced back to 1988, when the new Brazilian constitution redefined racial discrimination as a crime. The following year, the "Caó Law" (Law 7716), by Black congressman Carlos Alberto Oliveira, made obsolete the "Afonso Arinos Law" (Law 1390, from 1951), long the object of scorn, because it defined racial discrimination only as a penal infraction. The Caó Law "deals specifically with racial discrimination in jobs contracted by the public (article 3) and private sectors (article 4)" (DIEESE, 2000:10; my translation).

The 1988 constitution also promotes the preservation of ethnic diversity in Brazil. In that vein, it instituted the Palmares Cultural Foundation (Fundação Cultural Palmares), named after the most famous *quilombo*.[2] That entity is responsible for promoting all measures of cultural, economic, and political insertion of Afro-Brazilians into society. The sponsorship of Blacks into foreign service, mentioned above, is "the first concrete action of the Comitê Científico Palmares [Palmares Scientific Committee]" (Fundação Cultural Palmares, 2002; my translation). In addition, after discussions initiated during the Third World Conference against Racism, which took place in South Africa in 2001, the foundation has proposed that the government pay for tuition and all other expenses related to attending college, in an effort to increase the retention of Afro-Brazilians (Fundação Cultural Palmares, 2002); currently, only about 3 percent graduate from college (Ramalho et al., 1998:27). Also worth noting are the president's creation of the Interministerial Group for the Appreciation of the Black Population in 1995 and the identification of 511 communities of descendants of quilombo slaves, with the goal of granting them the deeds of the land; several communities have already received the deeds (Pereira n.d.:3-4).

In sum, the myth of racial democracy has had a rather colorful trajectory. It is interesting to note that it is based on the premise that class, not race, has a stronger effect on stratification, as Donald Pierson suggested in 1942 and reiterated a quarter-century later despite severe criticism (Skidmore, 1985:22). However, the longstanding myth of Brazil's racial paradise has finally crumbled under the official recognition of the need for affirmative action policies. In contrast to Brazil, as we will see below, according to Wilson the United States starts out by focusing on race, and now relies more on class.

### *The Declining Significance of Race*, Once Again

Nearly a quarter century after its original publication, *The Declining Significance of Race* still yields reflections such as the present one. In that book, Wilson defends the thesis that race is declining in social importance vis-à-vis class because it is no longer possible to "speak of a single or uniform Black experience," as there are clear class distinctions within the U.S. Black population (Wilson, 1980:144).

Despite what his critics may say, at no point does Wilson claim that racism in the form of racial discrimination and segregation has vanished altogether from American society, so much so that he devoted his subsequent book, *The Truly Disadvantaged* (1987), to the causes of persistent racism against underprivileged Blacks. But he maintains that, *in the economic sphere*, race has given way to class as a determinant of Black access to positions of power and privilege. At the same time that more Blacks are reaching influential posts comparable to Whites, "the Black underclass is in a hopeless state of economic stagnation, falling further and further behind the rest of society" (1980:2).

Wilson conceives the history of race relations in the United States as characterized by three distinct periods. The major characteristic of the first two periods (i.e., pre-industrial and industrial) was the hegemony of economic racial domination of Blacks by Whites, reinforced by political, juridical, and social discrimination. This pattern was sustained by ideologies of racial inferiority that influenced every intergroup interaction.

That, by the way, was not very different from the Brazilian situation, except for the absence of comprehensive segregationist laws there.

Also somewhat similar were some of the social circumstances surrounding the beginning of industrialization in both countries. Just as the U.S. allowed the mass immigration of Europeans specifically to work in the Northern and Midwestern factories, Brazil also opened its doors to European immigrants–first, to work in the coffee plantations after the abolition of slavery in 1888, and later, to work in the nascent factories in the Southeastern state of São Paulo. In both countries, Whites were preferentially hired for wage labor. To Blacks were left "the most modest jobs, which required minimal specialization and were poorly paid" (Ramalho et al., 1998:5; my translation). Wilson is, therefore, mistaken when he argues that, after the abolition of slavery in Brazil,

> the large Negro and Mulatto population was not thrust into competition with the much smaller white population over access to higher-status positions because, as Marvin Harris notes, 'there was little opportunity for any member of the lower class to move upward in the social hierarchy.'... The Mulattoes, Negroes, and poor Whites were all in the same impoverished lower-ranking position" (Wilson, 1980:15).

If that were true, how could we explain the relatively rapid rise of European immigrants in the economic, political, and social spheres? Wilson's argument only works if we ignore the power of the whitening ideology on race relations in Brazil. Poor Whites (e.g., recent European immigrants) had over Blacks the advantage of their higher racial status, which led to preferential hiring practices.

Preferential treatment by race resulted in similar housing patterns in the two countries. In Brazil, Blacks' economic marginalization, coupled by mass rural-to-urban migration, resulted in the formation of *cortiços*, or slum-tenement houses, that were the precursors of the *favelas* of today

(Ramalho et al., 1998:5). In the U.S., the formation of urban Black ghettoes is also associated with Blacks' great migration north in search of better-paying jobs and less racial segregation, only to be relegated to inferior socioeconomic conditions (Massey and Denton, 1999). Even the few Blacks who had been able to acquire an education and more prestigious occupations were restricted in their practice and their choices of residence. Therefore, for all intents and purposes, race was still more important than class status; the larger U.S. society did not yet truly differentiate among Blacks on the basis of social status.

The U.S. situation started to change during the 1940s. First, the legal ban on discrimination in government agencies and subsidized training programs allowed Blacks to get manufacturing and some clerical jobs. Later, in 1954, institutionalized segregation was abolished by law. This period, which Wilson labels "modern industrial," marks the onset of higher political resources for Blacks; the civil rights movement and the successful state intervention to eliminate discriminatory laws contributed to Black occupational mobility. Those job opportunities eventually led to greater occupational differentiation in the Black community.

For Wilson, with the expansion of white-collar jobs and affirmative action in the U.S., access to the means of production and the possibility of better jobs came to be based on education—those who are talented and educated have more opportunities of upward mobility than it was ever possible before; those who are poorly educated become trapped in low-paying jobs outside of the corporate sector.

Thus, if we accept Wilson's argument that past racial oppression (i.e., up until the late 1940s) was responsible for the creation of ghettoes and an underclass, it is not fair to say that race still has the same influence on the life chances of African Americans as a whole. Certainly since the 1970s, "as race declined in importance in the economic sector, the Negro class structure became increasingly a consequence of class affiliation" (Wilson, 1980:153).

At first, the situation in Brazil appears to be the opposite of that in the United States because of the absence of *de jure* discrimination and the presence of the whitening ideology there. Upon closer scrutiny, however, we notice the similarities between the two societies: not only is *de facto* discrimination present in both, but race relations in Brazil are only harmonious as long as Blacks are "kept in their place,"[3] i.e., at the bottom of society, away from meaningful competition with Whites. Keeping Blacks in their place, a paternalistic policy, was also used in the United States, especially during slavery and in the South.

In that respect, the main difference between Brazil and the United States is that paternalism seems to have dominated race relations in the former country for a much longer period than in the latter. To this day, it is common for Brazilians to differentiate the "good" Black from the "bad" one: the "good" Black is well-mannered, affable and subservient, and has a "White" soul (Ramalho et al., 1998:6). Another major difference between the two countries is that Brazil expressly promoted miscegenation as a way of absorbing its Black population, whereas the United States, with its segregationist policy, sought to keep Blacks as such. Consider the telling–albeit unfulfilled–prediction of Mário Pinto Serva, a Brazilian educational reformer from the 1920s:

> a century from now the United States will have between twenty and thirty million strong and vigorous Blacks in a system of complete social segregation and will therefore face the gravest ethnic problem within the country. Not so in Brazil. A century from now we shall have one hundred and fifty million inhabitants, almost all white, but having peacefully accomplished the absorption of the other elements (in Skidmore, 1993:276n).

There is an irony to this comparison. Through most of its post-slavery history, Brazil has condemned the United States' practices of racial exclusion. Now, not only is Brazil finally facing its own legacy of exclusion, but as a result, it is adopting affirmative action policies that rather resemble those of the United States. Those policies are justified in view of the blatant inequalities between Whites and Afro-Brazilians, as I show below.

## The Price of Race

Brazil ended the 20th century older,[4] but in much better social shape: a more educated population with a longer lifespan, smaller families, lower infant mortality rates, lower illiteracy rates, and lower rates of child labor (IBGE, 2002a; IBGE, 2002d). Changes in educational attainment were manifold and noteworthy: more children between the ages of seven and 14 remained in school, up from 84 percent in 1989 to 96 percent ten years later; the proportion of high-school graduates among persons above nine years of age increased from 15.5 percent to 19 percent; the overall illiteracy rate went from 17 percent in 1992 to 13 percent in 1999 (IBGE, 2002a:2), whereas the illiteracy rate among 10- to 14-year-old children in 1999 decreased to nearly a third of the 1989 figure of 14.8 percent (IBGE, 2002d:2); finally, functional illiteracy decreased 7.5 percentage points, to a low of 29.4 percent, between 1992 and 1999 (IBGE, 2002a:2).

Arguably, these changes in educational attainment are most significant because they correlate with so many other transformations. For example, while overall employment grew by 2.4 percent, the proportion of employed children between the ages of 10 and 14 shrank from about one-fifth to less than 17 percent (IBGE, 2002a:3). Moreover, while fertility rates declined remarkably from 5.8 children in 1970 to 2.3 children per woman in 1999, the decline was, not surprisingly, more pronounced among women with at least a high-school education–1.6 children–than among grade-school dropouts–3.1 children (IBGE, 2002a:1). Educational attainment is also correlated with infant mortality: in 1999, there were only 29.7 deaths per 1000 children of mothers with at least a middle school education, as opposed to an astounding 93 deaths per 1000 children whose mothers had only finished grade school (IBGE, 2002a:2).

On the other hand, such aggregate data mask profound racial inequalities, for if it is true that Brazilians as a whole are more educated, Whites tend to stay in school longer than do Mulattoes and Blacks, as Table 10.2 shows (IBGE, 2002a:2).

**Table 10.2**
Average Years of Schooling
for Persons 10 Years of Age or Older by Color, 1999

| Average Years of Schooling | | | |
|---|---|---|---|
| Brazil and Great Regions | Total | White | Black & Mulatto |
| Brazil | 5.7 | 6.6 | 4.6 |
| North | 5.7 | 6.7 | 5.4 |
| Northeast | 4.3 | 5.3 | 3.9 |
| Southeast | 6.5 | 7.1 | 5.2 |
| South | 6.2 | 6.5 | 4.7 |
| Center-West | 5.9 | 6.8 | 5.3 |

*Source:* Pesquisa Nacional de Amostra de Domicílios (PNAD, Instituto Brasileiro de Geografia e Estatística (IBGE, 2002f).

While the illiteracy rate of 20 percent for Blacks and Mulattoes impressively decreased ten percentage points since the early 1990s (IBGE, 1992: Table 22.3), it is still seven percentage points above the current national average and over twice as high as that of Whites (IBGE, 2002a:2). Moreover, not only are Brazilians of African descent much less likely than Whites to go to college,[5] but they may also be subjected to crippling prejudice on their way. For instance, a report from 1998 documented the following:

> On the entrance exams for the Federal University of Mato
> Grosso, the more than 15 thousand candidates faced a sentence on
> the Portuguese exam with explicit color prejudice. The sentence
> 'She is beautiful, but she is Black. Although she is Black, she is
> beautiful' generated protests by some candidates, who felt ill at
> ease, and members of the Unified Black Movement (MNU), who
> alleged that the ill feeling that the incident created in the
> candidates made the competition unequal. They started a motion,
> headed by the State Council of the Rights of Blacks, based on
> Law 7716, which punishes crimes resulting from discrimination
> or prejudice on the grounds of race, color, ethnicity, religion, or
> national origin with one to three years in prison (Ramalho et al.,
> 1998:6; my translation).

Not only are Whites much more likely than Afro-Brazilians to get an education, but when there is educational parity between the races, Whites reap twice as high wages from their educational gains as do Blacks and Mulattoes. The other side of the coin is no less bleak. An analysis of the 2000 Survey of Employment and Unemployment (PED) covering six major metropolitan regions reveals that "When Blacks in all regions finish high school or reach college, their unemployment rates decrease, but continue to be significantly higher than those registered among non-Black workers" (DIEESE, 2000:5; my translation).[6] Curiously, as we can see on Table 10.3, the highest rates of unemployment for all regions, regardless of race, are among high-school dropouts; as expected, the college educated fare best. Still, that Blacks have higher unemployment rates than non-Blacks at all educational levels is particularly perverse, given that the former have higher rates of labor force participation in all metropolitan regions than the latter (DIEESE, 2000:4, Table 11).

**Table 10.3**

Total Unemployment Rates, by Race and Schooling,

Brazilian Metropolitan Regions, 2000

| Metro Regions | Race | Illiterate | Some Grade School | Grade School Grad | Some High School | High School Grad | College |
|---|---|---|---|---|---|---|---|
| Belo Horizonte | Black | 16.7% | 21.3% | 20.3% | 26.6% | 15.7% | 6.9% |
| | Nonblack | 13.4 | 19.9 | 19.6 | 25.4 | 14.3 | 6.7 |
| Brasília | Black | 24.8 | 28.5 | 26.4 | 34.3 | 19.0 | 6.8 |
| | Nonblack | 23.6 | 27.0 | 24.6 | 31.8 | 18.4 | 7.2 |
| Porto Alegre | Black | * | 28.9 | 26.9 | * | 19.6 | * |
| | Nonblack | * | 21.1 | 19.9 | 26.6 | 15.0 | 8.9 |
| Recife | Black | 19.3 | 24.6 | 26.1 | 32.5 | 21.3 | 10.5 |
| | Nonblack | 15.0 | 23.8 | 22.2 | 28.9 | 19.1 | 9.2 |
| Salvador | Black | 24.0 | 32.9 | 32.6 | 40.7 | 23.3 | 12.2 |
| | Nonblack | * | 29.4 | 30.0 | 33.0 | 20.2 | 11.6 |
| São Paulo | Black | 22.6 | 25.1 | 27.3 | 33.6 | 19.2 | 10.4 |
| | Nonblack | 18.1 | 19.5 | 20.7 | 27.2 | 15.8 | 8.0 |

Source: Departamento Intersindical de Estatística e Estudos Sócio-Econômicos
(DIEESE, 2000, Table 13).
* Not enough data to disaggregate.

In effect, higher labor force participation does not yield higher income for Afro-Brazilians. Compared to them (see Table 10.4), Whites earn at least R$210 more yearly (in metropolitan Recife, in the Northeast) and as much as R$467 more (in the Southeastern metropolitan region of São Paulo, the wealthiest in the nation).[7]

**Table 10.4**
Average Annual Income of Employed Persons, by Sex and Race,
Metropolitan Regions, January-June 2000[a]

| Metro Regions | Blacks | | | Nonblacks | | |
|---|---|---|---|---|---|---|
| | Total | Men | Women | Total | Men | Women |
| Belo Horizonte | 485 | 595 | 358 | 756 | 914 | 563 |
| Brasília | 909 | 1,120 | 675 | 1,329 | 1,574 | 1,077 |
| Porto Alegre | 369 | 442 | 292 | 684 | 823 | 505 |
| Recife | 365 | 433 | 268 | 575 | 682 | 436 |
| Salvador | 416 | 503 | 320 | 963 | 1,154 | 760 |
| São Paulo | 515 | 612 | 393 | 982 | 1,178 | 714 |

[a]In 2000, US$1=R$1.721 (Conselho Universitário, 2002).
*Source:*PED, Departamento Intersindical de Estatística e Estudos Sócio-Econômicos (DIEESE, 2000, Table 14).

Disaggregating men from women, we see that Black women have the lowest earnings in all metropolitan regions. As Table 10.5 shows, Black women earn only about a third of what White men do per month; White women, who earn about 60 percent of their male counterparts' income, fare much better than Black women or men, which suggests that, in Brazil today, race may have a higher impact on individuals' life chances than gender.

As a consequence, Black families are much more likely to be poor. nearly a third of them, compared to about a quarter of Mulatto families, but less than 15 percent of White families, must do with only half the per capita minimum wage. That is not surprising, given the much higher rate of Blacks who are domestic servants (14.6 percent, compared to 8.4 percent of Mulattoes and 6 percent of Whites) and are employed in other "vulnerable" job situations, i.e., those without working papers, the self-employed who "work for the public,"and those who work with their families for no pay (DIEESE, 2000:7). On the other hand, Whites are close to six times more likely than Blacks and thrice more likely than Mulattoes to be employers (IBGE, 2002a:3).

**Table 10.5**
Index of Average Monthly Earnings of Employed Persons, by Sex and Race, Metropolitan Regions, January-June 2000[a]

| Metro Regions | Blacks | | Nonblacks | |
|---|---|---|---|---|
| | Men | Women | Men | Women |
| Belo Horizonte | 65.10 | 39.17 | 100.00 | 61.60 |
| Brasília | 71.16 | 42.88 | 100.00 | 68.42 |
| Porto Alegre | 53.90 | 35.61 | 100.00 | 61.59 |
| Recife | 63.49 | 39.30 | 100.00 | 63.93 |
| Salvador | 43.33 | 27.73 | 100.00 | 65.86 |
| São Paulo | 51.95 | 33.36 | 100.00 | 60.61 |

[a]In 2000, US$1=R$1.721 (Conselho Universitário, 2002).
*Source:* PED, Departamento Intersindical de Estatística e Estudos Sócio-Econômicos (DIEESE, 2000, Table 15.)

What emerges, then, is a picture of racial-class inequality that all but guarantees limited life chances to non-Whites. In other words, centuries of inequality based on racial status have stuck most Afro-Brazilians in the lower social classes; in turn, descending from persons in the lower social classes makes it more difficult for Afro-Brazilians to experience upwardly social mobility or to survive at all. Let us make no mistake: at the rate of 34 percent (down from 40 percent in 1995), poverty is widespread in Brazil. The shocking point is the disproportionate incidence of poverty among Blacks: of the poor, over twice as many (68.9 percent) are Black than are White (30.7 percent). As Roberto Martins, the president of IPEA, put it, "poverty in this country has a color, and that color is black" (Farid, 2001:1; my translation).

**Table 10.6**
Mortality Rates for Infants and for Children
Younger than Five Years of Age by Color

| Brazil and Great Regions | Infant Mortality Rates/1000 | | | Mortality Rates for Children Younger than Five/1000 | | |
|---|---|---|---|---|---|---|
| | Total | White | Black & Mulatto | Total | White | Black & Mulatto |
| Brazil | 34.8 | 37.3 | 62.3 | 60.7 | 45.7 | 76.1 |
| North | 32.7 | -- | -- | -- | -- | -- |
| Northeast | 52.8 | 68.0 | 96.3 | 96.4 | 82.8 | 102.1 |
| Southeast | 25.7 | 25.1 | 43.1 | 36.7 | 30.9 | 52.7 |
| South | 22.8 | 28.3 | 38.9 | 35.2 | 34.8 | 47.7 |
| Center-West | 26.1 | 27.8 | 42.0 | 41.1 | 31.1 | 51.4 |

*Source:* Instituto Brasileiro de Geografia e Estatística (IBGE, 2000), Departamento de População e Indicadores Sociais.

On the issue of survival, of pressing importance are Afro-Brazilians' high infant mortality rates. As Table 10.6 above shows, Black and Mulatto children are at much higher risk of dying before age six than Whites and Brazilian children as a whole. That is particularly true of children who live in the Northeast, simultaneously the poorest region in the country and the one with the largest proportion of Blacks (see Table 10.1): the national average for the mortality rate of White children younger than five is 60.7 per 1000 births, whereas it reaches an alarming figure of 102.1 for Northeastern Blacks and Mulattoes. Comparing that figure to the

White rate of 82.8, we conclude that the disadvantage that Northeastern children in general face because of the dismal economic resources of that region is exacerbated by their nonwhite status. Adding to the interaction between race and socioeconomic resources, we also notice an interesting pattern: nonwhite children of any age experience the lowest mortality rates in the South, whereas White children do so in the Southeast, which also happens to be the region with the highest educational attainment, as is evident on Table 10.2 (IBGE, 2002a:2).

Those who survive early childhood must often live under unsanitary conditions, which may shorten their life expectancy. Table 10.7 indicates that, once again, Afro-Brazilians fall behind Whites in all regions of the country regarding the basic sanitation of their homes. Over 80 percent of Whites, but only two-thirds of Blacks and Mulattoes, had running water in their homes. The situation is worse for the sewerage system: fewer than two-fifths of Blacks and Mulattoes, as opposed to nearly two-thirds of Whites, resided in homes with a septic tank. As is true of other social indicators, Afro-Brazilians are best served in the Southeast, where close to twice as many of them have adequate sanitation as Blacks and Mulattoes in general.

In sum, one hundred and fifteen years after the abolition of slavery, and despite harmonious intergroup relations on the surface, Brazil continues to be dominated by unambiguous inequities based on race. From the moment of birth, through the years spent in school–or not–to entrance, rewards, and permanence on the labor market, it pays to be White in Brazil. None of that is new information, however; similar results were found using data from 1960 and the 1970s (Silva, 1985). What is new is the level of awareness of racism and the volume of debate about the need for radically rectifying measures in the population at large (see, for example, Bento, 2000; Pereira, n.d.). The myth of racial democracy seems to be finally dead; it will be probably laid to rest when affirmative action policies are thoroughly implemented.

| Table 10.7 Households by Condition of Sanitation according to the Color of the Reference Person, 1999 | | | | |
|---|---|---|---|---|
| Brazil and Great Regions | Running Water and General Distribution | | Sewer and Septic Tank | |
| | White | Black & Mulatto | White | Black & Mulatto |
| Brazil | 82.8% | 67.2% | 62.7% | 39.6% |
| North | 68.8 | 57.5 | 19.2 | 12.7 |
| Northeast | 66.7 | 55.1 | 28.7 | 19.8 |
| Southeast | 90.0 | 82.5 | 83.9 | 71.0 |
| South | 79.8 | 77.3 | 46.4 | 34.0 |
| Center-West | 75.2 | 66.4 | 38.7 | 31.3 |

*Source:* PNAD, Instituto Brasileiro de Geografia e Estatística (IBGE, 2002f).

## Conclusion

Where formerly there was the delayed fear (born of slavery) that the treatment of racial inequalities could be a factor of national fragmentation, today there is an understanding that our consolidation as an emerging nation depends on creating mobility for blacks, a human segment that accounts for an extremely significant portion of the population and which, being immobilized by such inequalities, fails to produce and consume wealth (Pereira, n.d.:4).

For most of Brazil's history since the abolition of slavery, race (or color) has been so enmeshed with class as to suggest the concept of "social races" (Pitt-Rivers, 1987:298). Because of the large Black contingent among the poor and the predominance of Whites in the elite, the class structure in Brazil cannot be fully comprehended without its racial overtones. One consequence of such hierarchy has been the production and perpetuation of stereotypes according to which middle-class Blacks are reclassified as Mulattoes or brunettes, or described as "Black, but efficient and cultured" (Fundação Cultural Palmares, 2002; my translation). Following the politics of whitening, the implication was that anything Black was negative and, thus, an insult, and also that educated Blacks must per force be on their way to whiteness. The alternative was conspicuously to ignore the race of Afro-Brazilians who had "made it" and to discourage all discussions of racial inequality, for fear, as the quote above notes, of social conflict.

However, ignoring race in no way erases its effects on the social structure in general and on individuals' life chances in particular. Nor has the "peaceful" coexistence of racially diverse groups guaranteed equal opportunity for those who are not White. Brazil has started to face up to that reality, thus putting an end to its ill-deserved reputation as a racial democracy. Now that Brazil has begun to adopt affirmative action as the weapon against centuries-old racial inequality, it remains to be seen whether class will actually assume greater importance for the social status of its citizens, as the Brazilian elite claimed nearly a century ago, and Wilson argued about the social situation in the United States. Also, as affirmative action policies are implemented and, as a consequence, being labeled "Afro-Brazilian" may become economically advantageous, it will be fascinating to see whether more Brazilians will start to think of themselves as such.

## Endnotes

*The author wishes to thank Jeff Mellow for comments on an earlier draft of this chapter.

1. In Brazil, the official designation for the Black race or color is "preta," even though Blacks prefer the term "negra." "Mulato(a)" (i.e., the offspring of Black and White parentage) is treated by the Census as "parda," the color of brown paper

bags, and an older classification of all Blacks in birth certificates. In this chapter, in addition to "Blacks" and "Mulattoes," I also use the term "Afro-Brazilians" to refer to the two groups as one.

2. *Quilombos* were nuclei of resistance to slavery in Brazil, formed by slaves who had escaped their plantations. The most famous of them was Palmares, led by Zumbi, in the 17th century. In 1995, President Fernando Henrique Cardoso declared November 20, the day of Zumbi's assassination, "National Day of Black Consciousness" (Maio, 1999).

3. For example, even after having been elected congresswoman, senator, and vice-governor of Rio de Janeiro, Benedita da Silva, the minister of social assistance and promotion in the current government of president Luiz Inácio Lula da Silva, observes that she still confronts racism "all the time" (Ribeiro, 2000). As a dark-skinned Black person in the spotlight, Benedita has been the target of numerous racial slurs, from being called a "monkey" during one of her earlier campaigns to, more recently, being cited as a metaphor for an extremely ugly distortion. Criticizing Congress, a businessman stated, "In Congress, you know what something is like when it goes in, but no one knows how it will come out. A picture of Marilyn Monroe goes in and comes out as a picture of Madonna. Actually, Madonna is too good a comparison; it's more like Benedita" (ISTOÉ, 1996; my translation).

4. April 22, 2000 marked the 500th anniversary of the arrival of the Portuguese in Brazil.

5. According to the Institute of Applied Economic Research (Instituto de Pesquisa Econômica Aplicada–IPEA), only 2 percent of Blacks between the ages of 18 and 25, in contrast to 11 percent of Whites, had ever been to college as of 1999 (Farid, 2001:1).

6. The Interunion Department of Statistics and Socioeconomic Studies (Departamento Intersindical de Estatística e Estudos Sócio-Econômicos–DIEESE), the author of the study, defines "Blacks" as Blacks and Mulattoes and "Nonblacks" as Whites and "Yellows," i.e., Brazilians of Asian descent (Boletim DIEESE, 2000:1).

## References

Bento, Maria Aparecida. 2000. "Racismo no Trabalho: O Movimento Sindical e o Estado." In *Tirando a Máscara: Ensaios sobre o Racismo no Brasil*. São Paulo: Paz e Terra.

Conselho Universitário, Universidade Federal de São Paulo. 2002. "Relatório de Atividades." http://www.unifesp.br/admin/relativid/intro.html. Retrieved August 09, 2002.

Degler, Carl N. 1971. *Neither Black nor White: Slavery and Race Relations in Brazil and the United States*. New York: The Macmillan Company.

*Der Spiegel.* 2002. "Bush's General Educaction: Do you Have Blacks in Brazil?" May 19. http://gwbush.com/copies/trans.shtml. Retrieved June 4, 2002.

Departamento Intersindical de Estatística e Estudos Sócio-Econômicos (DIEESE). 2000. "Edição Especial--20 de Novembro: Dia Nacional da Consciência Negra." *Boletim DIEESE* November. http://www. dieese.org.br. Retrieved July 15, 2002.

Departamento Intersindical de Estatística e Estudos Sócio-Econômicos (DIEESE). 2000-2001. "T15. Salário Mínimo: Brasil 1940-2000." *Anuário dos Trabalhadores* http://www.dieese.org.br/anu/2001/3/ pg48-50.pdf. Retrieved July 16, 2002.

Farid, Jacqueline. 2001. "Brancos São 2,5 Vezes mais Ricos que os Negros". *O Estado de São Paulo* 8 July. http://www.estado.com.br/ editoriais/2001/07/08/ ger014. html. Retrieved June 19, 2002.

Fontaine. 1985. "Introduction." Pp. 1-10 in *Race, Class, and Power in Brazil*, edited by Pierre-Michel Fontaine. Los Angeles: Center for Afro-American Studies, University of California, Los Angeles.

Frazier, E. Franklin. 1992 [1942]. "Brazil Has no Race Problem." Pp. 121-130 in *African-American Reflections on Brazil's Racial Paradise*, edited by David J. Hellwig. Philadelphia, PA: Temple University Press.

Freyre, Gilberto. 1946. *The Masters and the Slaves: A Study in the Development of Brazilian Civilization*. New York: Knopff.

Fundação Cultural Palmares. 2002. "Notícias." http://www.palmares. gov.br. Retrieved July 17, 2002.

Gilliam, Angela M. 1992 [1970]. "From Roxbury to Rio–and Back in a Hurry." Pp. 173-181 in *African-American Reflections on Brazil's*

*Racial Paradise*, edited by David J. Hellwig. Philadelphia, PA: Temple University Press.

Gonzalez, Lélia. 1985. "The Unified Black Movement: A New Stage in Black Political Mobilization." Pp. 120-134 in *Race, Class, and Power in Brazil*, edited by Pierre-Michel Fontaine. Los Angeles: Center for Afro-American Studies, University of California, Los Angeles.

Hasenbalg, Carlos A. 1985. "Race and Socioeconomic Inequalities in Brazil." Pp. 25-41 in *Race, Class, and Power in Brazil*, edited by Pierre-Michel Fontaine. Los Angeles: Center for Afro-American Studies, University of California, Los Angeles.

Instituto Brasileiro de Geografia e Estatística (IBGE). 1992. "Seção 2: Característi-cas Demográficas e Socioeconômicas da População." *Anuário Estatístico do Brasil*. Rio de Janeiro: Fundação Instituto Brasileiro de Geografia e Estatística.

Instituto Brasileiro de Geografia e Estatística (IBGE). 2002a. "Síntese de Indicadores Sociais." http://www.ibge.net/home/presidencia/ noticias/0404sintese.stm. Retrieved June 18, 2002.

Instituto Brasileiro de Geografia e Estatística (IBGE). 2002b. "Censo Demográfico–2000–Tabulação Avançada. Tabela 2.1.1: População Residente, por Cor ou Raça, segundo as Grandes Regiões e as Unidades da Federação." http://www.ibge.gov.br/home/ estatistica/ populacao/censo2000/ tabulacao_avancada/tabela_brasil-1_1_1.stm. Retrieved July 11, 2002.

Instituto Brasileiro de Geografia e Estatística (IBGE). 2002c. "Indicadores Sociais Mínimos: Conceitos." http://www.ibge.gov.br/home/ estatistica/populacao/condicaodevida/indicadoresminimos/ conceitos.shtm. Retrieved June 5, 2002.

Instituto Brasileiro de Geografia e Estatística (IBGE). 2002d. "Pesquisa Nacional por Amostra de Domicílios--PNAD 1999: Destaques." http://www.ibge.gov.br/home/estatistica/populacao/trabalhoeren

dimento/pnad99/destaques.shtm. Retrieved July 11, 2002.

Instituto Brasileiro de Geografia e Estatística (IBGE). 2002e. "Indicadores Sociais Mínimos: Aspectos Demográficos–Informações Gerais: Taxa de Mortalidade Infantil e de Menores de 5 Anos de Idade por Cor e Sexo." http://www.ibge.gov.br/home/estatistica/ populacao/ condicaodevida/indicadores minimos/tabela1.shtm. Retrieved June 17, 2002.

Instituto Brasileiro de Geografia e Estatística (IBGE). 2002f. "Indicadores Sociais Mínimos: Educação e Condições de Vida–Média de Anos de Vida das Pessoas de 10 Anos ou mais de Idade por Sexo e Cor, 1999." http://www.ibge.gov.br/home/estatistica/populacao/ condicao devida /indicadores minimos/tabela3.shtm. Retrieved June 5, 2002.

*ISTOÉ.* 1996. "Publicidade a Pleno Vapor." December 4. http://www. terra.com.br/ istoe/economica/141825. Retrieved July 17, 2002.

Maio, Marco Chor. 1999. "Against Racism: in Search of an Alliance Between Afro-Brazilians Jews in the Early 1990's". *Estudios Interdisciplinares de América Latina y El Caribe* 10 (2):109-130.

Massey, Douglas S. and Nancy A. Denton. 1999. "The Construction of the Ghetto." Pp. 178-202 in *Majority and Minority: The Dynamics of Race and Ethnicity in American Life*, 6th ed., edited by Norman R. Yetman. Needham Heights, MA: Allyn and Bacon.

Mitchell, Michael. 1985. "Blacks and the *Abertura Democrática.*" Pp. 95-119 in *Race, Class, and Power in Brazil*, edited by Pierre-Michel Fontaine. Los Angeles: Center for Afro-American Studies, University of California, Los Angeles.

Penha-Lopes, Vânia. 1996. "'What Next?': On Race and Assimilation in the United States and Brazil." *Journal of Black Studies* 26, 6 (July): 809-826.

Penha-Lopes, Vânia. 1997. "An Unsavory Union: Poverty, Racism, and the Murders of Street Youth in Brazil." Pp. 149-168 in *Globalization and Survival in the Black Diaspora: The New Urban Challenge*, edited by Charles Green (SUNY Press).

Pereira, Dulce Maria. n.d. "The Black Face of Multicultural Brazil." http://www.mre.gov.br/revista/numero06/ingles/facenegra-i.htm. Retrieved June 19, 2002.

Pitt-Rivers, Julian. 1987. "Race, Color, and Class in Central America and the Andes." Pp. 298-305 in *Structured Social Inequality: A Reader in Comparative Social Stratification*, 2nd ed., edited by Celia S. Heller. New York: Macmillan Publishing Company.

Ramalho, André, Daniel Machado, Emília Carneiro, Fernanda Almeida, Jaqueline do Carmo, Regina Marques, and Sheila Nunes de Oliveira. 1998. "Racismo no Brasil: As Dificuldades do Negro no Mercado de Trabalho." Departamento de Relações Internacionais, Faculdade de Ciências Sociais, Universidade Católica de Brasília. http://www.geocities.com/CollegePark/Lab/9844. Retrieved July 11, 2002.

Ribeiro, Wal. 2000. "Benedita da Silva: Sucesso na Política e no Amor." *Raça*, August. http://www2.uol.com.br/simbolo/raca/0800/entrevista.htm. Retrieved March 19, 2003.

Silva, Nelson do Valle. 1985. "Updating the Cost of not Being White in Brazil." Pp. 42-55 in *Race, Class, and Power in Brazil*, edited by Pierre-Michel Fontaine. Los Angeles: Center for Afro-American Studies, University of California, Los Angeles.

Skidmore, Thomas E. 1985. "Race and Class in Brazil: Historical Perspectives". Pp. 11-24 in *Race, Class, and Power in Brazil*, edited by Pierre-Michel Fontaine. Los Angeles: Center for Afro-American Studies, University of California, Los Angeles.

Skidmore, Thomas E. 1993. *Black into White: Race and Nationality in Brazilian Thought*. Durham and London: Duke University Press.

Wilson, William Julius. 1980. *The Declining Significance of Race: Blacks and Changing American Institutions*, 2nd Edition. Chicago:

University of Chicago Press.

Wilson, William Julius. 1987. *The Truly Disadvantaged: The Inner City, the Underclass, and Public Policy.* Chicago: University of Chicago Press.

# Chapter 11

# From Biracial to Tri-Racial:
## The Emergance of a New Racial
## Stratification System in the United States

**Eduardo Bonilla-Silva**
Texas A&M University

R ace relations in the United States are slowly but surely becoming "tri-racial," much like they are in Latin America, South Africa, and other regions of the world. The biracial system typical of the United States has been the exception in the world-racial system. In the 21st century, the United States is becoming like the "norm." It is evolving into a complex racial stratification system. Specifically, the U.S. is developing a tri-racial system with "Whites" at the top, an intermediary group of "honorary Whites"–similar to the coloreds in South Africa during formal apartheid, and a nonwhite group or the "collective black" at the bottom. The "White" group will include "traditional" Whites, new "White" immigrants and, in the near future, assimilated White Latinos and other groups. The intermediate racial group or "honorary Whites" will comprise most White middle class Latinos (e.g., most Cubans and segments of the Mexican and Puerto Rican communities) (Rodríguez, 1999), Japanese Americans, Korean Americans, Asian Indians, Chinese Americans, and maybe Arab Americans. Finally, the "collective Black" will include Blacks, dark-skinned Latinos, Vietnamese, Cambodians, Laotians, and maybe Filipinos. Figure 11.1 presents this tri-racial map.

**Figure 11.1**
**Preliminary Map of the Tri-Racial System in the U.S.**

**"Whites"**
Euro-Americans
New Whites (Russians, Albanians[1], etc.)
Assimilated White Latinos
Some multi-racials
Recovered memory[2] & Assimilated urban Native Americans
A few Asian-origin people

**"Honorary Whites"**
White middle class Latinos
Japanese Americans
Korean Americans
Asian Indians
Chinese Americans
Arab Americans

**"Collective Black"**
Filipinos
Vietnamese
Hmong
Laotians
Dark-skinned and poor Latinos
Blacks/African Americans
New West Indian and African immigrants
Reservation-bound Native Americans

[1]For an example of the whitening of Albanians, see Howard
Pinderhughes' book, *Race in the Hood* (1997).

This map, however, is heuristic rather than definitive. Hence, the position of some groups may change (e.g., Chinese Americans, Asian Indians, and Arab Americans) and, at this early stage of analysis, the map is not inclusive of all the groups in the United States (for instance, Samoans, Micronesians, etc., are not on the map). More significantly, if this tri-racialization thesis is accurate, there will be categorical porosity–fluidity in racial categories such that individual members of a racial strata will more easily move up (or down) the stratification system (e.g., a light-skin middle class Black person marrying a White woman and moving to the "honorary White" strata). There will also be a "pigmentocracy" in which the rank ordering of groups and members of groups will occur according to phenotype and cultural characteristics (e.g., Filipinos being at the top of the "collective Black" given their high level of education and income as well as high rate of interracial marriage with Whites).

Race relations in the United States are becoming tri-racialized for several reasons. First, the demography of the nation is changing. Racial minorities are up to 30 percent of the population today and, as population projections suggest, may become a numeric majority in the year 2050. And these projections may have underestimated the growth of racial minorities, as early data releases from the 2000 Census suggest that the Latino population was about 12.5 percent of the population. This is almost 1 percentage point higher than the *highest* projection and the proportion White (77.1 percent White or in combination) was slightly lower than originally expected (Grieco and Cassidy, 2001).

The rapid darkening of the United States is creating a situation similar to that of many Latin American countries. For example, Puerto Rico, Cuba, and Venezuela in the 16th and 17th centuries, and Argentina, Chile, and Uruguay in the late 18th and early 19th centuries all experienced a darkening of their citizenry. When these countries realized their citizens were becoming "Black," they devised several proposals (unsuccessful in Puerto Rico, Cuba, and Venezuela, but successful Argentina, Chile, and Uruguay) to whiten their populations (Helg, 1990). Although whitening the population through immigration or by classifying many newcomers as White (Gans, 1999; Warren and Twine, 1997) is a possible solution to the new demography of the United States, for reasons discussed below, this is not likely to occur. Hence, a more plausible accommodation to the new racial reality is to (1) create an intermediate racial group to buffer racial conflict, (2) allow some newcomers into the White racial strata, and (3) incorporate most immigrants into the collective Black strata.

Second, as part of the tremendous reorganization that transpired in America in the post-civil rights era, a "new racism" that is a kinder and gentler version of White supremacy emerged (Bonilla-Silva and Lewis, 1999; Bonilla-Silva, 2001. See also Smith, 1995). In post-civil rights America, the maintenance of systemic White privilege is accomplished socially, economically, and politically through institutional, covert, and apparently non-racial practices. Whether in banks or universities, in stores or housing markets, "smiling discrimination" (Brooks, 1990) tends to be the order of the day. This new White supremacy has produced an accompanying ideology of color-blind racism. An ideology is the "broad mental and moral frameworks, or 'grids,' that social groups use to make sense of the world, to decide what is right and wrong, true or false, important or unimportant" (Bonilla-Silva, 2001: 62). Color-blind ideology is one in which social groups believe that racism and discrimination have been replaced by equal opportunity; that one's qualifications, not one's color or ethnicity, are the main methods by which upward mobility is achieved. This ideology denies the salience of race in America, scorns those who talk about race, and increasingly proclaims that "We are all Americans" (for a detailed analysis, see Chapter 5 in Bonilla-Silva, 2001).

Third, race relations have become globalized (Lusane, 1997). The once almost all-White Western nations have now "interiorized the other" (Miles, 1993). The new world-systemic need for capital accumulation has led to the incorporation of "dark" foreigners as "guest workers" and even as permanent workers (Schoenbaum and Pond, 1996). Thus today European nations have racial minorities who are increasingly becoming an underclass in their midst (Castles and Miller,1993; Cohen, 1997; Spoonley, 1996). As a consequence, these nations have developed an internal "racial structure" (Bonilla-Silva, 1997) to maintain White power, and they have developed a curious racial ideology that combines ethno-nationalism with a race-blind ideology similar to the color-blind racism of the U.S. today (for more on this, see Bonilla-Silva, 2000). This new global racial reality, therefore, will reinforce the tri-racialization trend in the U.S.

Fourth, the convergence of the political and ideological actions of the Republican Party, conservative commentators and activists, and the so-called "multi-racial" movement (Rockquemore and Brunsma, 2002), has created the space for the radical transformation of the way we gather racial data in America. Possible outcomes of the Census Bureau's decision to include the "check all that apply" instructions for racial and ethnic classifications are either the dilution of racial data or the elimination of race as an official category (for more on the multi-racial "movement" and its implications, see Farley, forthcoming). Ward Connerly–a "multiracial" Black man who spearheaded the drive to abolish affirmative action by appropriating the language and symbols of civil rights activists–gathered signatures to place the California Racial Privacy Initiative on the ballot in November 2002 to forbid California from classifying individuals by race.

Lastly, the attack on affirmative action, which is part of what Stephen Steinberg (1995) has labeled as the "racial retreat," is the clarion call signaling the end of race-based social policy in the U.S. Although it is still possible to save a watered-down version of this program, at this point, this seems like pie in the sky. Again, this trend provides support for the tri-racialization thesis because the elimination of race-based social policy is predicated on the notion that race no longer affects minorities' racial status.

## How Race Works in the Americas

Racial stratification systems operate in most societies without races being officially acknowledged (Bonilla-Silva and Lewis, 1999). For example, although racial inequality is more pronounced in Latin America than in the United States, racial data in the former is gathered inconsistently or not gathered at all. Yet, most Latin Americans, including those most affected by racial stratification, do not recognize that inequality as being racial in nature. Latin American nation-states, with the exception of Argentina, Chile, Uruguay, and Costa Rica, are thoroughly racially mixed. Racial mixing, however, in no way challenged White supremacy in colonial or post-colonial Latin America since: (1) the mixing was between White men and Indian or Black women, maintaining the race/gender order in place, (2) the men were fundamentally poor or working class, which helped maintain the race/class order in place, (3) the mixing followed a racially hierarchical pattern with "whitening" as a goal, and (4) although most marriages historically have been within-strata, they still have produced phenotypical variation because of within-group phenotypical variations, members of the strata can try to "marry up" by choosing light-skinned partners within strata.

Although Portuguese and Spanish colonial states wanted to create "two societies," the demographic realities of colonial life superseded their wishes. Because most colonial outposts were scarcely populated by Europeans, all these societies developed an intermediate group of "Browns," "Pardos," or "Mestizos" that buffered socio-political conflicts. Even though this group did not achieve the status of "White" anywhere, it nonetheless had a better status than the Indian or Black masses and, therefore, developed its own distinct interests.

Another layer of complexity in Latin American racial stratification systems is that the three racial strata are also internally stratified by "color" (i.e., skin tone, phenotype, hair texture, eye color, culture and education, and other markers that indicate the degree of "Europeaness"). A phenomenon known in the literature as pigmentocracy or colorism (Kinsbrunner, 1996) has been central to the maintenance of White power in Latin America because it has fostered: (1) divisions among all those in secondary racial strata, (2) divisions within racial strata limiting the likelihood of within-strata unity, (3) mobility viewed as individual and conditional upon "whitening," and (4) White elites being regarded as legitimate representatives of the "nation" even though they do not look like the average member of the "nation."

As a social practice, whitening "is just not neutral mixture but hierarchical movement . . . and the most valuable movement is upward" (Wade, 1997: 342). Thus, rather than showing Latin American racial flexibility, racial mixing oriented by the goal of whitening shows the effectiveness of the logic of White supremacy. In the Latin American context, a formidable ideology forged around the myth of national unity crystallized. This ideology hides the salience of race and the existence of a "racial structure" (Bonilla-Silva, 1997; 2001), unites the "nation," and better safeguards White power than Hispanidad (regarding oneself or one's country as Spanish), an ideology that still exists among White elites in Latin American and which causes problems for the maintenance of nonracialism (For Puerto Rico, see Negrón, 1997 and Torres-Saillant, 1998. For Venezuela, see Wright, 1990). Thus, most Latin Americans, even those obviously "Black" or "Indian," refuse to identify themselves in racial terms. Instead, they prefer national (or cultural) descriptors such as "I am Puerto Rican." This has been the subject of much confusion and described as an example of the fluidity of race and racism in Latin America (For examples, see the otherwise superb work of Clara Rodríguez, 1991; 2000). However, defining the nation and the "people" as the "fusion of cultures" (even though the fusion is viewed in an Eurocentric manner), is the logical outcome of all of the factors mentioned above. Nationalist statements such as "We are all Puerto Ricans . . . " are then the direct manifestation of the racial stratification peculiar to Latin America rather than evidence of nonracialism.

### The Objective Standing of "Whites," "Honorary Whites," and "Blacks"

If tri-racialization is occurring in the United States as it has in Latin America, gaps in income, poverty rates, education, and occupational standing between Whites, "honorary Whites," and the "collective Black" should be developing. The available data suggest this is the case. In terms of income, "White" Latinos (Argentines, Chileans, Costa Ricans, and Cubans) are doing much better than dark-skinned Latinos (Mexicans, Puerto Ricans, etc.). In particular, according to data from the 1990 Census, Argentines had average incomes that were more than twice as large as those of Mexicans. Moreover, the lowest income "White" Latino group (Costa Ricans) had incomes that were more than 45% higher than those of Puerto Ricans.

Similar patterns exist among honorary White Asians (Japanese, Koreans, Filipinos, and Chinese) relative to those who are among the collective Black (Vietnamese, Cambodian, Hmong, and Laotians). Japanese have average incomes that are more than four times greater than those of Cambodians, and more than 13 times greater than the average incomes of the Hmong. The lowest income "honorary White" Asian group (Koreans) had incomes that were more than 145% higher than the median income for those Asians who are part of the collective Black.

There are similar patterns in terms of education. White Latinos have between two and two-and-half years of educational advantage over dark-skinned Latinos. Honorary White Asians have up to seven years of educational advantage over Black Asians.

Substantial group differences are also evident in the occupational status of the groups. White Latinos are more than 50% more likely to be represented in professional, managerial, and technical jobs than are dark-skinned Latinos. Costa Ricans are almost twice as likely as are Mexicans to hold professional, managerial, and technical jobs. Along the same lines, honorary White Asians are even more likely than those among the collective Black to be hold professional, managerial, and technical jobs.

## Social Identity

Social psychologists have amply demonstrated that it takes very little for groups to develop a common view, and to adjudicate status positions to nominal characteristics (Tajfel, 1970; Ridgeway 1991). Thus, it should not be surprising if objective gaps in income, occupational status, and education among various groups is contributing to group formation. That is, "honorary Whites" may be classifying themselves as "White" or believing they are better than the "collective Black." If this is happening, this group should also be in the process of developing White-like racial attitudes befitting of their new social position.

In line with the tri-racialization thesis, we expect Whites to be making distinctions between "honorary Whites" and the "collective Black," specifically, exhibiting a more positive outlook toward "honorary Whites" than toward members of the "collective Black." Finally, if tri-racialization is happening, the "collective Black" should begin to exhibit a diffused and contradictory racial consciousness as is the case of the bottom group (Blacks or Indians) in Latin and Iberian America (Hanchard, 1994).

Historically, most Latinos have classified themselves as "White," but the proportion of Latinos who self-classify as such varies tremendously by group. Table 1 shows that the overwhelming majority of Latinos from nationality groups we regard as honorary Whites classified themselves as White, and less than half of Latinos from nationality groups we regard as belonging to the collective Black considered themselves White. As a case in point, whereas Mexicans, Puerto Ricans, and Central Americans are very likely to report "Other" as their preferred "racial" classification, most Costa Ricans, Cubans, Chileans, and Argentines choose the "White" descriptor. These Census 2000 data mirror the results of the 1988 Latino National Political Survey (de la Garza et al., 1992).

The incorporation of most Latinos in the U.S. has meant becoming "nonwhite." For a few, however, it has meant becoming almost White. Nevertheless, given that most Latinos experience discrimination in labor and housing markets as well as in schools, they quickly realize their "nonwhite" status. This leads them, as Nilda Flores-Gonzalez (1999) and Suzanne Oboler (1995) have shown, to adopt a plurality of identities that signify "otherness." The identification of most Latinos as "racial others" has led them to be more likely to be pro-Black than pro-White. Latinos who identify as "Black" express the most positive affect toward Blacks.

Regarding how Whites think about Latinos and Asians, not many researchers have separated the groups that comprise "Latinos" and "Asians" to assess if Whites are making distinctions. However, the available evidence suggests that Whites regard Asians highly and are significantly less likely to favor Latinos (Bobo and Johnson, 2000). Although for political matters, Asians tend to vote pan-ethnically (Espiritu, 1992), distinctions between native-born and foreign-born (e.g., American-born Chinese and foreign-born Chinese) and between economically successful and unsuccessful Asians are developing. Leland Saito (1998), in his *Race and Politics*, points out that many Asians have reacted to the "Asian flack" they are experiencing with the rise in Asian immigration by fleeing the cities of immigration, disidentifying from new Asians, and invoking the image of the "good immigrant." Thus, when judged on a host of racial stereotypes, Whites classify Asians and themselves almost identically (favorable stereotype rating) and a negative rating (at an almost equal level) of both Blacks and Latinos.

## Conclusions

This chapter has presented a broad and bold thesis about the future of race relations in the United States. However, at this early stage of the analysis and given the serious limitations of the data on "Latinos" and "Asians," it is hard to make a conclusive case because much of the data is not parceled out by sub-groups, and hardly anything is separated by skin tone. Nevertheless, almost all the objective, subjective, and social interaction indicators point in the direction of tri-racialization. For example, the objective data clearly show substantive gaps between the groups we labeled "White," "honorary Whites," and the "collective Black." In terms of income and education, Whites tend to be slightly better off than honorary

Whites who tend to be significantly better off than the collective Black. Not surprisingly, a variety of subjective indicators signal the emergence of internal stratification among racial minorities. For example, whereas some Latinos (e.g., Cubans, Argentines, Chileans, etc.) are very likely to self-classify as Whites, others are not (e.g., Dominicans and Puerto Ricans living in the United States). This has led them to develop a racial attitudinal profile similar to that of Whites.

If the predictions presented here are right, what will be the consequences of tri-racialization for race relations in the United States? First, racial politics will change dramatically. The "us" versus "them" racial dynamic will lessen as "honorary Whites" grow in size and social importance. They are likely to buffer racial conflict–or to derail it–as intermediate groups do in many Latin American countries.

Second, the ideology of color-blind racism will become even more salient among Whites and honorary Whites and will also impact members of the collective Black. Color-blind racism (Bonilla-Silva, 2001), an ideology similar to that prevalent in Latin American societies, will help glue the new social system and further buffer racial conflict.

Third, if the state decides to stop gathering racial statistics, the struggle to document the impact of race in a variety of social venues will become monumental. More significantly, because state actions always impact civil society, if the state decides to erase race from above, the social recognition of "races" in the polity may become harder. We may develop a Latin American-like "disgust" for even mentioning anything that is race-related.

Fourth, the deep history of Black-White divisions in the United States has been such that the centrality of the Black identity will not dissipate. The research on even the "Black elite" shows that they exhibit racial attitudes in line with their racial group (Dawson, 1994). That identity, as argued in this chapter, may be taken up by dark-skinned Latinos as it is being rapidly taken up by most West Indians. However, even among

Blacks, we predict some important changes. Their racial consciousness will become more diffused (see Chapter 6 in Bonilla-Silva, 2001). Furthermore, the external pressure of "multiracials" in White contexts (Rockquemore and Brunsma, 2002) and the internal pressure of "ethnic" Blacks may change the notion of "Blackness" and even the position of some "Blacks" in the system. Colorism may become an even more important factor as a way of making social distinctions among "Blacks" (Keith and Herring, 1991).

Fifth, the new racial stratification system will be more effective in maintaining "White supremacy" (Mills, 1997). Whites will still be at the top of the social structure but will face fewer race-based challenges. And, to avoid confusion about our claim on "honorary Whites," let's clarify that their standing and status will be dependent upon Whites' wishes and practices. "Honorary" means that they will remain secondary, will still face discrimination, and will not receive equal treatment in society. For example, although Arab Americans should be regarded as "honorary Whites," their treatment in the post-September 11 era suggests their status as "White" and "American" is very tenuous.

Although some analysts and commentators may welcome tri-racialization as a positive trend in American race relations, those at the bottom of the racial hierarchy will discover that behind the statement "We are all Americans," hides a deeper, hegemonic way of maintaining White supremacy. As a Latin America-like society, the United States will become a society with more rather than less racial inequality but with a reduced forum for racial contestation. The apparent blessing of "not seeing race" will become a curse for those struggling for racial justice in years to come.

## References

Bobo, Lawrence, and Devon Johnson. 2000. "Racial Attitudes in a Prismatic Metropolis: Mapping Identity, Stereotypes, Competition, and Views on Affirmative Action." Pp. 81-166 In *Prismatic Metropolis*, edited by Lawrence Bobo, Melvin Oliver, and James

Johnson, and Abel Valenzuela,. New York: Russell Sage Foundation.

Bonilla-Silva, Eduardo. 2001. *White Supremacy and Racism in the Post-Civil Rights Era*. Boulder, CO: Lynne Rienner Publishers.

Bonilla-Silva, Eduardo. 2000. "This is a White Country": The Racial Ideology of the Western Nations of the World-System." *Sociological Inquiry* 70:188-214.

Bonilla-Silva, Eduardo. 1997. "Rethinking Racism: Toward a Structural Interpretation." *American Sociological Review* 62:465-480.

Bonilla-Silva, Eduardo, Amanda E. Lewis. 1999. "The New Racism: Toward An Analysis of the U.S. Racial Structure, 1960s-1990s." Pp. 55-101 In *Race, Nation, and Citizenship*, edited by Paul Wong, . Boulder: Westview Press.

Brooks, Roy L. 1990. *Rethinking the American Race Problem*. Berkeley: University of California Press.

Castles, Stephen and Mark Miller. 1993. *The Age of Migration: International Population Movements in the Modern World*. Hong Kong. MacMillan.

Dawson, Michael C. 1994. *Behind the Mule: Race and Class in African American Politics*. Princeton: Princeton University Press.

de la Garza, Rodolfo O., Louis DeSipio, F. Chris Garcia, John Garcia, and Angelo Falcon. (Editors).1992. *Latino Voices: Mexican, Puerto Rican, & Cuban Perspectives on American Politics*. Boulder, San Francisco, and Oxford: Westview Press.

Farley, Reynolds. Forthcoming. "Identifying with Multiple Races: A Social Movement that Succeeded but Failed?"in *The Changing Terrain of Race and Ethnicity*, edited by Maria Krysan and Amanda Lewis. New York: Russell Sage Foundation.

Flores-Gonzales, Nilda. 1999. "The Racialization of Latinos: The Meaning of Latino Identity for the Second Generation." *Latino Studies Journal* 10:3-31.

Gans, Herbert J. 1999. *The Possibility of a New Racial Hierarchy in the Twenty-First Century United States*, edited by Michele Lamont. pp. 371-390. Chicago: The University of Chicago Press.

Grieco, Elizabeth M., and Rachel C. Cassidy. 2001. *Overview of Race and Hispanic Origin 2000.* Washington: U.S. Government Printing Office.

Hanchard, Michael. 1994. *Orpheus and Power: The Movimiento Negro of Rio de Janeiro and Sâo Paulo, Brazil, 1945-1988.* Princeton.: Princeton University Press.

Helg, Aline. 1990. "Race in Argentina and Cuba, 1880-1930: Theory, Policies, and Popular Reaction." Pp. 37-69 In *The Idea of Race in Latin America, 1870-1940,* edited by Richard Graham. Austin: University of Texas Press.

Keith, Verna M., and Cedric Herring. 1991. "Skin Tone and Stratification in the Black Community" *American Journal of Sociology* 97: 760-778.

Kinsbrunner, Jay. 1996. *Not of Pure Blood: The Free People of Color and Racial Prejudice in Nineteenth-Century Puerto Rico.* Durham, NC and London: Duke University Press.

Lusane, Clarence. 1997. *Race in the Global Era: African Americans at the Millennium.* Boston: South End Press.

Miles, Robert. 1993. *Racism After Race Relations.* London and New York: Routledge.

Mills, Charles W. 1997. *The Racial Contract.* Ithaca and London: Cornell University Press.

Negrón-Muntaner, Frances. 1997. "English only Jamas but Spanish only Cuidado: Language and Nationalism in Contemporary Puerto Rico." Pp. 257-285 In *Puerto Rico Jam: Essays on Culture and Politics,* edited by Frances Negrón-Muntaner and Ramón Grosfoguel. Minneapolis: University of Minnesota Press.

Oboler, Suzanne. 1995. *Ethnic Labels, Latino Lives: Identity and the Politics of (Re)Presentation in the United States*. Minneapolis: University of Minnesota Press.

Ridgeway, Cecilia L. 1991. "The Social Construction of Status Value: Gender and Other Nominal Characteristics." *Social Forces* 70: 367-386.

Rockquemore, Kerry Ann and David L. Brunsma. 2002. *Beyond Black: Biracial Identity in America*. Thousand Oaks, CA: Sage Publications.

Rodríguez, Clara E. 2000. *Changing Race: Latinos, the Census, and the History of Ethnicity in the United States*. New York: New York University Press.

Rodríguez, Clara E. 1991. *Puerto Ricans Born in the U.S.A.* Boulder, San Francisco, and Oxford: Westview Press.

Saito, Leland T. 1998. *Race and Politics: Asian Americans, Latinos, and Whites in a Los Angeles Suburb*. Urbana: University of Illinois Press.

Schoenbaum, David and Elizabeth Pond. 1996. *The German Question and Other German Questions*. New York: St. Martin's Press.

Smith, Robert C. 1995. *Racism in the Post-Civil Rights Era: Now You See It, Now You Don't*. Albany: State University of New York Press.

Spoonley, Paul. 1996. "Mahi Awatea? The Racialisation of Work in Aotearoa/New Zealand." Pp. 35-77 In *Nga Patai: Racism and Ethnic Relations in Aotearoa/New Zealand*, edited by Paul Spoonley, David Pearson, and Cluny Macpherson. Palmerston North, New Zealand: Dunmore Press.

Steinberg, Stephen. 1995. *Turning Back: The Retreat from Racial Justice in American Thought and Policy*. Boston: Beacon Press.

Tajfel, H. 1970. "Experiments in Intergroup Discrimination." *Scientific American* 223: 96-102.

Torres-Saillant, Silvio. 1998. "The Tribulations of Blackness: Stages in

Dominican Racial Identity." *Latin American Perspectives* 25: 126-146.

Wade, Peter. 1997. *Race and Ethnicity in Latin America*. London and Sterling, VA: Pluto Press.

Warren, Jonathan W. and France Winddance Twine. 1997. "White Americans, the New Minority?: Non-Blacks and the Ever-Expanding Boundaries of Whiteness." *Journal of Black Studies* 28: 200-218.

Wright, Winthrop R. 1990. *Café con Leche: Race, Class, and National Image in Venezuela*. Austin: University of Texas Press.

# Index

# Index

# Index

# Index

**About the Contributors**

## Editors

**Cedric Herring** is Professor in the Department of Sociology at the University of Illinois at Chicago and in the Institute of Government and Public Affairs at the University of Illinois. Dr. Herring is former President of the Association of Black Sociologists, and he was the Founding Director of the Institute for Research on Race and Public Policy at UIC. He has published widely on topics such as social policy (e.g., social welfare and affirmative action), political sociology, labor force issues and policy, stratification and inequality, and the sociology of African Americans. He is the author of *Splitting the Middle: Political Alienation, Acquiescence, and Activism* and he is the editor of *African Americans and the Public Agenda: The Paradoxes of Public Policy* and co-editor of *Empowerment in Chicago: Grassroots Participation in Economic Development and Poverty Alleviation.* He has also authored several research monographs and more than 50 journal articles and book chapters in scholarly outlets. He has also received support for his research from the National Science Foundation, the Ford Foundation, the MacArthur Foundation, the Joyce Foundation, and others. Dr. Herring has shared his findings in community forums, at press conferences, in newspapers and magazines, on radio and television, with community groups, and before legislators and other government officials.

**Verna Keith** is Chair of the Department of Sociology at Arizona State University. She has two main areas of research interest: (1) the study of how stress affects health and emotional well-being among African Americans and the elderly, and (2) issues related to minority access to health care. She is currently investigating gender differences in the effects of chronic stressors such as marital problems on the mental health of African Americans. She also has a project that focuses on skin-color, gender, and self-concept among African Americans. In addition, she recently completed a project that investigated socioeconomic status and use of health care among African Americans. She is a co-editor of *In and Out of Our Right Minds: African American Womenís Mental Health.*

**Hayward Derrick Horton** is Associate Professor of Sociology at the State University of New York at Albany. Professor Horton specializes in demography and race and ethnicity. He has published over 20 articles on topics such as: the demography of rural Black families; differences in Black-White levels of home ownership; population change and the employment status of college-educated Blacks; race, ethnicity and levels of employment; the demography of Black entrepreneurship; and the feminization of poverty. Professor Horton developed the first and only sociological model of Black community development. He is currently co-authoring a book on the model entitled, *Rebuilding Black Communities: Black*

# About the Contributors

*Community Development in Contemporary America*. Professor Horton has held leadership positions in the American Sociological Association, the Southern Sociological Society, the Rural Sociological Society, and the Society for Applied Sociology. He is former Chair of the American Sociological Associationís Section on Race and Ethnic Minorities, and he is currently President of the Association of Black Sociologists.

## Other Contributors

**Eduardo Bonilla-Silva** is Associate Professor of Sociology at Texas A&M University. Currently, he is a Hewlett Fellow at the Research Institute for Comparative Studies on Race and Ethnicity at Stanford. Professor Bonilla-Silva achieved sociological recognition through his 1997 article in the *American Sociological Review* entitled, ìRethinking Racism: Toward a Structural Interpretation,î where he challenged sociology to move away from the individualistic understanding of racism as ìprejudice.î His first book, *White Supremacy and Racism in the Post-Civil Rights Era* (Lynne Rienner Publishers, 2001), received the 2002 Oliver C. Cox Award given by the Section of Racial and Ethnic Minorities of the American Sociological Association. His second book, *Racism Without Racists: Color Blind Racism and the Persistence of Racial Inequality in the USA* (Rowman and Littlefield), as well as his third book, *Whiteout: The Continuing Significance of Racism* (With Ashley Doane, by Routledge), are forthcoming.

**Phillip Bowman** is Director of the Institute for Research on Race and Public Policy, as well as Professor of African American Studies and Psychology at the University of Illinois at Chicago. He conducts research on the social psychology of role strain and adaptation. He has held joint appointments in Psychology and African American Studies at the University of Michigan, the University of Illinois-Urbana-Champaign, Northwestern University, and the University of Illinois at Chicago. His work on several national surveys of African Americans has resulted in numerous publications, including *Race-Related Socialization, Motivation and Academic Achievement; Joblessness and Discouragement Among Black Americans*; and *Post-Industrial Displacement and Family Role Strains*. He has received both Ford and Rockefeller Foundation Fellowships and is a very active consultant on the theoretical, methodological, mental health, organizational, and social policy implications of his ongoing research.

**David Brunsma** is Assistant Professor of Sociology at the University of Alabama at Huntsville. He is co-author of *Beyond Black: Biracial Identity in America* (Sage 2001). His current research examines geographic differences in racial identity development among multiracial people.

**Katrina M. Carter-Tellison** is a Ph.D. candidate in sociology specializing in race relations at the University of Miami. She is currently working on her dissertation entitled *Skin Tone and Perceptions of Discrimination among African Americans, Hispanics and Asian Americans: Evidence from the Multi-City Study of Urban Inequality*. Her research interests include issues and problems in race relations, social stratification and inequality, and race attitudes.

**Heather Dalmage** is a Professor of Sociology at Roosevelt University in Chicago. In her book, *Tripping on the Color Line: Black-White Multiracial Families in a Racially Divided World*, Dalmage explores through in-depth interviews and participant observation the racial thinking of interracially married, transracially adopted and multiracial people. She is the editor of the forthcoming anthology, *The Politics of Multiracialism*, in which the origins, discourse and outcomes of the Multiracial Movement are explored. She is also the Director of the Mansfield Institute for Social Justice and a board member at the Chicago Council on Urban Affairs.

**Kimberly L. Ebert** is a doctoral student in the Department of Sociology at the University of California, Davis. Her interests include racial inequality, race and ethnic relations, sociology of law, public policy, and comparative-historical methods. Ebert's current research includes an investigation of anti-affirmative action organizations and an exploration of color-blind ideology within Supreme Court decisions.

**Korie Edwards** is a doctoral candidate in the Department of Sociology at the University of Illinois at Chicago. Her dissertation is entitled *Beyond Segregation: Understanding How and Why Interracial Churches Work*. Her paper entitled ìAre Public Housing Residents the Catalyst for the Underclass?î was awarded first prize in the Association of Black Sociologistsí Graduate Student Paper competition. She is the co-author of *Against All Odds: The Struggle for Racial Integration in Religious Organizations*.

**Margaret Hunter** is Assistant Professor in the Department of Sociology at Loyola Marymount University in Los Angeles. Her research focuses on women of color in the United States through the intersectional lens of race, class, and gender. She has published several articles on skin color stratification and also has interests in racism and pedagogy. Hunter is currently working on a book comparing African American and Mexican American womenís experiences with regard to skin color and social status.

**Mosi A. Ifatunji** is a graduate student in the Department of Sociology at the University of Illinois at Chicago. He is also affiliated with the Institute for Research on Race and Public Policy at UIC. Broadly, Ifatunji is interested in the sociology of the African American experience. Within this unique cannon of race-, class- and gender-related issues, he focuses on the process of African American socialization and identity formation, urban education and urban community development.

**V,nia Penha-Lopes** is Assistant Professor of Sociology at Bloomfield College. A native of Rio de Janeiro, Brazil, she has a Bachelor's of Social Sciences from the Universidade Federal do Rio de Janeiro, and a Master's of Arts in Anthropology and a Ph.D. in Sociology from New York University. Her research and teaching interests focus on the sociology of the family, comparative race relations, sociology of masculinities, and social stratification. She is the author of "An Unsavory Union: Poverty, Racism, and the Murders of Street Youth in Brazil" (in *Globalization and Survival in the Black Diaspora*), "What Next? On Race and Assimilation in the United States and Brazil" (*Journal of Black Studies*), and "'Make Room for Daddy': Patterns of Family Involvement among Contemporary African-American Men" (in *American Families: Issues in Race and Ethnicity*). Dr. Penha-Lopes is currently at work on her manuscript, entitled *It's a Family Affair: Parenting, Domestic Participation, and Gender among Black Men.*

**Ray Muhammad** is currently a doctoral candidate in the Department of Sociology and a graduate research assistant at the Institute for Policy Research at Northwestern University. He was previously a visiting lecturer in African American Studies and graduate research assistant at the Institute for Research on Race and Public Policy, at the University of Illinois at Chicago, He specializes in research on family and urban life.

**Kerry Ann Rockquemore** is Assistant Professor of Sociology at Boston College. She is co-author of Beyond Black: Biracial Identity in America (Sage 2001). Her research focuses on racial socialization and she is currently completing a book entitled Raising the Biracial Child: From Theory to Practice (Altamira).

**Lori Sykes** is a doctoral candidate in the Sociology Department at the State University of New York at Albany. Sykes is also Assistant Director of the Critical Demography Project. Her areas of specialization are race and ethnicity and demography. She recently published an article entitled, "Wealth Inequalities Among and Between Asian, Black, Hispanic and White Women." She continues work on her dissertation, "Income Rich, Asset Poor," which examines the simultaneous effects of race and gender on the spatial assimilation of Black females.

**Maxine S. Thompson** is Associate Professor of Sociology at North Carolina State University. Her research interests include Mental Health (Caregivers of Person with Severe Persistent Mental Illness), Social Inequality (Race and Gender), and Social Psychology (Coping, Self-esteem, and self-efficacy).